HOW TO INTERPRET
DREAMS & SIGNS

KAYA

UCM
NON-PROFIT ORGANIZATION

UCM

Non-profit organization
Publishing House
51-53, Saint-Antoine Street
Sainte-Agathe-des-Monts, QC
Canada J8C 2C4

Administrator: Jean Morissette, lawyer
Business and Administration: 819-321-0072
Fax: 514-352-5272
E-mail: publishing@ucm.ca
UCM's Website: www.ucm.ca

KAYA's Website: www.kaya.fm
Facebook: KAYA (official)

English translation: Blánaid Rensch, Micheline Marcotte, Nicole Beaulieu
Revision: Christiane Muller, Joanie Boux
Proofreading: Anne-Marie Marko
Photographer: Anthony Di Benedetto
Editing: Edith Lacroix
Cover Design, Illustrations: Jimmy Greco, Dominique Grelot, Christophe Guilloteau, Anthony Di Benedetto

Transcription, structuring and revision of original French version, *Rêves et Symboles, La Matérialisation de la Vie*: Andrée Hamelin
Transcription and proofreading in French: Sophie Chansard, Claire Fortin, Sonia Gagnon, Ginette Nadon, Florence Pichonnaz, Johanne Pomerleau, Janick Quenet, Marie-Hélène Ruaux, Francine Stricos
Coordinators: Caroline Chabot, Martine Thuillard

Legal deposit of French version: 3rd term 2007
National Library of Quebec
National Library of Canada
National Library of France
ISBN: 978-2-923097-14-5

Legal deposit of English version: 4th term 2011
National Library of Quebec
National Library of Canada
National Library of Switzerland
National Library of France
National Library of Ireland
ISBN-13: 978-2-923654-11-9
ISBN audio version: 978-2-923654-12-6
ISBN eBook version: 978-2-923654-13-3

Printed in Canada

Printed on Rolland Enviro100, which contains 100% recycled post-consumer fibre, is EcoLogo, Processed Chlorine Free and FSC Recycled certified and manufactured using biogas energy.

FOREWORD

"I remained silent for years. In my solitary hermit life, I finally found peace of mind through the answers that I discovered and that I share with you in this book.

I dedicate this book to God and to all the Angels who always guide me in my continual, eternal learning process...to my dear wife & lover Christiane—I love you with all my soul...to my daughter Kasara and my spiritual son Anthony, to our wonderful life of apprenticeship on Earth all together...to all the UCM team who help and support this Mission...and to all seekers of the Parallel Worlds... this book is for you and for all generations to come.

For me, as a pioneer, it was a long and very intense journey to rediscover all these answers...now with this knowledge, I hope with all my heart that this book will help you understand that dreams & signs are the beginning, the source code of who you are and who you will become. We are all born under the star of change, that's the purpose of life, of evolution..."

KAYA

KAYA endorses the UCM Foundation and has agreed to give all the revenue from this book to charity.

*This book contains transcriptions of workshops
that took place in various cities
around the world.*

*The reader will better appreciate the language
used in this book if he bears in mind that
this is an oral teaching.*

"Life is a process of continual transformation. If you do not like your life…remember…you can always change it…"

KAYA

HOW TO INTERPRET
DREAMS & SIGNS

INTRODUCTION TO THE WORKSHOPS

Welcome to this workshop on the interpretation of dreams and symbolic language. This workshop will allow you to share a dream that you would like interpreted or to ask questions concerning your path towards self-enlightenment. For those of you who have come for the first time, you will see that the workshop takes place in all simplicity, as though we were together in a living room, sharing our experiences.

What is the purpose of workshops on dreams? Essentially, it is to make us aware of the great importance of dreams and symbolic language.

Dreams inform us about what is about to happen or what is in progress in our lives. They announce the fact that a program has been initiated. We become aware of this by observing our frame of mind the day after a dream. For example, if we dream of *a beautiful sunny prairie*, the next day we will be infused with a beautiful feeling of capacity to create abundance, of completeness. If we dream that *we are walking down the back streets of a poor neighborhood*, the next day we will feel poor and sad. We will experience the state of conscience symbolized by the images in the dream.

Generally speaking, people who do not know how to interpret dreams believe that they are essentially abstract and that only some, occasionally, are premonitory. However, all dreams are premonitory; they all come true. In some cases they actually come true on the physical level, and in others they only come true on the emotional level, or on the level of concepts or understanding. They always come true, however. That's for sure; it's an absolute truth.

Dreams also give us the best answers to our questions. Why? Because they come from our unconscious. Their message is pure and direct, in the sense that it is not filtered or distorted by the conscious self — by desires, expectations, and preconceptions.

This is why we are sometimes quite surprised by what we see in dreams. We could be living a quiet, peaceful, orderly life and yet wake up in the morning after a dream filled with violence, where people were fighting, setting fire to homes, etc. Or scenes of sexual violence… all sorts of things are possible.

Where does this come from? Our unconscious is made up of reservoirs or storage trunks full of memories that are susceptible to being reactivated at any moment. These constitute all kinds of memories: aggression, happiness, jealousy, love, poverty, anguish, etc. In short, all kinds of actions, emotions and thoughts that are part of our being and that come not only from this life but also from our *eternal life*, from many other lives.

Through the course of our existence, of our lives, we have developed personalities that remain more or less conscious facets and tendencies of our being. We have been men, we have been women, we have lived in various countries, and we have participated in all kinds of enterprises, individual as well as collective, some right and fair, others not. This is why, sometimes, certain behaviors re-emerge that we do not recognize as our own. Our preferences, our temperament, our talents, our fears, and even our way of saying *I love you* are all determined by our past experiences.

Day after day, following certain situations that we must go through, these memories appear in the form of a frame of mind or a state of conscience that can last for a few seconds, a few minutes, a few hours, or even entire weeks. The situations activate states of conscience according to registered memories.

For example, when we were children, our aunt would serve us a certain type of cake when we went to her house. The atmosphere in her house was not very good. And when we hesitated to accept the cake, our mother would look at us with such intensity! We could read in her look, *Say thank you to your aunt now, and look at her when you are talking to her. And eat up that cake!* Later on in life, every time we eat that kind of cake, we get a stomach ache without knowing why or else we just don't like it at all. It is simply because, with regard to that particular type of cake, we have registered memories that have become unconscious. One day, we must transcend such memories. We must be aware that it's not the cake that is difficult to digest, but rather the atmosphere in the home that the cake reminds us of.

Memory functions by instant recall. An object or a person that we see, a perfume in the air, or a tune playing on the radio awakens in us an array of memories, most of which are unconscious. Such small triggers can cause us to plummet into states the scope of which often surprises us, since the emotion is so out of proportion to the exterior situation we are experiencing.

In order to understand dreams, we must remember that all the elements and all the symbols that we see represent states of conscience or fields of conscience that are parts of our being. Behind a flower lies a particular state of conscience or state of mind. When we say that someone is as beautiful as a flower, that he's blossoming, or that a mother-to-be is blooming, in truth we mean beautiful softness, a beautiful feeling emanates from them, because the person releases such a *perfume*. We are used to this language with our poets and our singers. They express themselves with symbols that represent states of mind. The same idea applies to symbols that appear in dreams.

When dreams actually corroborate concrete, material reality, it is because even in the physical world, in an awakened state, everything—absolutely everything—is created with states of conscience and fields of conscience. In actual fact the whole Creation of the Universe—from the smallest to the largest thing, from the microcosm to the macrocosm—operates through states of conscience.

Everything that exists in the Universe—cars, boats, rockets, planets, wind, police officers, firefighters, tsunamis, volcanoes, etc.—also exists within us as states or fields of conscience. All objects, all colors, all people, all animals represent forces that exist within us. In reality, everything that is created exists first and foremost on the metaphysical level, within our being, as a state of conscience. We shall see how.

States of conscience and fields of conscience as such constitute the *vocabulary— the alphabet*—of Creation and they are presented to us in the form of symbols, as much in concrete reality as in our dreams.

Quantum physics has demonstrated that when we delve into the infinitesimal, when we go beyond the particles that constitute matter, there is only energy—there is no longer any matter. Matter is therefore an illusion, in the sense that what we believe to be an object, an animal, or a person, in reality is an assemblage of vibrations, of many states of consciousness, of forces and/or weaknesses sometimes.

Matter is an illusion, but oh, how intelligent! because everything holds and works together. The human body, with its organs and metabolism, is able to function—it lives. Vegetation reproduces itself: the seed gives birth to a plant that resembles its creator. The planets follow their course around the sun in a predictable manner. Everything is held together in this immense assemblage of vibrations, of forces that we perceive as matter.

So how are objects created? How do situations occur? According to what *information*, so to speak, because these vibrations are necessarily formed—therefore informed? Situations are created by a universal phenomenon of resonance in which *like attracts like*. Thoughts and emotions of abundance attract abundance, thoughts and emotions of gratitude attract happy events, and thoughts and emotions of deficiency contribute to the creation of more limitations in our lives.

It is a well-known fact that emotions affect the physical environment. For example, indoor plants are healthier when the people who care for them are joyful or peaceful rather than sad or aggressive. This idea also applies to our thoughts, and this has often been demonstrated: the results of concrete experiments are modified by the presence of observers.

Creation also proceeds in stages of materialization. We have an idea for a project and we would like to carry it out. Therefore, if the conditions are favorable, it will eventually be implemented. All multinational companies begin as an idea; decades later, they manage billions of dollars. We see that thought is just as creative as action or emotion; it even *precedes* action and emotion.

However, in this creative process, there exists a level that is even more *causal* than that of thought. It is the level of the intention or of the spirit, the one we call the metaphysical level of reality.

When we really want something, our intention seems oriented towards this objective; we are aware that we want that thing.

However, our being harbors so many intentions that are not conscious, that totally escape our conscious self. These unconscious intentions are just as creative as those on the conscious level; they attract situations and people of a certain type in our lives, in our environment. And with the unconscious being just that—unconscious—we are very often surprised by what happens in our lives. The world of our spirit is actually the world of causes.

Our spirit has a program all of its own, the broad outlines of which are established before we are born. And, barring modifications from Central Programming, it will materialize. This is an absolute truth. This is because our life program is inscribed in the metaphysical dimension of our being, in the actual structure of our spirit, just like computer software conceived to run precise operations at prescribed moments.

The analogy of the computer is quite useful to help us understand our being. We can compare our spirit to electricity that circulates in our personal computer, according to trajectories that are dependent on internal circuits and the functioning of our programs. Similarly, our soul is comparable to the whole of the memory already registered on the hard drive. Our soul is, in a way, the *home* of our spirit, of this intelligent energy that circulates inside it. The two merge, just as our physical body merges with our spirit.

The spirit activates the soul's memories according to its life program, much as intelligent energy acts inside a womb. Of course, this womb is the sum total of our actions, of the emotions and feelings we have nourished, and of the thoughts we have maintained throughout *eternal life*, or throughout our many lives if we believe in reincarnation.

Countries took centuries to build their main structures— social programs, banks, judicial systems, etc. Their history has definitely prepared today's events. Similarly, everyone has a story, and everyone has a structure of memories that determines the situations they experience and will experience in the future.

We are so intelligent in terms of our spirit! Its intelligence is infinite. Everything that the spirit does, it does *via* symbols. Our body is actually conceived via symbols. If we have short legs or a long nose, if we have weak kidneys or a sensitive liver, it all has meaning. If we wear red one morning and blue the next, that too has meaning. We can understand the meaning if we know how to decode symbols. We must not forget that our spirit is what creates our body, that dresses it, that makes it move, etc. It is our spirit that creates all the situations that appear in our life.

We can use the image of the computer to go further. Our *personal computer* subscribes to an Internet *service provider*. It has access to other *personal computers* and to the immense Living Computer that is God, Cosmic Intelligence. Because of this link, we can have access to all the information contained in the Universe and to all Programs — those of every being, every group, every country, etc. We cannot help but feel humbled in the face of such greatness.

The goal of every spirit is to be continually connected to this Great Intelligence, to actually merge with It, because the spirit wholeheartedly aspires to rediscover its Celestial Origin, which is comprised of Qualities, Virtues, and Powers in their purest state — Love, Truth, Justice, Beauty, etc. Thus — most of the time without being aware of it — everyone is trying to integrate these Divine Qualities. Throughout this process, we travel many paths, experimenting with all kinds of distortions such as selfishness, lying, and so many other attitudes. Eventually, we find ourselves at an impasse because these attitudes will only have served to bring us actual states or inner feelings of poverty, isolation or ill-being. A person takes all of these detours with one goal in mind: to integrate Knowledge, which, in the Tradition, we refer to as the Knowledge of good and evil.

Evolution is God's one and only objective. The same goes for us, for our being, whether we are aware of it or not. As human beings, we would like to be rich and improve our lot in life. We would like to have a house, maybe even a summer cottage, a new car, etc. And of course it is possible to get these things. But God and our Higher Self view these acquisitions simply as ways of experimenting with specific states of conscience. Having a summer cottage generates a certain state of conscience, driving a new car generates another state of conscience, etc. Our life scenario is worked out within this dynamic and the frame that holds it all together: the country and family we are born in, our spouse, our children, our work, etc. Through these conditions, a person can experiment with certain qualities and distortions—good and evil.

One day, when the person has experimented with distortions for a while, a program is activated that allows him to review his distorted memories so that he can rectify them. Then, it becomes necessary to clean the *hard drive*. This is what we call initiation or depression: generally difficult periods where the person, destabilized by exterior events or inner blockages, or both, has no other choice but to question his existence. Many are going through initiation on this Earth at the moment, because so many old souls have reached this stage in their evolution.

Earth is the land of experimentation of states of conscience, as much in their pure or angelic form as in their distorted form. Earth is also a school, since this is where we learn about the consequences of the past actions of our soul.

The profound meaning of existence—which is to develop qualities, virtues and powers in their pure state—is the sole perspective from which dreams are conceived. Consequently, it is only in reference to this meaning that we can begin to understand the deep meaning of dreams. This fact can never be repeated enough. If you try to analyze and to understand the messages you receive in your dreams without coming back to this fundamental fact, you will never succeed.

To develop qualities and virtues is not an abstract or disconnected process. On the contrary, it is very concrete. Among other things, it is kindness, love, respect, honesty, integrity, etc. If we apply ourselves to the development of qualities through all of our actions, emotions, and thoughts, inevitably we move toward happiness and abundance. Because we attract people who are respectful, honest, and kind with whom we can associate to materialize projects and develop friendships, we create a healthy and harmonious environment for our loved ones and for ourselves.

This is what it means to learn to materialize in a divine way, to develop our spirituality. It is to marry spirit and matter, intention and action by developing qualities and virtues.

In this process, dreams are a most precious key because they show us, as we progress, what we must learn and all the stages we must complete in order to integrate Qualities, Virtues, and Powers.

The symbols we see in dreams are not just images: they are the icons of programs that have begun. All those who understand computer technology know that behind an image or a movement on the screen there is an entire sequence of hidden operations on the electronic circuit level. The same applies to dreams: they truly are motors of life.

Dreams are the leading pulse of Creation. If you receive a dream one night, you will inevitably experience — or you are already involved in — a vast array of scenarios associated with this dream, whether physical, emotional, or mental. Everything we see in dreams represents parts of ourselves, states of conscience and fields of conscience that constitute our being on the most essential level and that are activated during the dream. The following is an example.

Recently, a friend had a dream in which *he was in a city, which was prey to civil war and social disorganization. In his dream, he was trying to maintain order and to limit the damage so that the conflict would not become generalized.* That day, when I was with him, I could feel this conflicting energy. When he was talking with people — when he was giving information or whatever he was doing — he was doing it with greater intensity than usual and it seemed as if he saw conflicts everywhere. At the same time, we could feel that he was trying to contain this conflicting energy. He was doing his best but he was not yet in full mastery of those forces. However, he was actively working on his inner conflicts and if he perseveres, one day, in accordance with his Program, he will master them and integrate great harmony.

Dreams show us the hidden dimension of what we are in the process of living and of what is being activated within us. Through dreams, we go to the heart of our memories and we understand what we are experiencing, whether it is positive or negative. We can even modify the course of the materialization process: if we are aware of destructive forces in the works, we can stop them before they manifest on the physical level.

Sometimes we put too much emphasis on a problem we are experiencing. We exaggerate it. It is a question of seeing the glass half full or half empty. When we see the glass as half empty, we say, "Ah! I've hardly any left," whereas when we see it half full, we are happy, because we know we still have some resources left. By giving us an *overview* of situations, dreams help us take the drama out of our difficulties. We are aware that we are going through a stage that is part of a process. It's another step on the path towards Knowledge and Enlightenment.

No therapist can help us understand what we are experiencing as well as our dreams can. Of course, therapists have their place; they can inspire us and help us find our way. But the more we understand our dreams, the more we develop our autonomy; for not only are we able to *read* the programs being implemented, we are also able to see how we react to them on the deepest level of our being. In a relatively near future, children will learn the language of symbols before learning to do math. They will understand the meaning of life and their reason for being on Earth.

Through our dreams, we also have the possibility of receiving answers to our questions. Once again, we must remember that answers are always given in order to develop qualities and virtues, even when the questions are of a material nature. We'll talk about this later.

It is Spiritual Guides from the Parallel Worlds who script our dreams. Guides are particularly evolved beings who have responsibilities concerning life on Earth. They are, in a way, public servants of the conscience and each assumes a very precise role on behalf of Celestial Government. Some take care of a group of souls, others of the climate or the cycles of animal or vegetable life, others of economic or political processes. Their Work is always in line with That of Creation, which consists in guiding beings on the path towards Universal Consciousness.

Guides organize, among other things, the general outlines of events that we experience, with great precision, infinite sensitivity, and often, great humor! Always with the goal of helping us evolve. These responsibilities are part of their own learning.

There exists a complete hierarchy of these beings—a hierarchy of responsibilities—because through them God makes sure that the

Divine Plan is achieved. God acts with the Guides in the same way we act with our children. As our children grow up, we give them ever-greater responsibilities so that they may continue to learn. God builds the Universe in this manner. Responsibilities are given to spirits who are deeply involved in their own development, and Divine Intelligence reserves the right to intervene at any moment, like a good father or mother.

All of this tells us that, when we learn to decode our dreams, we truly provide ourselves with the means to participate in our evolution.

And so, throughout this workshop, we shall study symbolic language. Through this *state-of-conscience* language, we are all united and involved—consciously or unconsciously—in our evolution towards the Light.

We sometimes think that symbols can only be subjected to a more or less superficial interpretation, that they are vague and indistinct and that for this reason we cannot trust them. This impression derives from not knowing the structure and logic of dreams.

Symbolic language is very precise. To understand its structure and logic, all that is required is to apply to it the logic of our material world. For example, to identify the symbolism of an object, we need only ask ourselves, "What is the use of this object here on Earth? Why was it made? What state of mind does it inspire?"

A municipal court does not serve the same purpose as a house. Therefore, they do not have the same symbolic meaning: the former represents justice, whereas the latter refers to the intimacy of family life. Following the same reasoning, fire does not have the same symbolic meaning as air or water; we wouldn't think of using them for the same purpose. A person dressed in lovely white, or beautifully colored garments does not represent the same state of conscience as a tramp in rags. Lying in a hospital bed does not inspire the same state of conscience as lying in our own bed at home.

Because of this very familiar, common logic, it is easy, even for a child, to identify the symbolism of just about any object. As for the characters that appear in our dreams, we only need to ask ourselves, "What does this person represent for me? What does he inspire in me?" If we know him, we ask ourselves, "What type of behavior or attitude does he have?" If we have recently had news of this person, we ask, "What is he going through at the moment? What is his present situation?" The first image that comes to mind — the most immediate idea — is the one we must retain. If the character is unknown to us, we simply analyze his dress, his line of work, behavior, features, mood and the part he plays in the dream.

We must remember that even if we see other people in a dream, they always represent parts of us. The character always refers to a facet of our being. This is so even if we are visiting his soul — because this can happen: our spirit merges with the state of conscience of this person at the time of the dream.

If we see an animal in a dream, we analyze its behavior. Let's take a lion for example. The lion is said to be the king of the jungle because it has no predators. This is why it is so calm. Large felines are very calm because they have a lot of confidence and, when they need something, they simply go and get it. The lion is often associated with businessmen who have a certain amount of power and with people who have great presence. This is the energy that the lion represents and it can be either positive or negative — the lion can be calm while also radiating great power, or it can roar and behave aggressively.

When we use symbolic language, we must always remember that all symbols have positive and negative symbolism. This is exactly why dictionaries of symbolism are generally so simple, because they do not take this double value into consideration. Under a given item there generally appears either positive or negative symbolism. It will be written, for example, that a tiger symbolizes aggressiveness. Of course, characteristically the tiger has great potential for aggressiveness but it also has positive symbolism, which, as it happens, is the ability to master this great aggressive force.

Generally, people who write dictionaries of symbolism only use a psychological approach; they do not have a spiritual perspective. As a result, these dictionaries are not complete and cannot really help those who wish to develop deep understanding of the language of dreams.

Sometimes, we must begin with an animal's negative symbolism in order to understand its positive symbolism; this is generally the case when it is culturally associated with something negative. If, in a dream, we were to see the most poisonous, dangerous spider, it could still signify something positive if it were in the right place and not aggressive. If it is calm and mastered, any negative force can be transcended or represent a power.

For example, if we think of a peacock, the symbolism that immediately comes to mind is vanity and pride. However, if the peacock we see in a dream is beautiful and luminous, it means that we are in the process of transcending this aspect, that is to say, we are putting the aspect of appearance back in its rightful place within our personal values. If, in a dream, we see a beautiful, polite bear that talks, the dream indicates that we have transcended our boorish side or our coarseness, our tendency to grab and be gluttonous in various situations. We are in the process of developing sophistication and good manners and mastery of our forceful, instinctual needs.

This reminds us of the important concept that distortions stem from the same energy as qualities. They are simply reversed. We distort the pure energy, which is the quality. Thus, lies and truth come from the same force, except that in lies the energy is distorted or crooked whereas in truth it is right and pure. This is why we use the term *distortion* when we speak of weaknesses or faults. For example, if we want abundance for ourselves and only for ourselves, we create an imbalance in the pure State of Consciousness of Abundance and we distort It, making it selfish and distorting its altruistic aspect or its purity.

The universal aspect of symbols clearly has a system of gradation; some are more universal than others. For example, the four elements — fire, air, water and earth — and the kingdoms — mineral, vegetable, animal, etc. — truly have a universal character. In themselves, they incorporate everything that exists on Earth. The same goes for colors with which we can associate every part of the visual field. These symbols have the same meaning for everyone, which is part of their universal aspect. On the other hand, other symbols have a meaning that varies according to personal, family or ethnic experience or culture. For example, our sister does not represent the same thing to everyone who knows her. To her co-workers, for example, she is a reminder of professionalism because, as a nurse, she is very conscientious, whereas to her spouse she might represent severity and rigidity.

Now, let's see how we proceed when interpreting dreams.

First of all, we must remember that a dream is like a story with a beginning, a middle and an end. We treat the beginning as an introduction that announces the theme, then we analyze all the symbols in the order in which they appear. The changes of scene (the development) indicates that we are delving deeper, since in the first scene, we are shown the cause of what is expressed in the final scene.

Let's take an example. In a dream, *a police officer gives us a ticket, we feel bad*, and all of a sudden there is a change of scene: *we are confronted with a roaring tiger*. This change of scene reveals to us that the reason we feel bad in situations where justice is being served is that we harbor memories of aggressiveness with regard to justice. This change of scene reveals that our inner rebels — who would like to do as they please without consequences — are at the origin of our ill-being.

If the dream is made up of many scenes or many elements, it is useful, especially at the beginning of our apprenticeship, to make a list of the elements of the dream. Some dreams are so elaborate that we have the impression that they fly off in every direction. Making a list of each element allows us to examine the symbols one by one, as if we were going through the dream in slow motion to view the details with precision. All the details are important; they give a particular *color* or *tinge* to the other symbols. We will have an opportunity to use this method later.

How do we interpret a symbol? The first thing to do — and we need to reflect on this — consists in asking ourselves if the symbol represents a quality or a distortion. Because dreams serve only to help us evolve, the symbols are either positive or negative. They represent either qualities or distortions.

Let us suppose that we were shown a tornado in a dream. Our first reaction is to think that this is a negative symbol since tornadoes generally destroy everything in their path. It would certainly be true if we had seen a tornado that was uprooting trees and demolishing homes. However, if the tornado were in the center of our left hand and we had a good feeling, a feeling of calmness, then the dream would be a positive one… and a very powerful one. Wind belongs to the air domain; in terms of consciousness, it therefore concerns the world of thoughts. As for the left hand, it symbolizes fabrication and the act of giving and receiving on the inner level, since the left represents the inner world. Therefore, the tornado in the center of the left hand represents great mastery over negative thoughts in everything concerning giving, receiving and the fabrication process of our lives.

Here is another example. If we see a heater in a dream, we immediately think of the positive side, of the heat that this object can bring. We think of comfort because heat creates a state of mind we identify with well-being and with love. But if the heater in the dream were covered in graffiti, its presence would indicate a tendency to *heat* ourselves with destructive attitudes. What might this mean? We might think for example, 'Ah! People from this or that country are like this or like that. I have nothing to do with them, and I don't care about them,' and having these types of antisocial, destructive thoughts would *warm us up*. We would be in a similar state of mind as a terrorist plotting an attack — although on a less pronounced level, of course.

In order to know if a symbol in a given dream is positive or negative, we situate it within the context in which it appears, all the while considering the associated details — namely the other elements of the scene. If the context is not enough to determine if the symbolism is positive or negative, for example, we ask, "Was it a lovely chair? Was it clean? Was it solid? Such and such a character, was he behaving in a correct, right manner? Did he have nice eyes, a lovely expression? Was he lit up? Did he release good energy? The plant, was it in good health? The animal, was it gentle or aggressive?"

This interpretation — determining the positive or negative value of the symbol — is truly essential and is the first of all the steps. Even if we have 50 symbols in a dream, we must go through the same evaluation exercise for all of them. It is the same for each of our actions: we must evaluate them in order to know if they rank among qualities or distortions. This is how the Cosmic Computer and the Guides evaluate them, and it is this evaluation that determines the situations we will have to go through as we evolve.

The second step is to determine which of the four elements the symbol is associated with. When considering a symbol we ask ourselves, "Does it belong to the fire, air, water or earth element?" If we saw a flying fish, we know that it belongs to the element of water because fish live in the water and because it was flying, we know that the element of air is also implicated. The same elements would apply if we saw waves on a lake or if we saw rain falling; but of course, these images would not have the same meaning as the flying fish.

Let's see what the four elements symbolize.

Fire represents our spirit, our vital energy. The spirit is comparable to fire, in the sense that is not palpable. It is usually manifested as heat, energy or charisma. As we have already seen, the spirit is vivid intelligence that circulates within our being on all levels. It is, in reality, true intelligence: the one that, informed by our memories, creates our body, our emotions, and our thoughts. Therefore, when we see a positive fire in our dreams — for example a candle that lights up beautiful faces — we know that our spirit is positive, and when we see a forest fire, we know that our spirit or manifested energy is destructive or negative.

We have all felt at some point, as we approached a very critical or aggressive person, a negative energy or a type of black cloud around the person. This is like a black sun or a negative sun. When this happens, it is the spirit of the person that we perceive. We perceive his fire. We can also feel the positive fire in a person, the one that makes the eyes shine, that gives the face its beauty and that makes us feel good. This fire is also the spirit, a light we all have inside.

Air represents thoughts. Thus, when we see smoke, wind, airplanes, birds or any other image that corresponds to the element of air, we know that the symbol concerns our thoughts. If, in a dream, a scene is taking place in an airplane, it means that we are in the process of building something on the thought level. A project is underway, whether conscious or not.

Water represents emotions. Fish, liquid, boats or any other symbol that belongs to the world of water speaks to us of our emotions.

Earth represents our actions. If, in a dream, we see a solid object that can be found on Earth — the array of symbols is so vast! — we will know that the dream concerns our actions. The surface of the earth represents our everyday life, whereas the interior of the earth symbolizes memories from which our experiences stem. We always act according to what we are and what we have been.

Of course, a scene can be made up of more that one of these four elements — we have already seen a few examples. In such cases, we simply combine their meanings. If we see a plane that is landing, it means that our thoughts are preparing to materialize, that we are preparing to enter into action. If we see a bird that emanates a lot of joy, and at the same time, a glass of water that is spilling, it means we will have lovely thoughts — for example, good news — but that we will lose control of our emotions. Some people have trouble managing good news; when they receive good news, they are afraid that bad news will follow. It is as if, unconsciously, they believe that they do not have the right to happiness.

As I mentioned earlier, the kingdoms also constitute a universal set of symbols, and their meaning is the same for everyone.

Everything that belongs to **the mineral kingdom corresponds to memories registered in the unconscious**. Minerals come from the soil and soil contains what has been deposited throughout the centuries: layers of sediment, fossils and other objects. By studying what is found in the soil, we can uncover information concerning the climate and the animal species that once inhabited the land and we can have some idea of the lifestyle of ancient societies. Therefore, when we see stones or metal in a dream, we know that this symbol refers to ancient memories, great foundation or the capacity to concretize a situation.

Everything that belongs to **the vegetable kingdom refers to feelings and emotions**. This is because what is vegetable is mostly made up of water—also the symbol for emotions, as we have just seen—and green, its predominant color, is the color of the heart chakra.

Everything that belongs to **the animal kingdom**—animals, fish, insects, claws, etc.—**symbolizes instincts, needs or attitudes based on fear**—fear of not surviving, fear of suffering, or fear of lacking in some way, to name but a few—in their actual form or in their transcended form.

Before we go on to the human kingdom, I would like to mention—because it is very important—that acquiring control over our instincts occupies a central place within our spiritual development. Instincts that have not been transcended keep a person in a state of enslavement, and stop him from making choices that would help him evolve. As long as one's instincts are not transcended, vital energy manifests itself mainly in the inferior centers of consciousness, those linked only to matter, and the person—without even being aware of it—thinks a little like an animal. He thinks only of himself, of satisfying his needs, without regard for others.

The animal dimension of our being is what gives us physical strength, powerful feelings, and a bonding relationship with Earth. We saw earlier that each animal, in its positive aspects, represents specific qualities. As we go through the process of transcending an animal, we integrate the strengths that it represents—for example, quick reflexes, a certain ease to enter into action, etc. When it is well managed, the animal dimension brings a well-balanced vital energy that expresses itself as much in the superior centers of consciousness as in the inferior centers.

The symbols that belong to **the human kingdom represent an apprenticeship linked to qualities and virtues;** they refer to the awakening of conscience. The human kingdom represents, among other things, all of the great values such as altruism, integrity, justice, and love, which is what distinguishes it from the kingdoms we spoke of earlier.

The kingdom of the Guides. In dreams, we sense that the Guides are very evolved, very wise beings. If we see a Guide in a dream, we know that this denotes true spiritual guidance that we can trust. The fact remains, however, that Guides perform transfigurations—they can take on any form. An evaluation of whether the apparent guide in our dream is positive or negative is very, very important. We need to distinguish between a Wise, Heavenly Guide and maybe an overinflated, selfish ego, our personal needs pushing us to instinctual satisfaction rather than improved behavior, enlightening evolution. In the negative aspect of that kingdom, we encounter all sorts of entities that have the capacity to influence people who have a negative resonance within them. It is important to understand that, in the Universe, it is no coincidence if we attract negative forces, it is because we have them within ourselves.

The Archangel and Angel Kingdoms. When we speak of an Angel, we speak of greatly condensed Divine Energy, Consciousness in its pure state that represents specific Qualities and Virtues. When we call upon the Angel of Justice, it is as though we were asking our spirit, 'Talk to me, teach me about Justice.' When we call upon the Angel of Patience, it is as though we were asking, 'Talk to me, show me what I need to learn about Patience,' and so on. The Archangel and Angel Kingdom is in fact, the representation of God's manifestation.

This sums up the main categories of symbols. With this underlying foundation, the broad outlines of your dreams can be interpreted.

I mentioned earlier that it is possible for someone to visit another person's soul in a dream. In reality the more we evolve, the more we are able to leave our *personal computer* and visit the Program of other people, groups of people, even entire nations. Since such explorations come with great responsibilities, it is not given to everyone to have such dreams but what is absolutely certain is that they always serve to help the person understand something. We will discuss this if the opportunity arises during the workshop.

And now, does anyone have a question or a dream they would like interpreted?

WORKSHOP

That's the First Key

(Female dreamer: I have three fairly short recurring dreams from my childhood that really intrigue me. In the first one, *I am at the wheel of a car—I'm driving—and my father is sitting beside me. We go down a hill, and at the bend in the road, instead of turning, we fall down a ravine. I can feel that there is a link between my father and this ravine.* In the second dream, *I am with my father again. We take an elevator; a big hole opens up on the side of the elevator and we fall into it.* And in the third dream, *I am in a farmhouse with family members, an aunt and some cousins that I really like. The house changes and starts to get dark; the people there move away toward the back, and in the middle of the front wall a stone is missing. A golden light shines through the hole. I am attracted to this light but at the same time, it scares me. I move closer to the wall which then collapses, and there's a dragon behind it.*) Fine. Thank you very much.

Approximately how old were you when you had these dreams? (Dreamer: About five, six or seven years old.) OK. These were recurring dreams, were they? (Dreamer: Yes.)

Did you experience difficulties with your father in your childhood? (Dreamer: Yes, lots. He was very overbearing. I would even go so far as to say that he was a tyrant. I've always been afraid that I'd turn out like him, that I'd behave the way he did and do the same things he did.) All right. I understand.

What you have just said—*I've always been afraid that I'd do the same things he did*—is very interesting. This fear shows that you can feel this negative force within you. This is actually the reason why it is so important for you to be on a spiritual path. In the third dream, we can see that part of your destiny is to work on these tendencies; the difficulties you experienced motivated you to pray and to search for the Light.

In the first dream, you are the one driving the car. This is interesting because it is rare for a five- or seven-year-old child to be driving a car. This shows that your conscience was quite developed at a very young age.

1

This type of dream—where a child does things normally reserved for adults—is prevalent in children who experience great difficulties with their family. At an early age, the child must learn to conduct, to *drive* his life by himself, because his parents don't show any interest in his education or in their relationship with him. However, just as a five or six-year-old child isn't capable of driving a car, nor is he capable of taking charge of his life. So, this recurring dream shows that you were experiencing accelerated development because your parents were not taking proper care of you.

This scene could have had positive symbolism—indicating great leadership potential for example—but, since you fell into the ravine, it is obvious that this is not the case. Even if the scene had had a positive tendency, it would still have served as a warning; you would have been warned not to become an adult before your time.

No matter how fast a child learns, no matter how many tasks he can do by himself, no matter how independent he becomes, he has to go through all of the steps of psychological development. This subject is a real problem in our society today. Children are too often forgotten, left to their own devices by their parents. The teaching of values—the foundation of all education—is left to television, video games and friends. Young girls are wearing lipstick and nail polish at the age of seven—just one example among many others that attests to a deregulation pertaining to values. We must teach our children that, in life, values are the most important thing. It is imperative that we do so! This is a subject close to my heart and we will probably discuss it later. Now, back to the dream.

A car symbolizes the way that we conduct our life on the social level because, normally, we use it to go to work, to meetings, or for leisure activities. We use a car to go toward others. In a more general sense, a car represents the way that we conduct our life. When we are in a car, we more or less become the spirit of the car; it's a little like an extension of our own physical body. We must remember that all the symbols that appear in our dreams represent parts of us, in terms of states of conscience.

Therefore, at such an early age, and due to your great difficulties with your family, you already felt an urgent need to take your life into your own hands.

Your father was present in the dream. He represented the difficulties that you mentioned, but more generally he symbolized action or the concrete world. The father always represents concrete action while the mother represents inner action. These are symbols that often occur in dreams. When we see our father in a dream, we know that this signifies something concrete, a real situation in the exterior, concrete world. Therefore, the notion of being in charge of your own life did not simply apply to your inner world; it also applied to the exterior world.

When you had this dream, you were trying to get out of this difficulty, of the somewhat tyrannical atmosphere that surrounded you—with all the fragility of childhood, of course, since your family was your only reference point, your only measuring stick. Therefore, in terms of consciousness, you fell into a ravine. The child you once were was in great difficulty, in an abyss so to speak, and you didn't want to live anymore. It was as if you were sinking into oblivion. When we experience a lot of suffering, we sometimes experience emptiness in our life. This is what the dream was describing.

In the second dream, there is a similar idea, except that in it you were trying to rise up because of the elevator. Were you going up in the elevator? (Dreamer: No, I was going down.) Ah! You were going down. All right then, let me correct that. When we go down, it symbolizes incarnating in matter, like in the first dream, where you were driving down a hill. As you became incarnate—not only in the sense of being born, but rather of being in matter—you were in great difficulty and you didn't know where life would lead you.

It is also possible to receive this kind of dream during adolescence when the unconscious opens up and we don't know where we're going. This is due to lack of preparation. Parents should explain to a young person what is going to happen to him when he reaches the age of 12 or 13 years old. They should start preparing him when he is approximately 7 years old. They should inform him that his unconscious will open up, that forces that had been latent up until then will begin to manifest in his being, and that he will experience periods of instability and duality on many different levels. At the moment, here on Earth, there is so little information available to parents to help them guide young people on the metaphysical level! We are still in the Stone Age in this area. You, however, were not a teenager at the time of these dreams, so the difficulties you were experiencing with your family left you with a feeling of abysmal emptiness and also the feeling of wanting to die.

In general, the moment a person who has had a difficult childhood revisits his past, he begins to hold a grudge against his parents or other family members and to identify with the role of the victim. He fights the negative and ends up going round and round in circles in this role. It is important to understand, however, that in order to truly heal a wound, we have to get out of the victim role. Even though people who go for therapy are generally encouraged to do this—because this notion is now widely accepted in psychology and psychotherapy—it is a method, which in itself, cannot go very far. Why? Because we have yet to understand that a person does not get hurt by chance. We still haven't integrated the ideas of karma and Divine Justice.

As we grow spiritually and the more we work with the information we receive in dreams, we accept the idea that our parents represent parts of our soul. What you suffered because of your father, you yourself subjected your own children to in other lives and that's why you were born into this family with such a difficult father. You had to face your karma and do the required inner work in order never to repeat this pattern.

When we have been victimized and we do not resolve things, what happens is that, at some point, we ourselves become the victimizer. We adopt the same behavioral patterns as those who have hurt us. Any psychologist or psychiatrist would validate this statement. But, in reality, the reason goes much deeper: we become the aggressor because we have been one before, and our memories of aggression have not yet been cleansed; we go back to those states of conscience that are familiar to us and re-become the aggressor we once were, or, we simply experience aggression through other people. Other people's aggression in our lives means exactly the same because it's impossible for a person who has never been aggressive to encounter aggression unless he has been aggressive and/or committed aggressive acts in previous lives.

Therefore, if a person who was beaten as a child, does not revisit his memories to make peace with them, he could, in turn, in a moment of anger or despair, beat his own children. This is because violence has been directly inscribed in his soul and body; it has been inscribed directly into his cellular memories. If his father or mother — or another person close to him — assaulted or harmed him as a child, this has bred very contradictory feelings within him: love and the need to be loved is mixed with revenge, the need to control, and many other feelings. The person becomes so confused in this sea of contradictory emotions that he begins to identify love with violent behavior. When he himself becomes a parent, he may, out of impatience, lose his self control and hit his child. Even if he adheres to beautiful principles of non-violence and tolerance, if he has not cleansed the memories that are at the core of his suffering, he will have a natural tendency to repeat the patterns of violence.

However, a pattern can remain dormant, just like a virus, and later show up in the form of a disease — possibly in another life. Diseases can subsist in latent states in our being for long periods of time before coming out into the open. We may already have the disease when we are very young but have it awaken only toward the end of our life. It was already in our genes, inscribed in our cellular memory.

Scientists are just beginning to open up to the idea of non-material dimensions of the body and of disease. One day, they will agree that the origin of a disease lies beyond cellular memory. Advances in technology have introduced us to an era where it is conceivable that something other than matter truly exists. Some results are difficult for Cartesian minds to accept but it has always been a reality. It is fundamentally true, in the sense that, basically, we are energy. The spirit is energy; it is a form of light.

(Dreamer: To get out of the role of the victim, do we have to resolve things with the other person? For example, do I have to resolve things with my father?)

First of all we have to say to ourselves, "What this person has done to me, I too have done in another life. This is why it is being done to me." That's the first key, the first step to being able to let go and truly forgive. As soon as we begin to think like this, we begin the true healing process that, eventually, will allow us to free ourselves from this karma. This is fundamental work, because the memory surpasses the conscious self, it surpasses our conscious will to forgive.

As long as we haven't understood that the other person is not essentially at fault, i.e., that, in essence, it's we ourselves who caused this to exist in our lives, then we cannot help but hold a grudge in the back of our mind. Resentment can remain quietly hidden somewhere in our conscience and all it would take is a situation of survival for revenge to resurface. Resentment can also appear under the guise of erroneous concepts or negative feelings toward certain people or situations. It could pull away from the framework of the father or mother and could, for example, transpose itself onto all men, all women, or any other category of people without conscious awareness of this fact. These dynamics can follow us from one life to the next.

The concept of reincarnation is one that many people find difficult to accept. Most of you have already integrated this concept. It is familiar to you because the more we dream, the more we see things and connect with our past memories. And one day, we receive the capacity to see and visit our past lives in our dreams. These are extraordinary experiences and revelations that expose the depths of our beings. Reincarnation is the first key, the first opening to deeply understand all the symbols and all sorts of situations we experience in our dreams and nightmares. This was the case for me a long time ago. I couldn't understand why someone should be born into a dysfunctional family whereas I'd had a lovely childhood without ever having any major problems. Over time, with the understanding of all the experiences we have to face in order to evolve and develop qualities, it became inconceivable to me that we had only one life and that everything stopped at death. This made no sense. This awareness was the first trigger that took me to another level. It is pure logic: without reincarnation, life cannot be fair. There must be Divine Justice; otherwise, nothing can be true and nothing can be truly right.

If you believe in God through Divine Justice, no matter what difficulties you have experienced, you will be reborn in your dreams and in your concrete life; not only in the next life, but in this one. Already, simply by saying, "If this was done to me, it's because I did the same thing myself," we stop believing that our difficult time is caused by others. By directing our thought process in this manner, we become part of this evolution.

We waste so much energy looking for happiness on the outside! It is within us. The keys lie within us. The first consists in understanding why suffering exists, where it comes from, and understanding that it is generated by our own experimentations.

One day, with the concept that our life is like a dream, we have such an understanding of life gravitating around us that we no longer view anything as dramatic. It is as if evil had lost its foul-smelling or aggressive dimension. We understand things on a different level of consciousness, like God that sees good and evil as educational forces that everyone must experiment with. When we have achieved this, if we see a person assaulting another or if we know of someone who takes drugs or anything else for that matter, and we feel upset by it, we know that we still have delinquency within ourselves and, unconsciously, we fear that it might become active. With symbolic language, life can be understood like a dream and we can analyze any concrete situation just as if it were a dream and, through it, find a true lesson for our soul. That's what is called **The Law of Resonance**. What is good and bad with people and situations in our daily life resonates as in dreams where we are shown symbols and parts of ourselves. The Law of Resonance allows us to accelerate our individual evolution.

The day you are no longer bothered by the behavior of others is the day when you will be able to truly love, understand, listen and be close to them. They can be right up close to you, telling you in detail what they are going through and you'll be able to listen to them without tiring. Whenever you feel your energy has been sapped, analyze the person with whom you were talking and say to yourself, "The difficulty he's had in his life, all that he talked to me about, I have all this within me. It has resonated with some of my memories and makes me feel heavy and lacking in energy."

One day, we will have acquired such a capacity for loving another person that we will be able to give him a great sense of well-being simply by listening. We all do this at whatever level our resonance allows us to. We are all both a teacher and a student. There is always someone to help; everyone is involved in helping and supporting others. We all help and support ourselves and others. This is the true meaning of altruism.

Altruism is what allows us all to live together here on Earth. A baker makes our bread and a mechanic repairs our vehicle, etc. Whether or not we like it or are aware of it, we are constantly linked to others and we exchange energy with them exactly like in dreams.

Let us go back to your dreams, madam. Could you tell us the third dream once again? (Dreamer: Yes. *I was at a party organized by my family. It started to get dark and people moved away. On the front wall, a stone was missing and a light shone through the hole. I was attracted to this light but, at the same time, it scared me. I came closer. The stones came apart, the wall collapsed and there was a dragon behind it.*)

This dream is very important because it allows you to understand your life path. The house symbolized your intimate self. All of the family members who were there represented parts of you — personality traits and psychological facets of your being.

The interior of the home got dark. This, combined with the fact that family members were present, meant that great difficulties on the family level were darkening your inner world.

A stone was missing and this led you to see light. Stone belongs to the mineral kingdom, which represents ancient memories and inner potential. As for light, it symbolized spirituality and understanding. In dreams, light always represents a spiritual awakening or becoming conscious because light allows us to see. Therefore, the dream was revealing to you what existed very deep in your unconscious.

The wall collapsed and behind it there was a dragon. The walls of a house symbolize the structure of our intimate self. Therefore, the collapse of the wall meant that at the time of this dream, an old structure in which you felt locked up, a prisoner even, was going to begin transforming itself.

The dragon is a very powerful symbol of affirmation, which features in practically every civilization. Closely related to the serpent or snake—*dragon* comes from the Latin, *draco*, which signifies great serpent—it also symbolizes vital energy. Like the serpent, the dragon is associated with the elements of water and earth, but it is also associated with fire and air because of the fire it breathes and its wings that allow it to fly through the air. In Chinese tradition, it was a symbol that represented the emperor's power and capacity to make decisions. In myths and legends, the dragon is often associated with castles, powers, and combat. This is not a coincidence: the dragon is the most powerful symbol of the animal kingdom because of its link to all four elements.

In its positive light, the dragon symbolizes transcendence of vital energy, the rising of the kundalini. More specifically, and still in its positive light, it represents the transcendence of instincts linked to the desire for power and domination.

The negative symbolism of the dragon is of course submission to negative powers and instincts. We must remember that this is a very powerful force that can manifest itself on all levels of our being—because of its affinity with the four elements.

The fact that the wall collapsed in front of the dragon meant an overflow of repressed violence due not only to the many years of suffering within your family, but also to memories of violence recorded in other lives—the stone represents ancient memories. The dragon behind the wall represented a great force of affirmation and the will never to experience such suffering again.

You must be very careful with the force of the dragon, because you might find yourself wanting revenge and attacking others to try and dominate them. In doing so, you would activate a new karmic cycle. Because it is a desire for power and submission to your instincts in another life that created the difficulties that you experienced with your family.

We must pay attention to the animals in our dreams because the forces they represent play an important role in our lives. When an animal is hungry, it can become aggressive and grab the food it wants. When an employee is in the grip of his instincts and wants a promotion, he doesn't think of others: he will go to any length to obtain his promotion. This can go very far. Some people are

9

prepared to take their clothes off and prostitute themselves to get a job or ensure a contract.

The fact remains, however, that no matter what we've done —excessive ambition, prostitution, drugs or whatever—it's ok; it's not terrible or awful or dreadful. We can always be reborn and we can always cleanse our memories. Who has never gone adrift, made bad choices, done wrong? Who has not experimented?

We sometimes think that an evolved soul is one that only goes toward the Light, that it knows nothing but the Light. This is wrong. An evolved soul is a soul that knows darkness and evil for having experimented with it, but that will no longer engage in it. Like us, the spiritual Guides that we sometimes see in our dreams have walked their path, like all human beings, but this was thousands, even hundreds of thousands of years ago, and not necessarily on Earth.

This is why They are able to help people heal their *negativity*. The Guides have transcended the negative within Themselves. This is what true Knowledge is. The highest Knowledge is that of good and evil. And let me repeat myself, if we have done things that were negative, it's OK . We acquire experience and, with time, this experience becomes a force of understanding that we can draw on and use as much in this lifetime as in others. It is positive *baggage* that dwells in the soul and brings us closer to the Light.

Yes, madam. (Dreamer: What if we dream and we wake up but the dream continues, can you explain this? We're not really dreaming anymore, but it's still in the dream.)

When we have such experiences, we are able to understand that there really isn't any separation between dreams and reality. When we are awake, it is as if we were in a dream except that time is measured differently. Sometimes, when we awaken from a dream that lasted only two or three minutes, we feel as if we were away for an eternity.

(Dreamer: But what if the dream continues? Not long ago, I woke up and I could hear noises in my room. *I heard scratching. It sounded like little rodents eating seeds. I was still in the dream but I was awake with my eyes closed. I was afraid. Then I saw a friend of mine with her young daughter and both had great big smiles on their faces. My friend said, "Don't worry." Then I saw a dead person. Then my friend — the mother of the little girl — was very happy because the person who had died had gone into a light. Then a light came out of my forehead but it was distorted.* I experienced this last part with my eyes open and I was very impressed. I'd like to know if this is a dream.)

It's like a dream — it's the same as a dream. It's what we call a daydream or a waking dream. One day, we get to a point where we live our daily lives as if in a waking dream. We analyze the situations we experience the same way we'd analyze a dream. The same thing applies to visions. There is truly no border between these states; there is no clear-cut distinction between the physical and metaphysical worlds.

To understand this aspect, we need only think of people with psychiatric problems. They may have their eyes wide open yet they see, for example, a mouse. They say, "There is a mouse over there," when no one else sees a mouse. They truly believe that they see a mouse and they are truly frightened. Or they see a bear and run away. A sleepwalker experiences something very similar: his eyes are open and he is in a Parallel World experiencing very concrete situations on the level of his conscience. Hence, the same principle applies to waking dreams, except that in a waking dream, the person remembers what he saw, whereas a sleepwalker usually doesn't remember anything.

So, you could hear little rodents in your room. Your bedroom represented your intimate self. We don't invite just anybody into our bedroom. It is a very intimate place. Little rodents are animals that nibble and gnaw things. Therefore, when you received this dream, instincts related to fears or to a feeling of lack were *gnawing* at the resources in your life.

Then you saw a dead person. Do you know who it was? (Dreamer: I saw him. He was dead but I didn't know him. I asked who it was and I was only told that he had died in a bomb attack.)

This character represented a part of you. Some people see ghosts — I'm not saying this is the case here — but in reality, the ghosts people see are parts of themselves. They are in contact with old memories within themselves. This is why that person is the

11

only one to see the ghosts; other people don't see them. If we see ghosts, it's because some of our inner forces are trying to catch hold of us; we have memories that haunt us that are more or less conscious. Often they come from past lives.

(Dreamer: But they do come.) That's right. They come to haunt us, to scare us. We are afraid that these states of conscience will come back and that we will go back to being the way we used to be. (Dreamer: Yes, yes! Exactly!) This is what the phenomenon of possession is — there are degrees, of course. In extreme cases, where negative memories are really significant, the person is literally possessed by them.

I myself have been through very intense situations with people who were possessed. They are truly inhabited by energies — their eyes change and their energy changes. It is very powerful. They can become quite manipulative to ensure they are right and to get what they want. They can even become evil; an evil personality can introduce itself into their main personality.

(Dreamer: Could you explain that a little more? I'd like to understand.) The person has a large reservoir of negative memories in his soul and, at a given moment, this *negativity* takes on a personality and it moves into the person; the person is possessed by his *own negativity* — not by someone else.

(Dreamer: Basically, the person is invaded by his own memories.) Exactly. Certain types of memories agglomerate and form a force within the person, a force that generates a type of personality in their conscience. In fact, this is what happens with schizophrenics. With schizophrenia, a person has several very strong personalities because he has several large reservoirs of memories.

He switches from one personality to the other. Why? Because he wants to be right and because he wants to run away from his dark aspects, until one day he can't escape from his own negative worlds.

Schizophrenics always want to be right. They are rebels of the conscience in the sense that they absolutely refuse to accept the idea that evil could be a part of their being. This is the key to understanding schizophrenia. When the person feels cornered because he realizes—more or less consciously—that he is not correct, whoops! he switches personalities and, in the new context, he is correct. He hides within a personality—which has its own concepts and emotions—a personality that allows him to have both a good conscience and to be right. He could be hard and overbearing and then suddenly become fragile and vulnerable. He changes like this to get what he wants—fame or recognition, attention, affection, love, etc.

In reality, schizophrenics are people who harbor a lot of rebellion and who want to be perfect—they consider themselves beautiful, kind, the best—and the more they hang on to this image, the more they refuse to see their negative aspects, their darkness, their shadow. They project their negativity onto others and they feel that the whole world is against them.

We are all a bit schizophrenic: we all have multiple personalities. However, our main personality is strong enough to remain centered—so to speak—to stay in control. When we study our dreams, we see our personalities. We see parts that are not very pretty. We wake up in the morning and we think, "Come on! That's not me." It's too violent or selfish; it's too dreadful. We refuse to see ourselves. This is called being schizoid, which is a moderate form of schizophrenia.

In a dream, if a violent person attacks us, we can easily become this person in concrete reality if we lose control of our central personality. A schizophrenic who had such a dream could easily identify himself with the block of memories that emerge from his unconscious and commit a murder.

Therefore, the only difference between a *normal* person and a schizophrenic is that the latter has lost his main personality. The person has so often fled reality and gotten into the habit of changing personalities that he ends up losing his central identity, losing the stable home for his Self. He is a bit like a homeless vagabond of the conscience.

I've worked a lot with schizophrenics and this is an aspect that really interested me. I tried to understand what was going on within these beings. By studying their dreams, it is easy to see that their rebellion leads them to extremes.

13

When a person can't stop eating—I'm referring to bulimia—in a way, he too is going through an episode of schizophrenia. When this occurs, the person is controlled by an animal, instinctual energy that is stronger than his conscience and reason. Actually, this dynamic is at the root of all forms of addictions: a very powerful animal force in the unconscious invades the conscience and starts to create particular behavior and attitudes.

I know many people who worked with the interpretation of dreams and signs and who have healed themselves of these addictions, simply because they managed to recognize that some aspects of themselves were not correct, weren't right. It is not that someone told them this; they discovered it by themselves by analyzing their dreams and by accepting the idea that all the elements of a dream represent parts of themselves. Schizophrenics are very intelligent people with open minds; they have immense potential. However, the tendency to run away from their *negativity* has grown out of proportion.

Just recently, a man told me a very interesting dream that touches on this subject. He's a man who tends to be tired and yet we can feel that he has immense potential. In his dream, *there had been a storm in the forest and a lot of wood had been cut, ready to be used later. He drove off in his truck to go and get the wood. On the way, he entered a tunnel and had an accident; his truck toppled over.*

The day after we receive such a dream, we will probably feel tired because it's as if our spirit had not been fed—symbolically speaking, we were without the firewood needed to rekindle our fire. We have a lot of potential but we have inner blockages that stop the wood from getting to the hearth. So even if a person has many inner resources, if his spirit is not being fed, he feels tired.

This dream revealed the reason why this man gets tired so easily: he has a tendency to cause accidents, literally and figuratively. The tunnel represented the unconscious and the truck going through the tunnel, an unconscious way of acting or of conducting himself. The dream, therefore, revealed unconscious forces in this man that cause accidents and that prevent him from advancing and having access to his inner resources.

14

We must cleanse these memories that prevent our lives from developing well. When we have difficulties on the physical level —a problem at work or whatever—we tend to believe that it's other people's fault: the boss's fault, society's fault, etc. In actual fact we are facing a situation that represents parts of ourselves. Just like in a dream.

Yes, madam. (Dreamer: I had a dream when I was very young, maybe three or four years old. *I could see myself running and there was fire behind me. I was running and running and the animals too were running to save themselves. Then, an elephant crushed me. He crushed my head down into the ground.* I have never forgotten this dream. I, myself, have always been tired—by nature, I'm a very tired person. I wonder if there is a link with this dream.)

This is very interesting. With this dream, you have just given us a key, because in it we can see there are problems with your instincts. In the dream, the fire represented the spirit. We can see that even at three or four years old, you already had very powerful, strong energy. Of course, this could have manifested itself through a quick-tempered parent or people around you with very strong spirits. However, these were also inner forces. The role of these people—among other things—was to put you in contact with similar forces within yourself.

This dream truly provides the key to understanding your tendency to be tired, because it shows that your vital energy is busy fleeing your destructive spirit.

Our inner animals must be well. They must be harmonious because it is only under these conditions that they can provide us with the energy we need to advance. Animals represent the different facets of our vital energy. They are not very intelligent energies—unless we see them talking, thinking, etc.—but they are vital forces that allow us to act.

We must develop a conscience that is able to guide these animals; otherwise, they pull us in all directions. People who suffer from bulimia have dreams in which animals keep eating and eating—they cannot be satiated. After eating to excess, these people regret having done so. They start to cry and wonder, "What have I done?"

15

Momentarily a bear took over their personality. Therefore, this facet of their vital energy is distorted. This is how the conscience works. At a given moment, we identify the animal that is leading us by the nose and we talk to it. We purify the memories that are linked to it so that it will stop leading us into situations that destroy our life and our body.

Sometimes we wish to block these energies but in doing so we disconnect ourselves from part of our vital energy and our sensations. We often see this tendency in some of the people who follow ancient oriental spiritual teachings that hold the view that the world we live in is not important, that matter is a lost cause and that we need to get away from it as soon as possible to live in Nirvana. True spirituality is spirituality that is incarnated and that can be experienced in everyday situations that often generate tension. We should not flee this reality but rather learn to manage our inner forces and transform them.

An elephant crushed your head to the ground. Elephants are famous for their great memory. The fact that it crushed your head shows that, during that period — when you were three or four years old — your father, your mother or someone else close to you was crushing you on the level of your thoughts. For example, they didn't let you speak or made fun of what you said. We must remember, however, that everything that happens in our environment comes from within — because the metaphysical *precedes* the physical. Therefore, these were memories of needs, memories linked to your animal parts that were destroying your life.

Yes, madam. (Participant: Last night, I made a decision and before falling asleep I asked for a dream to show me if I had made the right decision. At the same time, I didn't want to be told that I hadn't. So, I could feel the conflict within me. (*laughter*) During the night, I woke up many times and I said to myself, "I must have confidence; I have to trust Up Above," and I asked for an image. When it comes down to it, I was only partially motivated to receive an answer. (*laughter*) It was very interesting to see the resistance. I know we have to be flexible but I don't always feel flexible.)

It is very important to follow your own rhythm. When we ask for a dream with the question: *Is this the right thing to do?* We enter the

16

Cosmic Computer and then the Program answers our question. Sometimes we don't receive a direct answer. People often tell us, "I made such a request but the dream I received had nothing to do with my question." We must understand that sometimes we receive only one angle of the answer. This is because Up Above, They want us to work on something before giving us a clear, complete answer. We have to learn to accept this. However, if we asked a question, the dream always relates to it, always—this is an absolute truth.

Above all, we must remember that the sole purpose of the answers we receive is to help us evolve. Up Above, They do not necessarily see the situations we experience in the same way as we do.

For Them, the material dimensions are simply toys that help to put the Divine Plan into action. For us, these situations are usually either factors of stress or objects of our ambition or desire. In order to understand the meaning of the answers we are given, we must always remind ourselves that life is a School.

(Participant: We might receive answers that are difficult to swallow.) Sure. (Participant: They're having a good laugh Up There but we're not.) Well, we need to understand that God and all the spiritual Guides are not having a good laugh because They truly have high levels of Compassion and Love. They also have Wisdom: They understand the meaning of pain and suffering and They can see and plan the end of it. They know that via pain and suffering we will achieve something beautiful. They never forget this. We, however, do forget: when we are experiencing difficulties we have the impression that they will never end. But they do end one day. Eventually, we go on to something else. It is very important to remember this.

One day, we will behave like the spiritual Guides. We will develop enough wisdom to help those around us, and ourselves, of course. We begin by orchestrating our own life in consultation with Heaven, by asking Heaven questions.

Just before this workshop, a lady told me what she'd experienced during her morning's meditation. *She was walking on water and she could see patches of ice.* She was surprised because she didn't expect to see this. In actual fact, she was visiting a part of herself where there is emotional coldness. It was only a part, of course—this is not all she is. Then, *she saw the expanse of water open up, and she thought*—while still meditating—'*I am a spirit.' The water immediately took on beautiful colors and became very clear—she could see deep into the water.* Through this image, she was being shown that, with the force of her spirit, she was capable of transforming her emotional coldness and experiencing very powerful, pure emotional states of being.

This was a simple meditation, but very real, in which she managed to modify her state of consciousness. Meditation is also like a dream. We interpret it the same way, with symbolic language.

Once on the water, she could have asked God, "What is it that is not working in my relationship with my spouse?" and all sorts of symbols could have appeared. She could have seen a mouse or anything else that would have given her some indications.

Meditation is so powerful! And so simple! We ask a question and God's Computer answers. One day, we can see our states of consciousness go by. If I ask, "How am I feeling at the moment?" and I see a white bird, it means that I am having beautiful spiritual thoughts—because a bird belongs to the element air and white symbolizes spirituality. By doing this, we can quickly analyze ourselves. We can analyze our state of being.

Sometimes I gather my thoughts and I ask, for example, "Is it time to call this person?" or "Is it time to go to this particular place?" Then, symbols come to me and I decide what to do according to the answer.

This, of course, is an aptitude that we develop with time. In the beginning, we must do some inner work, otherwise our fears and needs create interference. What's more, our clairvoyance is not activated—we see nothing, we have no images. In order for this function to be activated and for this spiritual power to always be available to us, in all circumstances, we must meditate every day and not just for two minutes a day. We must train ourselves to be neutral on the spiritual level. If we are not neutral within our spirit, we create interference and the reception will be blurred. A voice within us insists, "But I want to call her. I miss her. I want to tell her I love her." The voice of need or desire takes up so much room in our consciousness that it is impossible to receive an answer from Heaven.

Persistence with our inner work—on acquiring detachment for one—and understanding that we have a Program allows us to acquire neutrality and clarity with the result that answers come easily. If we are surprised by the image that we get, it means that we are truly in a meditative state and that we have activated the process. If the image does not surprise us, it is because we created it ourselves.

We can control the process at the beginning of our meditation —for example, we can create a mental image where we see ourselves walking along, then opening a door—and then, at a given moment, we are no longer in control. As of that moment, we are surprised by what we see. In our guided meditations, we help people reach a profound state of relaxation, then we say to them, "*Remove the veil*—or *Turn on the television* or *Open the door*—then you will see what it is you need to understand about a given subject." Thus, we begin by consciously activating the Program and then we let the Program provide the answers. You can do this exercise alone or with your family. One person serves as a guide and helps the others travel through their memories and receive answers from Heaven.

But we must remember—as I said earlier—that the answers are always conceived with the goal of integrating Qualities, Virtues and Powers in their purest state. If we ask, "Is it time to sell my house?" and, Up Above, They have decided that this situation will help us learn something, They will send us an image that might not necessarily seem to answer our question. We will think, "They could have made it clearer! They could have shown me a real estate agent: *Ding! Dong! Hello. Here is my business card*." Why isn't the answer as clear as this? Because we have fears, we want to succeed, we really, really want to go to a certain place and we want to start projects, but we have no intention of developing qualities and virtues through them.

This does not exclude the fact that we can grow in any situation. But there is logic in the spiritual path and an essential principle in the process of Divine Materialization: our intention must guide our action rather than the opposite. We must have the intention to develop spiritually and to learn through matter.

19

In the beginning, we must be careful. We mustn't trust what we receive during meditation. We must proceed gently, especially if the decisions we have to make are going to have a great influence on our life and the lives of those close to us. However, the answers we receive in dreams are absolute truths because fear and need cannot intervene in the transmission process. We work on ourselves, we ask a question in all sincerity and — it's an absolute fact — we will receive a dream that will tell us what decision to make.

If the question concerns an important decision that we must make, or if we truly want to reach a deep understanding of a subject — a difficulty or whatever — we ask the same question for seven consecutive days. During the night, They will give us an answer but not necessarily a simple, straightforward one. Sometimes we may receive only one angle of the answer. They might tell us for example, "You want to know if you should leave your spouse? Well, We're going to show you why your relationship is so difficult. You know, he is not the only one who is wrong: you also have something that you must understand. He represents a part of you. So, here is what you have to improve within yourself." Then, They will present us with a character whose behavior is distorted. The following night, if we continue to ask, They will show us another angle of the problem.

If we want answers without doing the Work, Up Above, They can lead us to situations that are even more difficult. Why? Because we don't have the necessary integrity and discipline to converse with Heaven. We only want results — we don't want to go through the various steps that lead to results. It would be the same as if a person wanted money but refused to work. Even if he presented himself at the bank in his finest clothes and said, "Give me some money," he would be told, "You know, that isn't the way it works." In the Universe, it is the same thing: we have to work. If we work and if we are good students of this infinite Greatness, with all the humility and discipline that this requires, we get results. This is an absolute fact.

If you try to play the lottery with dreams, you'll have quite an adventure! Up Above, They will certainly make you dizzy. They can make someone rich in an instant if it pleases Them. They will allow the person to live in abundance, and then he will have to live five lives in great poverty because he won't have used his wealth properly.

Some people ask Up Above, "Give me a parking spot, right here, right now!" The method can work in the beginning and the person will think he is a great magician. However, one day, he will have all the trouble in the world parking because Up Above, They will say, "That's it for your magic wand! We are breaking it." We must ask with respect, love and gentleness. We must understand that we are speaking with Forces that are infinitely more intelligent than we are.

So, we proceed at our own rhythm. We learn to ask properly. We say, "What is right for my evolution?" The goal is happiness and the capacity to communicate with Heaven allows us to advance in a conscious, concrete way toward this goal.

(Participant: If I understand correctly, the idea is to properly formulate the question. *Is it right for me?*) That's correct. *Is it right for my evolution to do this? Is it right for the evolution of my soul to stay with my husband? Is it right for my evolution to stay in this job?*

Is there another question or a dream?

Yes, madam. (Dreamer: I have a dream. *I was with my husband. We were to sleep in an abbey but to get there we had to go through a park that was rather dark. It was daytime but it was dark. The abbey was at the very end of the park, at the end of a path or lane. I went through the park and I entered the abbey, then I came back out and went back across the park again. I did this three times. The third time I crossed the park, I was an actress and there was an actor there too. We were to act in a play but I was completely naked. So I said to myself, "I have to go and put something on — a pair of panties and a bra at least — to go into town." We had to mount a horse. So I crossed the park once again and it wasn't lit up at all. I was a bit scared but I did it anyway. I went and got dressed and came back. Then I mounted the horse and left.*)

What type of park was it? (Dreamer: It was full of trees and flowers. It was really lovely. There were small hotels and little houses all around. I had to go to the end of the path, to the abbey.) The goal was for you to get to the abbey, is that right? (Dreamer: Yes.)

21

This is a very interesting dream because it shows that often, during our spiritual path, our conscience takes all kinds of detours. In the beginning, it doesn't necessarily go very deep. I say this because, in the dream, you had a role as an actress in an embarrassing situation. In a dream being an actress could be positive, but in this case it is not.

Of course, all the elements in the dream represent parts of you. You were with your husband, who represents your inner man. Walking to the abbey represents your search for spirituality, your inner journey, which is mixed up with your superficial social life, since you were a nude actress walking with the aim of reaching an abbey in the middle of small hotels and little houses. So this is what the dream was about.

You were in a beautiful park. From a positive point of view, a park is where we go to relax and sometimes to think over things and make decisions. Since it was nice, we'll retain the positive aspect.

You were naked and you had to play a part as an actress. This meant that, with regard to your spiritual path, when you speak of yourself, you're very authentic — psychologically, you lay yourself bare before others — but, at the same time, you're playing a role. We may play a role to create a good atmosphere, to put everyone in a good mood. But here, the Program said to you, "No, no, no, no! No more role-playing for you; this is for real now." (*laughter from the dreamer*) Up Above was telling you, "There is something more profound, more powerful for you to experience." Therefore, you are at the beginning of a stage that will lead you further in your evolution.

The fact that you could see small hotels and little houses on your way to the abbey shows that you orient your social life toward spirituality.

Then, you went to get some clothes and you got dressed. Nudity is important in dreams. It is a beautiful symbol of authenticity when it is correct and positive. However, if we are completely naked in an inappropriate place, it takes on a distorted meaning. If we walked around the city of New York totally naked, we wouldn't get very far — would we? Because nudity awakens sensations in others, it stimulates needs. Generally speaking, nudity as such symbolizes authenticity, hence a form of purity. Human beings live with all kinds of forces. Indeed, that's why we have laws — to keep our instincts on a leash otherwise they would lead us in all directions.

So, when it is not appropriate, nudity means that we open up too much to other people and that we need the love, affection and attention of others. And at some point, this can lead to misunderstandings. We must learn to open up at the appropriate moment, to speak at the right moment, to talk about dream interpretations, spirituality, Angels and so forth to people who are ready to hear.

(Dreamer: That's why I had this dream, isn't it?) That's right. (Dreamer: I knew it.) You were too open and, since you were playing a role, you overdid it a bit — you were putting too much into it to emphasize the message. So you were given a sign to stop.

Then, no longer being nude or an actress, you were able to mount a horse. A horse symbolizes the force of vital energy and we must remember that the objective is to reach the abbey. This is a force that allows you to go forward with great willpower to reach your objective. So, when you received this dream, it's as though something *clicked* regarding this question. It is as though you had moved on to another level in the way you are progressing along the spiritual path because spirituality is not just a piece of cake and a cup of tea. That's what this dream meant.

Yes, madam. (Dreamer: You mentioned a horse and vital energy. When we see *a horse come striding out of the fog, but we only see the head, chest and front legs*, what does this mean?) We only see the top part? (Dreamer: Yes.) This means that we have a lot of will and energy to start things off, but, concretely, we don't advance fully. With this sort of dream, we see that you, the dreamer, have the potential to advance. You want it intensely but your past is still creating obstructions that stop you from getting out of the fog that obscures and confuses your situation in life.

(Participant: And when *the horse has wings on its head*.) (*laughter*) Ah! Well then, it's beautiful. Wings are a great symbol. A winged horse represents an elevation of vital energy, and wings on the head indicate elevation on the thought level. You have immense potential; you have a vital force that generates spiritual elevation on the thought level; a great force to put your spiritual thoughts into action.

(Dreamer: I have another dream that often comes back. *I see water—I think it's a lake, but I only see the water. Someone comes out of the water. Except that, so far...* (*laughter*) This is terrible, isn't it? *The person doesn't move, the water doesn't move.*)

Given the presence of water, this dream is concerned with emotions and feelings. It is also concerned with inertia and failure to act since the person's movement is halted—the person doesn't come completely out of the water. The water itself doesn't move. So, there is difficulty on the level of emotional action. You lack the necessary energy to pull yourself out of an emotional slump.

There we are. This completes our workshop. Thank you very much for your receptivity and beautiful sharing.

WORKSHOP
Events Planned in Advance

Yes, madam. (Female participant: I dreamt of Pope John Paul II the day after he died. In my dream, however, he was in good health. *There was a low, white building, with a door and the Pope was walking toward this door. I was walking behind him and, to my right, a man was following him and hassling him to walk faster. So I said to him, "You can see he's moving along fine. Leave him alone!" I had to repeat this several times before he finally left. However, I didn't actually see this man; I felt his presence there rather than actually seeing him. When the Pope entered the building, I looked back—I turned right around. At that moment, I found myself in a large courtyard surrounded by a white wall with a large table in the center. I walked toward the table. Someone was sitting there. There was going to be a meal for a lot of people and this woman had already sat down. I approached her and said, "Couldn't you wait for the others to come for the meal?" She said no and began to eat. She was Chinese.*) Thank you for sharing this dream, madam.

To make it easier to analyze the dream, I suggest we make a list of all the elements. We'll write down the key words of the dream—the main symbols—in the order in which they appeared and then we'll analyze them one by one.

A dream is a little like a story, a novel or a film in the sense that it has a beginning, a middle and an end. We wouldn't dream of beginning to watch a film in the middle of it. We could, of course, understand some things, but to understand the storyline, the elements that happened at the beginning would be missing. The same thing applies to dreams. The symbols marry with each other and the meaning of each one influences the meaning of the others.

Of course, if we forget a scene, it's all right; we can still find meaning in the dream—we recognize parts of ourselves. In any case, it doesn't matter to what degree we understand a dream because whatever we've understood is useful.

As we analyze the symbols on the list, the logic of the dream reveals itself and we manage to understand it globally. We can analyze

25

our dream while meditating or thinking deeply about it, ideally as soon as we wake up. One day, the process of interpretation happens very quickly; we read the dream as easily as we speak, because a dream constitutes a language with its own vocabulary and its own rules of composition. We must learn to think in a metaphysical way so as to understand the nature of an object or a character, because — as we mentioned in the introduction — they represent states or fields of consciousness.

Every detail of the dream is important because it nuances the scene or the dream as a whole. But if you can't remember certain details, it's ok; it means you don't really need them.

Let's begin the list of the elements of this dream. First of all, there is *The Self*, since you were in the dream. The Self is that part of your being you identify with most easily. Then, there was *the Pope*. Was there a notion of death in your dream? (Dreamer: In concrete reality it was the day after the Pope's funeral. But no, there was no death in the dream.) Ok. The Pope was simply moving — he was walking. (Dreamer: Yes. And in my mind, he wasn't sad and neither was I.) All right, thank you.

The Pope was walking toward a white building. We write *Walking toward white building*. (Dreamer: He was walking toward the entrance door.) OK. *Toward entrance door*. (Dreamer: Everything was white and he was dressed in beige.) OK. *Dressed in beige*. Each detail is important. (Dreamer: I'd already seen him wearing this tunic once during a public appearance.) OK. Fine.

There was a man who was hassling the Pope. *Man hassles Pope. Then, The Self tells the man to stop because the Pope is moving along fine; the man doesn't listen*. There we are.

(Dreamer: It seemed to me that the man was dressed in darkish colors but I didn't actually see him. He was walking on my right.) *Man dressed in darkish colors; on the right of Self*.

Then, when the Pope entered the building, you turned right around. *Self turns around*. And there you were in a large courtyard surrounded by a white wall. Isn't that right? (Dreamer: Yes.) In the courtyard, there was a large table and a meal was being prepared. *White courtyard; large table; meal being prepared*. Then you saw a Chinese woman who was eating before the others arrived. *Chinese lady doesn't wait for others.* (Dreamer: I didn't see the others.) OK, I understand.

Often, when international events, or events that are given great media coverage occur, many people dream about these events. We regularly receive emails from around the world from people telling us about such dreams. A few days before September 11, 2001 — the day the World Trade Center towers collapsed — many people dreamed of airplanes crashing into buildings. In some cases, it was their living room that was hit by the plane or, for some, it was their place of work. There were many scenarios surrounding this theme.

How do we explain such a phenomenon — that, in dreams, people see events of a collective nature, similar to those that happen on Earth? This is because these events have been planned a long time in advance on the metaphysical level, and they correspond to the states of consciousness of the people who see them in dreams.

On the concrete level, the terrorists planned the attack of the Twin Towers long before it took place. Just imagine, then, how long in advance this event had been planned by Up Above!

Terrorist activity has a role to play in the Great Plan. The Guides make resources available to certain beings who are focused on destruction because evil has an educational function, exactly like in our dreams. Of course, these terrorists create karma for themselves; in other lives, they'll have to go through difficulties similar to those they have caused. Life is a great theatre that allows us to experiment and collective acts of destruction generate more significant karma than those that affect only a few people. Those who are chosen to commit terrorism have such anger in them, that the Guides need only program them for a particular action and they act like puppets. This is because they have given their power of decision to the mass of accumulated memories of anger and frustration stored within them ready to explode on the outside rather than be cleansed on the inside. Such guidance is always educational. The path of learning through consequences can be very difficult but it is always, always educational for the souls of all those affected, near and far. Evil serves Good at all times, in all circumstances, always.

27

In your dream, you saw the Pope, but the Pope in question was your inner Pope since there was no notion of death — even if you saw him in the news the day before. We must analyze only what is in the dream. So let's analyze what the Pope represents as a symbol.

The Pope is a spiritual leader of the Catholic Church and even if we are not affiliated with that Church, we can see him in our dreams as a symbol representing our spiritual leadership if we feel a positive affiliation with him. Of course, for people who are Catholic, it is normally a positive symbol while for others who are not and who have a historical perspective on the Catholic Church, it could be a negative symbol. But for you, madam, it is a positive symbol. So we will interpret it that way. He represents your spiritual leadership and power — the power to make decisions and to advance in your faith.

In your dream, the Pope was wearing a beige tunic. A tunic is a garment that is often associated with spirituality — and here, even more so, since it is worn by a Pope. It therefore constitutes a social affirmation of spiritual orientation. Beige is a mixture of brown and white. Brown represents action on earth and white represents spirituality. Thus, when combined, these two colors represent the spiritualization of matter — the development of spirituality in matter. So the beige tunic colors the symbolism of your sacred way to materialize your decision.

The Pope was walking toward the entrance door of a white building. An entrance door symbolizes a transition; in this case, a passage between the interior and exterior world. As for the color of the building — white — it symbolized spirituality.

So, the pope represented your leadership and your power to make decisions concerning your spiritual path, as well as your spiritual power itself.

We can see that these parts of your being were moving forward and that they were preparing to go through a passageway leading to greater interiorization, to the integration of a more profound, deeper inner spirituality.

In the dream, there was a man who was harassing your Pope. This man represented another part of your being, a part that is pushing you to advance, to pray more, to interiorize more. This means that you are pushing yourself to evolve. You are tough on yourself sometimes. You want so much to evolve that you are harassing your spirituality. This can directly manifest itself in your behavior or via a person in your immediate surroundings. So sometimes, you attract people who push you to go faster. This is because we attract what we are.

You may have had some bad experiences concerning this subject because you've got memories of this type in your soul, whether you are aware of them or not. Sometimes, you don't sufficiently respect the evolution of others. Therefore, you encounter your mirrors.

As an example, let's say you could find yourself with a therapist or a spiritual coach who is excessively motivated about your progress and who has taken it upon himself to ensure that you advance. Some therapists who have not completed healing work on themselves become exaggeratedly enthusiastic about healing others. So, there you are with this therapist and you ask more questions than usual and he starts *pushing* you, getting rather impatient because he would like you to have already understood certain things. These are the kind of dynamics you sometimes find yourself experiencing because you create them, although not necessarily consciously. So, in this dream, Up Above wanted to attract your attention to this tendency that you have of pushing others to go faster in their spiritual life, which causes you to attract people that push in the same way — even if you are not aware of it.

We must learn to develop our autonomy and to stop giving others our power. We can trust ourselves and ask Heaven for answers. Therapists have their place: they are there to inspire us and to share their knowledge and experience with us. But we must examine and digest the information they give us, decide whether we shall accept to apply it or not and, above all, know that we must respect our own rhythm by completing the stages one by one. We mustn't let ourselves be pushed around like the Pope in the dream.

Occasionally, you might also play the role of the one who does the pushing. For example, you might want your son to start out on a spiritual path and when you are attending a lecture or a workshop, you insist, "Come on! Why don't you come?" Sometimes, we talk about dreams and Angels but we are too emissive and so we scare people. We need to be receptive when we speak to others and be able to perceive how much information they can take at that particular moment.

You are the best person to understand this dream because you have experienced all kinds of situations regarding this state of consciousness or this attitude. A dream is an X-ray of the conscience. When I interpret a dream, I don't have to ask the person, "Do you think this is true?" I know what the person is experiencing because it is written in his dream. Very specific forces are present within the person at the time of the dream. You are the man who hassled the Pope and you are also the harassed Pope. So, sometimes you harass others and sometimes you are the one who's harassed. You can incarnate one or other character in the dream because they are linked by the fact that they are actually one and the same state of consciousness.

What is interesting in this dream is that the Self is starting to talk to these parts that push and are pushed. You have become aware of this force within you, and you have begun to heal yourself. In addition to this, you are giving yourself the time needed to complete each stage. Previously, you may have had a tendency to say to yourself, "Go on! You're not making progress fast enough," and be rather hard on yourself. Whereas now, you say to yourself, "I'll follow my rhythm. I'll take my time to complete the stages." This is why you tell the man who harassed the Pope to stop and you succeeded because he left.

Yes, madam. (Participant: I have a question. When someone in our circle is negative and we would like to help this person evolve, how do we go about it?)

Someone who is negative is generally closed. When we want to help someone who is not open to evolving spiritually, the first thing we need to realize is that he alone has the key to open his door. Because normally, when a person is locked in, the lock is on the inside. (*laughter*)

In any case, if a person is closed, we shouldn't try to open him without the permission of his soul. Because if we try to do that, the risks of him closing his mind are even greater. At any rate, if we manage to open them up, the opening will only be temporary—it won't last. I'll give you an example. An acquaintance tells us that he would like to change jobs but is afraid of making a mistake by leaving his current one. This person has reservations when it comes to anything that is not officially recognized. Let's say we personally give a lot of credit to alternative medicine. So we say to the person, all enthusiastically, "You see, I did it—I left my job—I became a therapist and things are going fine. You can do it too. All you have to do is take a course in massage therapy and, you'll see, you'll be able to help others." And we go on and on because we are enthusiastic for the person.

Despite his reservations, we manage to open him up a little and at a particular moment, in a *positive* flush, he decides to take a massage therapy course. Four months later he quits his job. But his plan doesn't work; he doesn't have the necessary talent to continue his training. So he loses confidence in himself and is completely devastated and even more closed than before. He wants nothing more to do with alternative medicine and starts up an association against people who practice massage therapy, all because he wasn't prepared and now bitterly regrets giving up his job.

Of course, this example is a bit exaggerated, but it helps us understand that we must respect each person's rhythm. In the area of spirituality, the idea is the same. We must always respect the other person's evolution. This is the principle condition if we are to be able to help him.

The goal of spirituality is first and foremost the development of qualities and virtues. When we are kind and gentle, and we always see others as parts of ourselves like in a dream, and we are not constantly trying to open everyone up to spirituality, then no one will feel as though they're being pushed. They feel loved just as they are.

As for myself, when I meet a person who is not open to dreams and symbols, I don't want them to open up. It isn't important to me. I love them as they are. I respect them and understand that they are in a certain frame of mind, that they are experiencing particular soul-states that are different than mine, and that's fine. With this attitude, I can communicate with everyone because

31

my energy is not the energy of someone who wants to convince people to transform themselves.

(Participant: Yes, but what if this person opens up and then closes himself up again? One moment he's open then, all of a sudden, he's completely closed up again.)

Of course, the person can ask us questions and we must allow him to experience this opening, but we have to respect him just as much when he closes up again — we must respect his reservations. When he is open, it's time to talk to him a little bit, to give him information, perspectives, but as soon as we feel him closing up again, we stop. We don't say too much — just enough. It is wise to allow others to transform themselves at their own rhythm.

Let's go back to the dream. We have seen that you have a tendency to *push* the Pope and that you are beginning to be aware of this. Rest assured that when you have cleansed the memories linked to this problem, no one will ever be able to push you — yourself included — and you will no longer have a tendency to insist that others follow the same path as you.

(Dreamer: Yes, I realize that it can change. But I haven't had this attitude for very long. It's after certain events that occurred in my life that I started behaving like this.) Ah, there you are! (Dreamer: But, I didn't know that my dream could be so clear.) So revealing?

(Dreamer: So, I have to stop talking about spirituality?) No, you simply have to be aware of these forces and learn to master them. We mustn't stop ourselves from sharing our experience — because, of course, we can go to the other extreme, and that isn't what I mean at all. You will see that by cleansing the memories linked to this imbalance, you will be able to communicate in a new way, in a way that is more respectful of others.

Then, in the dream, you turned around. Here, we have the notion of what is behind us, at our back. The back represents the past. An Asian woman was at the table and she didn't wait for the others before beginning to eat. Through this character, you were being shown what kind of memories are at the origin of your tendency to push others.

32

Like all other countries, China has both a positive and negative symbolism. In the dream, it was the distorted side that was being manifested, since the Chinese woman should have waited for the other guests before starting to eat. In China, for a long time, most people lacked material resources. This country is presently experiencing great expansion on the material level, but this is relatively recent. The materialistic philosophy as a cultural movement is also relatively new. This country has an extraordinary spiritual heritage, an ancestral philosophy imbued with spirituality. This is a resource of great richness. One day, when the materialistic phase has passed, this great ancestral wealth will resume its rightful place.

So the Chinese woman represented a part of you that manifests within—because it was a woman—and this part feels a certain lack, and it is this lack that pushes you to act too quickly. Here again is the idea of not respecting the rhythm of things. So, this part of your being has needs that are too great.

This is a problem that concerns many, many people. This dream is a good example of the fact that when we force others, when we push them, it's because we have a feeling of lack within ourselves. People who have memories of lack often eat or act too quickly, in a way that lacks refinement. These memories create a compulsion in the person and this has a clear influence on his behavior.

Some people are compulsive talkers. They do not listen enough. When we talk too much, we no longer hear anything and we can't feel or sense the state that the other person is in. Neither can we be in contact with our own state of consciousness. Why are silence and meditation so fundamental to spiritual development? Because they help us listen to our inner self. Also, because we have to be calm and listen to our own self in order to be able to use our subtle senses—to hear beyond words, to see beyond images, etc. When we are busy saying to ourselves, "I'm going to do this and then I'm going to do that," we don't have the necessary receptivity to be in contact with ourselves or others.

When we want to do things that affect other people, we don't even know if they are ready. We don't take the time to observe if they have reached that point, because we are led by our compulsions. So what happens is that we end up pushing everyone.

Our family travels a lot for the lecture tours. We have acquired good discipline and beautiful harmony with regard to being on the move. I don't wait until the last minute to say it is time to leave. I don't say, "I'm ready, let's go," forcing everyone around me to hurry. No, no. The night before, I tell everyone what time we have to leave and, 10 or 15 minutes before departure time, I remind them. This way, everyone feels peaceful while preparing their things. And when we leave, everyone feels good and everything flows harmoniously.

At work, the same thing applies. Many volunteers help our non-profit organization with the preparation of lectures and workshops. Again, I don't come up at the last minute and say, "Could you find a hall for tomorrow's lecture?" We need to plan projects well to avoid jostling people and to create beautiful harmony.

So, the idea of pushing, of not following the natural rhythm, is expressed a second time in the dream—through the character of the Chinese woman—except that in this scene we can see the reason for this attitude: a feeling of lack. In this dream, you were being told, "Accept your rhythm; respect it. Be careful not to push and not to hold back."

Everyone has their own rhythm and we must never compare ourselves to others. This is very important. When we compare ourselves to others we are in a great distortion: it is a feeling of jealousy or envy that motivates our attitude. When we advance in this manner—when we push ourselves to advance and make progress—the results don't last because the movement is artificial. In order to achieve great transformations, we really must proceed with our heart, with Knowledge and inspiration, and accept to advance at our own rhythm.

(Dreamer: Can the tendency to push oneself be provoked by different situations? By our surroundings, our environment?) Yes, but the environment is also you. It's the result of unconscious memories that manifest in this way. They are in the soul. (Dreamer: Since birth?) Well, we can experience situations in childhood but they are always linked to forces that already dwell in our soul, to memories of our other lives. A dream is an open door onto the whole of the unconscious, not just to what we have experienced in this life.

(Dreamer: I understand. A few years ago, I went through a difficult time and since then I've developed this tendency to push. I'm only just beginning to be aware of it. It's true that I don't put on the brakes.)

But we can see that you are trying to reason with this part of yourself: you told the man to stop pushing the Pope and you told the Chinese woman to wait for the others, to think of others. So, you are talking to this disorganized part that pushes, that doesn't listen to common sense. This dream bears witness to the fact that you are beginning to work on these forces.

(Dreamer: I can sometimes feel this restraint. It's as though there were two people in me and that one was trying to fight the other. But sometimes it doesn't succeed. I let go from time to time and then, at some point, it starts all over again.)

It's interesting when you say *I feel the two people in me*, when speaking of characters in a dream. In dreams, we are shown the forces that are activated. These are the forces that create our reality, the way we advance, speak, love, etc. A dream generates life; it is not simply a series of trivial images. (Dreamer: Thank you very much.) You're welcome.

Does anyone else have a question or a dream they would like interpreted?

Yes, madam. (Dreamer: May I use the mike?) Sure. (Dreamer: First of all I would like to thank you for manifesting all that you do because, partly through your existence, I discover truths of mine. I would also like to attest to the fact that, following my experience with disorders and illnesses such as fibromyalgia and others, while I was immobilized, my dreams showed me that I could heal myself, get back on my feet and run. This is something that I undertook four years ago, through different methods. Your teaching is new to me, because I didn't know of your existence even though I have read a lot. And about two years ago, I think, I came across one of your books and I closed it over—it probably wasn't the right time. Maybe it's because I couldn't have talked to you like this two years ago. I am experiencing a great awakening of consciousness—if I can call it that—through health, sickness, and also through the experience of death of members of my family. I have lost a dozen people in my close circle with an open heart that has led me to understand that death is not the end at all and that it holds a wealth of teaching. In fact, I have dreams telling me… In one of my dreams, *I was asked if I was the only one in France to mention certain words and whether or not I would have the courage to do so publicly. I was asked to choose and I replied, "Yes, I'll have the courage to speak out." Then I found myself in thin air and I was told, "Ok then, jump into the void." So I jumped. Then I found myself on a cloud. When I got through the cloud, I found myself on a raging seashore and I was asked, "Are you still sure or are you beginning to have doubts?" I said, "I have no doubts anymore." Then I was told, "All right then, walk." So I walked on the water. I put my foot on the water and my foot became a star. When I took the next step, my other foot became a star and my hand became a star. Then my other hand became a star. This is how I moved forward. All of a sudden the raging sea parted. It became very bright and there was a great beam of light. I suddenly found myself in front of the body of my best friend who had died of leukemia. And faced with this dead body, I simply put my hands on it and asked myself, "Carole, are you still afraid of death or are you no longer afraid of death? And have you understood well what's been explained to you?" And I answered my question, saying, "No, I am no longer afraid of death." Then I was told, "Well, since you are no longer afraid, We're going to give you a gift." And this gift was a very brilliant light above this body. Then I levitated—well, I rose. And there I saw a luminous being of great beauty—that had a deep resemblance to an image on one of your works—a being with a beard, all in white, who welcomed me into a kind of magical garden where I found everyone that I had lost—and my children as well. They were all there. The animals that I lost were there, in fact, everyone that I love. Then, over to the side, there was the celestial cinema and, also, all the actors writing the scenarios that are being experienced at this moment in time were there.* I've also got a lot of humor in relation to everything that's happened to me because I had a dream where *Coluche* (a famous French comedian, now deceased) called out to me, "*OK, great! Disease of the invisible. All right then, now create the treatment for the invisible. Go on then, Carole! Dare to write.*" And that's what I'm doing now, I'm writing. To continue my dream, *this luminous being had leather sandals on his feet. He also had a leather bag and, inside this bag, there was a book on which was inscribed Kassiopeia with a K. And he explained to me…* By the way, can I just say I'm encouraged that all my thoughts, everything that is inside me, comes true. And for me, this is a precious gift, since it is thanks to all those dreams that I am alive and well today, although a little out of phase as though in tune with a different wavelength, when I return from this dream world. Because, once we've received these precious gifts, we still have to be able to express them, whether through the voice, the written word, or through art or other ways. And again, its raison d'être has to be understood correctly—which is not always easy either, I believe. *The book was a very ancient leather-bound book. The man told me I could bring it back to Earth. Well, I was delighted because I thought to myself, 'Well, of course! This is the book that I have to write.'* I don't know what was in that book. I simply saw the title and I have some clues. It's *Kassiopeia* with a K—not with a C—to symbolize the Universe, of course. So, that's where I am at the moment. It is true that my writings have taken a certain turn. Well, what I'd like to say with all of this is that through my life, through this incarnation, I only have one beautiful message for you: death is for the body only, as for love, it is eternal. There you are. That's what I can tell you.) (Several voices: Thank you.)

Thank you for sharing this with us. This dream is very interesting. You'll see. We're going to go into its very advanced philosophical content.

In a dream, everything is symbolic and each symbol relates to the other symbols. Therefore, at the very beginning, you were being asked questions. You were asked if you were the only one in France who was able to say certain things. This is what the voice asked you and you said yes. Then, you went on to another level, so to speak. This beginning of the dream is a fundamental key to understanding what follows because, in terms of consciousness, it is as though you were the only one in the whole of France to have certain powers.

I too received this type of dream at the beginning of my spiritual path. These dreams showed me that, in the state of consciousness I was experiencing at that time, I was the only one who was spiritual on Earth, and that the rest of the Universe was not spiritual. I was experiencing the awakening of my spiritual self—of my true spirituality—but this Self was going to have to teach all of the different parts of my being, the entire population of my inner universe, to become spiritual too.

France has a positive and a negative symbolism, as do all countries. The positive aspects of France are its mental strength, refinement, a vast, widespread general culture, and abundance—there are a lot of resources and many different climates for a country that is relatively small. At the moment, France is on a very privileged axis of the planet.

However, the fact that you were the only one in France to have certain powers leads us to consider the negative aspect since such exclusivity is not positive. The negative aspects of France are its tendency to be hyper-rationalistic and to criticize, its complex social organization and culture of superficiality, its constant search for recognition, its insubordination and lack of spirituality. Also, a growing sense of aggressiveness.

In Canada, a lot more human warmth can be felt in the social environment. Of course, Canadians also have their weaknesses but in France we see a lot of aggressiveness and coldness that comes from critical thinking. Everywhere in public places—on the street, in stores, even at toll stations—when people say hello, it's feels as though they are punching us at the same time. There are exceptions, of course, including those who are on a spiritual journey. In a way, these people are new seedlings; the more we work on ourselves, the more we develop the positive forces of all the countries. In fact, that's our soul's goal.

So, in this dream, you were being invited to work on those inner parts that lack spirituality.

Then, you began walking on water; you had enough confidence and courage to move forward on the rough sea. The water represented your emotions and the rough sea, your emotional turbulence. You managed to move forward despite the turbulence but don't forget that—among the 60 million parts represented by the French—only one part of you has this courage and this confidence. It's the same idea as before. I too had dreams where I managed to do extraordinary, hyper-spiritual things, and I was sure that the rest of the Earth was less advanced than I was.

In the beginning, this belief gave me a feeling of superiority then, at one point, I realized there was a split: I felt cut off from people. I felt spiritual but totally out of phase with the rest of the world, with the entire planet. I used to watch TV and I felt both uncomfortable and a total stranger to everything people said. I was under the impression that nobody could understand me, understand who I was, what I was experiencing. This made me very sad, of course.

At the same time, I felt a need to be acknowledged and I felt frustrated about it. Often, without realizing it, we slip into distortions through the beauty of the message that we wish to bring. We can even distort the message—as beautiful as it might be—when we absolutely want to communicate it to others, because at that moment, we would do anything to accomplish this and, in order to do it, we can push and force others. A spiritual path is quite something!

Some people can neglect or abandon their children. They can totally disorganize their family to bring the message of spirituality to others. A classic example is the man who abandons everything to become a monk and cloisters himself up somewhere. That's all very well but his children are sad and they don't see him anymore. He believes he will reach the Light but he'll have to come back in another life to take care of his family, of the children he left behind who were sad and bewildered. This is because he won't have taken care of his works; he didn't know how to balance his life. He too will have to be abandoned by one of his parents and later by a spouse in order to be able to understand that it is not right to leave your children, to leave your family.

This is not what this dream is about, of course, but the example I have just given you illustrates that we can achieve certain levels of lack of responsibility when we experience splits of this kind.

So, you were able to walk on the raging sea. This attests to the fact that you have managed to maintain your balance and a high level of detachment throughout emotions and initiations. Of course, this has greatly strengthened you. You now have confidence in yourself and your healing powers. The fact that your hands and your feet became stars as you moved forward on the sea shows that your spiritual self has become very strong.

But once again, we have to reposition ourselves in the context of the dream—depicted by the idea that you were the only one in France who could say certain things. Despite all the positive aspects of this dream, it is the kind of dream that leaders of sects might receive, that could be sent to those people who convey a spiritual message from a sick ego and very powerful spiritual will. Therefore, you must remember that there are still many parts within you that need to be educated.

When you mentioned the book and, in particular, the need to express yourself, behind the word *understood*, I felt that you suffer from other people's lack of understanding. I perceived a kind of split or discrepancy such as we might feel when we wonder why the world isn't spiritual when we are convinced that everyone should be. There was a kind of ideological struggle with regard to ordinary, everyday life. The dream attests to this very eloquently.

Of course, you are experiencing more and more elevated states of consciousness and you are rediscovering a great potential—represented in the dream by the people who have died, that you see again. You are also trying to heal a part of your being which, in terms of consciousness, has leukemia.

What does leukemia represent? This is a disease that affects the blood. When we think of blood, we think of the color red, the color of the first chakra, the chakra of action and materialization. Leukemia is a form of cancer and cancer is a manifestation of anarchy, because cancerous cells are cells whose genetic code has been de-structured. So leukemia represents an accumulation of ancient memories that have created anarchy in the different ways we materialize. It is a purification process of memories of erroneous actions and an accumulation of inner conflicts from one life to the next that end up creating forces in a person that eventually result in leukemia. We can be a very good person, be very open spiritually but still harbor within us old reservoirs of memories that we haven't cleansed yet, and the disease appears for that purpose.

When illness occurs, we sometimes have to go so far as to die in order to attain the levels of detachment and experience the opening of our consciousness that is planned for our Program. Faced with our own illness and death, we either evolve spiritually or we rebel. A half-hearted attitude is difficult to maintain in such circumstances because we face the inevitable, which leads us to reflect upon things we never really thought about before.

40

In the dream, after having put your hands on the body of your friend, you rose up, you levitated. This shows that you have access to a higher level of consciousness, to a more Universal vision of life regarding death. Then you saw actors who were writing scripts or scenarios. So you are becoming aware that everything is organized, that everything is planned. We can see that your spiritual self that has become very strong, as we saw earlier, is creating a very concrete opening. The hardships that you endured through illness and the death of people you loved have led you to experience very powerful things and to greatly develop your spirituality. And this is wonderful; it's a great gift. But you must be very careful because you are now entering a universal dimension and this means new responsibilities for you. Your ego is still present and it can try to take all of the credit for this progress. You can also lose yourself in the Universe. So you must be twice as vigilant. As it happens, the name *Cassiopeia*—the name of a constellation—evokes universal dimensions. This symbol attests to the expansion of conscience you are experiencing and that you surely feel.

The man who offered you the book had leather sandals and a leather bag. The book itself was covered in this material. Well, leather belongs to the animal kingdom; it is linked to the instincts. Therefore, we see that some of the ways you advance and protect or keep your knowledge are controlled by personal needs because the animal side represents needs.

Now, with regard to Coluche who challenged you to write, you must remember that this character represented a state of consciousness—as is the case with all of the other symbols in the dream. Coluche was a happy-go-lucky type of person, a lovely person—he had lovely qualities—and he made France laugh. However, he was not a Heavenly Guide. It wasn't a being of Light who told you to write about the illnesses or diseases of the invisible: it is a part of you, a part that was shown through the character traits of Coluche.

In order to know which parts exactly, we only need to analyze the way this man communicated and the nature of what he broadcast through the media. If, in your writing, you are motivated by the challenge of your inner Coluche, you may become sarcastic. Based

41

on the fact that you are the only spiritual person in your inner France, that we saw earlier, you could be very hard on people that you consider as not spiritual enough and this would appear in your writing.

This dream is interesting because it shows that broadcasting forces have been activated in your program—you have a book in progress, all of that. But you must continue to cleanse the memories that create splits or discrepancies in your being. Bookshops all over the world are full of books. There are very nice books, very good books, but some are also full of distortions.

Very often what is written in books lacks wisdom and love. This is why, as a spiritual person, it is important to develop discernment. Not to eat anything without thinking. We must address people with love when we broadcast, we must be in a state of love, because knowledge without love is poison. Why is it poison? Because what is essential is absent. Qualities are what is important, not knowledge simply for the sake of knowledge.

It is relatively easy to become a doctor, a lawyer or an engineer. Four to ten years of university and there you are, that's it! But to learn kindness and respect for everyone can take many lives. Many doctors and surgeons aren't even capable of being nice to the nurses they work with. What happens when a house has no foundation, just a nice facade and nice curtains? At a given moment, pffft! the walls crack and the house collapses. The same idea applies to the world of the spirit: if the person doesn't make proper use of what he receives from Up Above, in another life he will have nothing—no more wealth, no more diplomas.

So, you were shown this spiritual intensity and these broadcasting forces in the dream, but you must continue to cleanse your memories. Otherwise, your writings will have an aura of leather rather than Light.

The book *Kassiopeia* represented Knowledge with a capital K, spiritual knowledge that you are now learning to integrate but that you have not yet integrated. Since it was an ancient book, the forces that are awakening within you come from other lives. It is as though you're in the process of reclaiming a certain potential to believe in the Divine and to reach people. However, you must make sure you don't go back to old forms of broadcasting and that you don't convey knowledge and concepts that you, yourself, haven't yet integrated. You must continue to cleanse all of your inner France so as to install therein lasting harmony and succeed in seeing spirituality in everyone, whether they are nice or not.

On the spiritual path, some people are in kindergarten and others are more advanced, but everyone is at the school of Life. If a person is aggressive or violent, there are things he needs to understand, which might take three or four lives, but one day he will succeed, one day he'll understand.

We know that we have integrated the Divine States of Consciousness when nothing or no one bothers us. The Law of Resonance that explains that Life is a dream leads us to the Highway of Knowledge and one day, we see God's Work everywhere, in everyone and in all situations.

WORKSHOP

Dreams are Parallel Worlds

(Participant: When you speak of dreams in which we visit Parallel Worlds, do you mean that we become disembodied, that we leave our carnal envelope in order to receive information? How does this happen?)

It all depends on the type of dream because there are many types. Generally speaking, in the beginning, our dreams are simply personal dreams that don't go beyond the limits of our personal computer. God or Universal Consciousness creates virtual spaces or Parallel Worlds for us that are sometimes so real that we might think we're on Earth. We see landscapes, we hear birds and we smell things, we feel. Everything is concrete.

The forces or powers that God uses to create these images already exist within us and once we have finished dreaming, the images disappear in the same way that they appeared. This is because we are visiting our own memories and forces that live within us. All in all, these dreams are not that different from what we experience on Earth—there, as here, we continue experimenting that leads us to experience positive and negative situations, to see the probabilities of what we will become if we behave this way or if we do not change.

Dreams are motors of life; they set in motion the program of what's going to happen in our life. It's amazing all that we can be led to experience after a dream that features something as simple as, say, a *light that has appeared in a bedroom.* After such a dream, we could find, for example, a letter among our wife's personal effects that proves she is having an affair with another man. The light has lit up our intimate life and it's not just a faint night light; no, no, it can be quite a spotlight! We begin to think and see things from a different perspective. We think, 'For some time now I've been feeling sad but I didn't know why. Now, I understand; my soul could feel this situation.'

This type of dream takes place within us, on the inside, so to speak; it's as if we were opening an application in our computer.

45

However, we can also visit other people's souls in our dreams. In such cases, it's as if we were connecting to a network that enables us to visit other people's computers. With this type of dream, we wouldn't need to find the actual letter in our spouse's personal effects—we would see our spouse in the arms of his/her lover because we would be *visiting* his/her soul. But I have to say that we must be very careful before thinking we are visiting others. Because most of the time, we are in our own program and we can see our own memories related to infidelity through the image of our spouse and an eventual lover. People who have memories of infidelity within themselves will have these dreams and it will not mean their spouse is having an affair.

It's also possible to visit the Program of whole communities; in this case it's as if we were connecting to the Internet and accessing a whole load of information from all over the world. Thus, we can also know the Program of a city, a region or a nation. We can even go into the Universal Server and see the movements of Creation.

It's not necessary to have achieved Enlightenment to visit other people's souls. It's possible, in the same night, to have a dream about our sister where she simply represents aspects of ourselves, and then have another one where we visit her soul.

How do we make sense of all this? In the beginning, as I mentioned earlier, we stay in our personal computer, then, as we gradually integrate wisdom, we can go beyond the solely personal and visit others. When we visit other people's souls in a dream, we don't visit as mere tourists—there is always something for us to learn about ourselves. This allows us to develop wisdom, since being made aware of certain things can awaken negative forces within us. On visiting a friend's soul, if we realize that he has negative thoughts about us, this is not necessarily easy to cope with—we could feel like putting an end to this relationship, this friendship.

Imagine if you knew everything that your friends and family think about you! Thoughts have a hidden side—we don't tell others everything that we think about them. Even our spouse; we love her very much but sometimes she gets on our nerves but we don't necessarily tell her—we behave as if everything's fine. Therefore, the more we evolve, the more we have the possibility to see, in dreams, exactly what others think, what they feel and what they are going through or are to go through. When we work with the Law of Resonance—always referring back to ourselves when we are bothered—we often experience an increase in this type of dream.

In fact, to develop this habit, it is recommended to always refer back to ourselves when we dream of someone we know; we should always say to ourselves, "Ah! He represents a part of me."

Referring to computers is really useful to help us describe the world of the spirit. The school subject referring to this is called I.T., which means Information Technology. In French we say *informatique*, which has the same root as *inform, information*. Similarly, for the spirit, information leads to power. Information gives us the possibility to act successfully, to deal with matter and to materialize. The first thing the Prime Minister or the President of a country sees when he walks into his office in the morning—the file at the top of the pile—is the Secret Service file. In it he finds out what's going on behind the scenes that no one else knows about. In that secret file, information is condensed so that he can grasp what is going on as quickly as possible. The same applies to dreams: information is condensed and it reveals the kind of program that's been activated, in the form of its previous history, its present manifestations or its results.

Initiates have the possibility to go behind the veil, have true access to the collective unconscious and hence know the movement toward materialization before it reaches the concrete or material level. And, like the Guides, they can intervene if they receive permission to do so.

So, we begin in our own laboratory. We study ourselves, we say, "Ah! This force is manifesting itself within me. There's a storm. There's water and things are being stirred up. So, I must work on my emotions." Then, later on, when we've acquired a certain level of stability and harmony, we can develop our spiritual powers and help our friends and family in dreams.

Is there a dream or another question?

Yes, madam. (Dreamer: I had a dream about two years ago or more, and it had to do with transport. *I had to take a plane headed for Canada or Quebec. The plane was in two parts—a front part* and a back part. It was huge. At first, I was in the back part where there were a lot of people—crowds of people. It was a bit like the main hall in an airport. At one point, a steward told me that I wasn't to stay there, that I was well used to being there, and that now I had to go to the front part of the plane. I started to move toward the front but to get there I had to go through a very difficult passage. In this passage, there was a sort of big porthole window in the floor that let in a lot of light. Around the outer rim of the window, the ledge was quite solid but I wasn't so sure about the middle. An inner voice was saying to me, "But you have to go across it." With a little help and encouragement, I managed to cross over to the other side. There, we could sit down and we had a great view. It was vast because there were great big picture windows. The view was truly magnificent. It was really obvious that the other people there were more at ease than I was. That's all I remember.) That's fine. Thank you, madam.

We'll make a list of the elements of this dream.

First of all, *The Self*, since you were in the dream. *The Self must take a plane; huge plane*—this is important. *In two parts: front and back. The Self in the back; a lot of people.* There were more people in the back than in the front, isn't that right? (Dreamer: Oh, yes! There was hardly anyone in the front section.)

Then one of the cabin crew said to you…(Dreamer: He said, "It's straight ahead, just go straight ahead!") Was it a man? (Dreamer: Yes.) That's an important detail. (Dreamer: He was a bit annoyed. Rather than being friendly, he seemed to be saying, "You can fend for yourself." Actually, he more or less sent me packing.) All right. *Steward rather annoyed.*

Then you had to go through a passageway to get to the front. (Dreamer: It was a bit like having to cross from one railroad car to the next.) OK. And there was a kind of window in the floor? (Dreamer: Yes. I either had to walk across it or go around the side. I didn't feel very safe. There was a lot of light.) All right. So, we write *Passageway; glass floor; light; fear.* There we are.

Then, you managed to get across thanks to encouragements, and you joined people who had already gone through that passageway. *The Self manages to cross; difficulties but encouragement; other people.* Then *Magnificent view.*

Did you know right from the beginning that the plane was leaving for Canada? (Dreamer: Yes, I did, but I truly realized it once I was in the glass-window part because of the magnificent view. For me—since I live in France—Canada represents immense space, an endless, unlimited horizon.) All right. That's fine.

Let's begin. To understand the symbolism of the airplane, we simply need to remember that it flies in the air. What does the world of air correspond to? (Participant: Thought.) That's right. Therefore the huge plane represented a very powerful, concentrated thought-form that you had at that time.

We have to go back two years because you have changed since you had this dream. Some dreams focus on long periods of time but this one described your state of mind on that day only.

Therefore, on that day, a thought-form within you was very strong. And that thought concerned—symbolically speaking—a trip to Canada. When we travel by plane, we leave from the ground, we go up into the air and we fly toward a destination. Therefore, in terms of consciousness, to travel by plane consists in leaving a concrete situation, going into our thoughts and heading toward a new part of our conscience, sort of like we were going from one continent to another.

In terms of consciousness, the entire planet Earth is part of our being and we can go from one *country* to another in our thoughts. Each country represents a state of consciousness with its positive and negative aspects. Each person must one day transcend the *negative* of every country and *incarnate* the major, essential quality of each one.

So, on that day, your mind was chockfull of thought—it was very intense—and those thoughts were leading you in one direction, symbolically to Canada. We will see what this meant a little later.

At first, you were in the rear of the plane. When we find ourselves in the front of a vehicle, we see where we are going, and if we have access to the controls we can control, we can command and master the movements of the vehicle. Whereas, when we are at the back, we are more or less at the mercy of the person driving and we can't see much. The numerous people who were in the rear with you represented those parts of you that were *following* the idea of going to Canada.

Then, the passageway you went through from the rear to the front of the plane represented a movement on the thought level, where you went from the attitude of someone who follows an idea — like a child following his parents — to a person who understands and so can be in command of his path, his progress. You were shown this change in attitude and your willingness to be more conscious of what you were experiencing.

The steward was a bit annoyed when he told you to go to the front. This character represented a part of your being that knew you were ready to move to another level and who thought you were not going fast enough. Therefore, in your will to change your attitude, you were a bit impatient, and this impatience was going to manifest itself on the action level because the steward was a man.

Then, *Passageway; glass-floor; light; fear.* That day, you wanted to reach a better understanding of your life and, indeed, you experienced an opening on the thought level. However, when the opening occurred, you had a feeling of vertigo, as if the ground could drop away under your feet. We sometimes get this feeling during initiations when we're getting ready to move to another level. We have lovely thoughts, we truly wish to evolve, but we can see the extent of the changes the transformation will lead to on the material level — symbolically speaking, we look down through a window — and this is very scary. We say to ourselves, "Yes, I want to make some profound changes in my life but if I do change, this or that is going to happen," and we really feel destabilized.

Because of the characters that were already at the front of the plane, we can see that some parts of you had already gone through this passageway. These parts gave you the necessary courage to continue advancing. Therefore, you managed to get through the difficulties associated with this type of thought. All of this was going on in your head that day.

Once you'd negotiated the passageway, you had a magnificent view. So, that day, the minute you crossed over, you became aware of the place you were headed for, aware of the states that you now had access to.

What does Canada indicate in terms of conscience? The positive aspect of Canada—because it was the positive aspect that was present in this dream—is its vastness, its large spaces. You said this yourself. It is also the aspect of the heart.

In Canada, we can feel more warmth and love; it's more heartwarming than here in France. When we come to France, we notice the intellectual side of things is more developed. The French are more refined and have a much greater general culture than Canadians. Of course, this can be positive or negative; it all depends on the degree of evolution of the people living in this beautiful country. I'm French myself—I have dual nationality, French and Canadian—and I love France as much as I love Canada.

In truth, I love all the countries in the world, because a country is like a child. We love all of our children but this does not stop us from evaluating them—from seeing their strengths and weaknesses. The more we are aware of our children's strengths and weaknesses, the better we can help them grow and surpass their limits. The same applies to countries.

On the negative side, France has the faults of its qualities. A lot of French people put too much emphasis on culture and knowledge, and sometimes a person can get lost because things can get so complicated when the intellect is cut off from the heart. For some people, if we have cheese with strawberry jam, goodness me! This is just terrible according to certain French people! (*laughter*)

I'll always remember a story one of our friends told us. He's a man who helps us a lot; he's a great philanthropist in our Canadian organization. This great humanist is an executive in a multinational corporation and his work involves traveling to many different countries. Once he was in a restaurant in Paris and he asked for butter. The waiter looked down his nose at him in disdain as if putting butter on bread was a terrible thing to do, as if this practice was solely responsible for all the obesity in America. Our friend could feel the waiter's prejudice on the subject and his lack of openness to others.

Not all of the French are like this of course. This is the negative, reverse side of the great refinement that we find in this beautiful country and it is manifested mostly in people whose minds are closed to other cultures.

We've also noticed a lot of aggression in France — at least a lot more than in Canada. Here in Alsace (French department or state), however, it's as though we were in another country. I'm not saying this to flatter you. In a way Alsace is a mixture of France, Switzerland and Germany. The *structure* aspect that you've developed generates energy that is very different than the one we feel in the rest of France. You have a whole *baggage*, a whole collective history that has led you to develop this structure because your ancestors experienced rather difficult situations. In moments of great distress, we have to get organized and this results in profound changes that take place in the collective consciousness. For example, before criticizing this or that, we think a little and we say, "We're happy to have what we have. We could have nothing." We've also noticed a positive German influence since the war didn't only bring negative aspects — people learn lessons and draw knowledge from such experiences.

A region can be compared to a person: it has its unconscious, its mentality and other individual characteristics that it has developed from its experiences. The collective memory creates an egregore, a form of intelligent energy that resides in the people who come from the country, the region or the city or town in question.

In fact, it's the basis of these egregores upon which the place and date of people's incarnations are decided. Each person has specific experiences to go through and specific states of consciousness to cleanse in his lifetime because he has to transcend certain weaknesses and cultivate certain strengths — this is his Program. So, he is born in the country and region that will best allow him to encounter these situations and states of consciousness. Up Above, They say, "Such and such a soul will be born in India, this one will be born in Africa, and this other one in Australia."

For example, someone who is hyper-structured or too rigid might reincarnate in Africa where social life is rather disorganized. He will have to learn to live in a relaxed manner and by applying structure — that lovely quality that he acquired in previous lives — he will help other Africans get organized and become more structured. Of course, for a while, he will feel really torn, as if his previous personalities, now unconscious, keep telling him, "Everything is upside down here. We need to do this, we need to do this and this and this!" and his more recent personalities answer, "It's ok. Did you see how beautiful that bird is?" (*laughter*) Throughout his life he will spend his life trying to resolve his great inner divide and through this process he will integrate the positive side of Africa.

One day, we have to be able to contemplate nature while maintaining a well-organized life. The general idea is to come to a point where we integrate the qualities of all of the countries in our conscience and thus become a free spirit, a universal spirit.

(Participant: Could you tell us the positive and negative aspects of Switzerland and Germany?) Of course. In Switzerland, wherever we go, we truly have a feeling of abundance. It is one of the rare countries where money is dealt with as if it were simply paper.

(Participant: That's because it's other people's money.) Yes, but that's a different question. I'm talking about the positive aspect. Abundance is a quality; it is one of the Divine, Angelic Qualities. Of course, the distortion of this Quality is very present in Switzerland, and I totally agree with you, sir.

Generally, the positive and negative aspects of a country come from the same *department*, from the same nature, in the sense that, pushed to the extreme, a quality generally begins to lean toward the negative side.

Switzerland is a neutral country because it does not take political sides. Yet it welcomes the money of a great number of people whose activities are not always *clean*—this is no doubt what you were referring to. It's a well-known fact that numbered bank accounts camouflage a lot of illicit activities. It's as if the problems of the entire world, often generated by atrocious activities, were concealed under the carpet because of this so-called neutrality.

There can also be a certain rigidity linked to this. When we wish to project an image of cleanliness on the outside and we are not clean on the inside, we become rigid in order to maintain credibility.

In Switzerland, tidiness and order is also quite remarkable. I, myself, am married to a Swiss woman, so I've been able to observe this particular aspect. For example, Christiane used to wear her slippers even when there was no need to. She liked cleanliness so much that in the beginning she couldn't stand the least speck of dust or the slightest stain on anything. If you come to our house, you'll see, it's very clean. (*laughter*) At home, it's Swiss quality with my dear wife. (*laughter*)

As for Germany, its positive aspects are structure, discipline, respect for law and order and thoroughness: all the great qualities that ensure solidity, continuity and durability. When we buy a product made in Germany, we know it will last a long time because it is well constructed—it is built to last.

The negative side of Germany is extreme structure. We may think in particular of the emotional problems that rigidity can create. When Germans drink they can really go over the top; they can be so excessive and completely lose their structure! Why? Because a force that retains or maintains a structure that is not natural, which does not come from Angelic Qualities—such as Love, Gentleness, etc.—inevitably creates blockages and extremes. In such cases, as soon as we open the floodgates, the forces held back in the person are unleashed and the result is not very positive.

The languages spoken reflect the qualities of the country. For example, we notice the structured and very precise, rather blunt aspects of German, whereas French is noticeably soft-sounding and poetic or negatively haughty.

Yes, madam. (Dreamer: I have a dream I would like interpreted but before I tell it to you I would like to explain what happened to me. Six months ago, I witnessed an assault. A group of men were assaulting a person and I intervened to help. Following that event, I had many nightmares. In these nightmares, my life was almost always in danger and I would often get killed. Of course, through all of this, I made some spiritual progress; I tried to understand why I'd had such an experience and this awakened hidden memories. During this period, I decided to buy a book on spirituality and, finally, I bought your book. It was the first time I read one of your books. So I'm a novice. I started reading and I had a dream, which was actually a nightmare, but which I consider to be a super-beautiful nightmare. In my dream, *I was a heart, a big heart. I was the big heart, but it was a bit like a Valentine's Day*

54

box of chocolates. It was a flat heart—not rounded like a real heart. There was a marksman on my left. I couldn't see him but I could tell everything he was thinking. I knew he was going to fire at me until I died because he absolutely wanted me to die. Then the man shot me many times and every time a bullet hit me, instead of making a hole, a stream of light came out. The more he shot, the more I soared away like an airplane, flying faster and faster. I was happy and I felt totally fulfilled. It was the first time since I had helped the woman that I felt liberated by being killed. When I woke up from this dream, I felt wonderful. I said, "Ah! I think my Angel has just answered me." But I would like to have it interpreted.) That's fine. Thank you, madam.

This is an interesting dream because it attests to the beautiful work you've done raising your consciousness.

If we're given a situation to experience, it's because we harbor within ourselves memories that correspond to this situation. Therefore, if we're assaulted, it's because in other lives we were the ones who assaulted. If we are led to help someone, in actual fact, we're helping ourselves. We're helping a part of ourselves, which is represented by that person. There is no such thing as coincidence. The person that you helped harvested what she had sown in her garden. This is Divine Justice, an absolute Law of the Universe.

When you rescued that person, it awakened memories within you that were connected to situations of assault. Everyone has memories like this, because humanity has a history of great violence.

It must have been very difficult for you to experience this dramatic event. Before you can understand the situation and defuse all of the tension generated by these memories, you must have experienced all kinds of upsets, hence the nightmares.

In the dream, the heart represented a part of your being. It symbolized your love, your way of loving. The marksman also represented a part of you. You were visiting aggressive memories that were destroying love in your life.

The woman experienced aggression on the physical level, whereas you experienced it first as a witness and then in your dreams. You

55

experienced it on the metaphysical level by encountering your memories. The advantage of encountering our memories and cleansing them at the root, at their source, on the metaphysical level, is that we don't have to experience them in the concrete world. If you hadn't gone deep down to the source of the event, if you had simply rescued the woman, thumped the assailants and criticized them, saying, "Agh! They're rotten, sickening this and that!"—you really wouldn't have cleansed anything. Justice would have judged them and maybe imprisoned them. But, as far as you were concerned, you would not have made any progress on the level of your soul.

So, this dream gives evidence of true evolution. Your love was in the process of transforming itself; it was becoming more powerful.

Was it your body that was in the form of a heart? (Dreamer: I was that heart. It was I who was the heart.) You had a head and arms...? (Dreamer: No, I was really just the big red heart.) Ok, I understand.

So we can see that the entire emotional aspect was affected. What is interesting, however, is that the Work you did led you to understand things, to say to yourself, "I am upset by what happened to this woman. This means that there are parts within me that are aggressive." This led you to encounter your memories of aggression and your love became stronger than these negative forces.

In the nightmares that you had following this event, did you respond with aggression? Were you afraid? (Dreamer: No. My life was in danger but something always happened to save me. I remember that when I went to defend the woman, there were about 10 young men who had started to assault her with sticks and bottles. The Angels must have helped me because I managed to stop all those people. When I thought about it afterwards, I couldn't believe that I'd managed to master them. I said to myself, "It wasn't me who did this." It's certain that there was aggression and repressed anger within me, because if I was able to react to this aggressiveness, it's because I had it within me.) Yes, that's right.

So, you faced the situation. You were given the necessary strength to allow you to resolve this situation. If, in the dreams where your life was in danger, you had feared for your life, that would have indicated that you hadn't yet integrated the concept of Divine Justice. However, in the dream, the heart responded to aggression with streams of light, which symbolized understanding. This testifies to the fact that you did some very deep inner work.

What happens on the concrete level following a dream such as this one is that we cease to respond to violence with violence. If a person is not nice to us, we're able to do some alchemy; we say to ourselves, "Ah! He's not very nice. Ok, so I refer back to myself and I work on that energy." The more we do this, the more we develop truly powerful love.

In the beginning, the heart resembled a box of chocolates, which symbolized the type of love where we nourish people with sweet things, with affection, whereas now your love is deeper, it's more spiritual. The opening you experienced on the emotional level transformed your heart: it can now radiate Light. This is truly wonderful!

(Dreamer: The more the man fired at me, the farther up I soared.) In a dream, flying represents an elevation of consciousness. Among other things, it is the Angelic notion of rediscovering the capacity to travel in multiple dimensions. On a more earthly level, flying means we can remain in elevated states of consciousness even when we're surrounded by negative energies.

(Dreamer: I have another question to ask you. Someone told me that I'd interfered with that woman's karma by rescuing her. He told me that she had something to learn and that, by intervening, I had harmed her because she hadn't been able to live out her karma. I replied, "Well, maybe I was a little spark of light that showed her that love still exists in this world.") Exactly, that's right.

(Dreamer: Should we intervene in situations such as this one? She would probably be dead if I hadn't intervened—at least that's what the police said. Should we just stand and watch as someone is killed?) No, on the contrary. Of course there's no set recipe in these situations but, most of the time, if we are able to do something, if we can help, it's our duty to do so.

In actual fact, it's as if you rescued yourself because the woman represented a part of you. One day, we no longer have the notion of strangers. Everyone that we meet on our path represents parts of ourselves. When we are able to help, we do so. Of course, if we follow this logic, as we watch the news on TV, we might say, "I'm going to overthrow the dictator of that country." We could set off on a crusade to help people—there certainly are enough causes out there. That would be another set of dynamics. However, if we are close to a situation and it is within our capacity, we must help. The notion of interfering with a person's karma by saving him is erroneous. If this woman really had to experience greater karma, first of all, you wouldn't have been in that place at that time and secondly, you wouldn't have had either the idea or the strength to save her. In general, if we leave when we could help, we can create important karma for ourselves.

(Dreamer: I've been on a spiritual path for quite some time and I still had drawers that were closed. This event helped me to go deeper, to go and find out what was at the bottom of the drawers.) Yes, I understand.

If you were confronted with this situation, it's because you had forces of aggression within you. However, your force of love and justice—unconscious for the most part—manifested itself and brought the conflict to an end because you didn't fight the assailants. You had a feminine presence of wisdom and, just like in your dream, you emanated a powerful Light that managed to disarm the negative forces.

(Dreamer: Well I did actually have to intervene physically to grab their weapons. I still can't believe that I am the one who disarmed them. There are parts that I don't even remember. I have to appear in court this week; it will make for a strange testimony. It was no longer my physical body that was there. It was probably my Angel.) That's right. You were in a very elevated state of consciousness during the assault and your dream showed you that you are in the process of integrating this high level of love and compassion permanently.

You must also remember that you had a karmic link to this aggression because we don't encounter a situation such as this by coincidence. It was there to teach you something. It's as if you disarmed yourself; you disarmed the parts of yourself that had a tendency toward aggression and assault. Of course, when something like this is experienced on the physical level, the sensation, the feelings are very strong and so the teaching is deep because to defend another person in such a situation demands courage. Courage is not just for men; it's also for women.

(Dreamer: I came out of it all right but I believe that my spiritual opening helped me a lot because these past months have been very difficult.) Yes, I can imagine. What you went through is very powerful. You visited your memories of aggression and that's why you feared for your life in your nightmares. You opened compartments where memories of aggression and violence had been registered since God knows how many lives.

(Dreamer: I find what you're saying quite special because my ex-husband was violent. Now, he's part of a group that campaigns against violence to women.) You see, this fact shows you that you're in the process of cleansing important parts of your inner man.

During the event, you had a positive impulse of courage and afterwards your unconscious brought back to the surface memories that hadn't yet been cleansed. Sometimes, we can be traversed by positive fields of courage, strength and power because the Universe sends us metaphysical energies that enter our physical body and lead us to act in an almost supernatural way.

(Dreamer: In any case, I've retained two important lessons from all of this. First of all, I have a better understanding of compassion. When I accept the idea that I had all that violence within me, I say to myself, "This is where those people are at on their path. I have no right to judge them because I once did the same thing." Then, I have a better understanding of my ordeals as learning experiences, part of my apprenticeship. Despite the difficulties I experienced in the last few months, in the end, everything is totally positive. I tell myself that if Life sends me things, it's because It thinks I'm ready to go further. So, it's positive. It is a school. And it really helps me to talk about myself and what I'm experiencing.) What you are saying is beautiful and wise.

One day, when we understand the Law of Disturbance — the Law of Resonance — and we invariably come back to ourselves as soon as we feel upset, we can attain very high levels of consciousness. The Law of Resonance is extraordinary in helping to cleanse the distorted memories in question.

What you've just said is so beautiful because it's true that the Earth is a school. We are here for the sole purpose of learning. And one day we'll die. Death is part of everyone's destiny. We are here for a few years only and we carry our baggage, our memories—the positive as well as the negative—from one life to the next.

Oh! How time flies when we feel good! It's already the end of this workshop. I thank you with all my heart for your beautiful sharing.

WORKSHOP

In Dreams, Symbolism is very Precise

Yes, madam. (Dreamer: I have a dream I would like interpreted. My dreams always concern water; I suppose that this is in continuity with work on my emotions. In my dream, *I was in my car. I was leaving the city of Montpellier to go home to Aix. But I wasn't paying attention and I went to Nice instead. Then, once in Nice, it turned out that in reality I wasn't in Nice: I was by a little creek by the sea, a lovely little creek with pine trees and a little road that skirted the creek. The creek was very calm and there were two large, solid, 2-3 ton rocks. There was a thin vein of rust encircling these rocks. I was in my car and I said to myself, "I'll take this little road." So I took the road that skirted the creek and I looked at the water as I drove along. At one point, the sea swelled and rose up and the water came onto the road, but not in a violent way. I'd say there was about 10 centimeters (approx. 4 inches) of water on the road. So, I turned around, quite calmly, and came back to my point of departure at the creek. It was weird: I felt that I was both on a road and on a sidewalk at the same time, and there was water. As I arrived at the parking lot, I looked at the water in the creek and it had become calm and clear. And then, in the water, I saw steps going down. They were beautiful steps, a bit like very wide ancient Roman steps. I looked around and I was feeling good.* It felt as though Up Above wanted me to go down somewhere.) That's fine. Thank you for your dream.

You live in Aix, France, is that right? (Dreamer: Yes.) In your dream, were you aware that you lived in Aix? (Dreamer: Yes, absolutely.) Ok, fine.

What do the cities of Montpellier and Nice represent to you? (Dreamer: I am a sales representative and that is the sector I work in.) Ah, I see! Ok. So, Montpellier and Nice simply represent your work? (Dreamer: Yes.)

In dreams, symbolism is very precise. We must always be sure not to go beyond the symbol, not to extrapolate; we must concentrate on the essence. Since Nice and Montpellier represent your work, we know from the start that the dream concerned an attitude you have toward your work.

Let's go ahead with the analysis. At first, you were in your car. What does a car represent? What is it used for? As I said in the introduction, a car allows us to go to work, to go shopping, to go see people, etc. In general, we head toward the social dimension when we use a car. Therefore, a car and the way we drive it indicate how we behave in life and how we advance toward others. We must always refer the symbol back to ourselves, because it represents a state of consciousness or a field of consciousness.

It is quite clear that this dream was related to your work in the concrete world, to your way of working in matter. Otherwise, you'd have been somewhere else. You wouldn't have been given Nice or Montpellier as symbols; you would simply have been by the seaside or some other symbol would have referred to a different area of your life—evoking something emotional or to do with the family, for example. This dream definitely pertained to that part of your life that involves your work and the concrete way in which you work because there's no other symbol leading you in another direction. There can be many directions in a dream; many aspects can be brought to light but, in this one, everything focuses on work.

You were leaving Montpellier and you wanted to go home to Aix. The idea of wanting to go home indicates that we wish to go within in order to find new resources. However, you were inattentive and you found yourself in Nice rather than Aix. This was a *misaction** because normally when we want to go somewhere that is where we should end up. This means that when you're at work, you sometimes have a tendency to forget your intimate life represented by your home town. You are constantly focused on work and on exterior action and this stops you from coming back to yourself and resting and finding resourcement.

What does a rock represent? Rock belongs to the mineral kingdom. It therefore corresponds to the unconscious, to unconscious memories related to ancient actions. Rocks also represent the basic structure of the foundations of the soul as well as memories.

---

* misaction is our translated version of the French expression 'acte manqué' and it encompasses the idea of a slip-up, a mishap, a mistake, a blunder, an oversight, forgetting to do what we'd intended to do, a lapsus, an act of omission, any act or non-action that isn't right, isn't divinely harmonious.

A vein of rust encircled each of the rocks. It's as if old rusted memories were manifesting themselves in your way of working, as if you began your work with rusty dynamics. When we see a rusted vehicle, we immediately think of deterioration and corrosion.

The actual work that you do — the product of your work — is not necessarily affected because that idea is not part of the dream, but the way you work is affected by ancient memories that, symbolically, are rusted. When we think of rust, we think of something that's been abandoned to the mercy of the elements and that has eroded.

Because the scene took place in a creek, emotions are at issue — and strong emotions at that, because the sea was swelling and water flooded the road. Therefore, strong emotions hinder your work and create blockages. For example, you could be in the middle of Nice and say to yourself, "Ah! I've had it up to here! I've had enough of work, work work!" It is as if you lose your vitality and you feel great fatigue due to these old emotional memories that erode and use up your energy.

Then, you went back to the creek, the water was calm and clear and you saw steps going down into the water. This is very positive. Up Above wants to take you down into your emotional world so that you will transform your emotions concerning your work. This is why you saw the steps.

They were ancient-styled steps — you said Roman style. This means that you have taken this road before; you have already been down into your emotional unconscious. So, you have already acquired a whole potential that will facilitate your purification work. Eventually, you will develop a new way of working in matter, a new way of manifesting yourself, because you will have integrated a new vision.

So, at the moment, you are in a state of mind where you want to find new meaning in your work and a way of working that will renew your motivation. This is what the dream explains. There you are.

(Dreamer: Things are starting to *unrust*?) Yes, this is what is happening because of the presence of the stairs at the end of the dream. With rust, the problem comes with the fact that we don't do anything; we just let things go. This was you before. And now you are entering a phase where you're going to enter your old memories and go down into the emotions that are eroding and corroding your energy. And as you cleanse these memories, you will understand new things; you will find new meaning and new motivation in your work. Your life will have more meaning.

You know, this rather rusty way of working is to be found in many people. If we haven't found the spiritual meaning of our work and if we haven't integrated spirituality in our way of working, there will necessarily come a time when we will feel tired. No matter what type of work we do, even if we like our work, after 10 or 15 years, we will have the impression of fully explored the job—we will know every facet of the job, all of the ins and outs, the nooks and crannies of the firm, and we'll lose our enthusiasm.

If we don't have a spiritual foundation, insecurity, ambition and greed keep us in our job, but we start rusting on the inside, and eventually we encounter a blockage. We feel tension and we continue to work with these dynamics, a little like a workaholic who never has enough resources, never enough money, and who's always afraid of not having enough.

Alternatively we develop a feeling of belonging to the firm which has nothing to do with sharing spiritual values and which, in fact, is simply an emotional dependency; it's as if the business had become our reason for living.

Of course, even if remaining in a job for the money or because of dependency is a distortion, it has an educational value—we continue to learn about ourselves and about life. However, the fact remains that one day we must integrate the spiritual notion of work, that of developing qualities and virtues through our work. When we smile at a customer, we don't do it because we want to close a sale, and when we are nice to a colleague, we don't do it to obtain a favor.

We should also question ourselves about what we encourage through our work and, if necessary, look for another way to earn our living and advance spiritually because some jobs, some products and some services are very distorted. If our work has something positive, just and inspiring for humanity, this is what should motivate us.

In any case, our conscience transforms itself constantly through the gestures we make, the actions we do, the emotions we feel and the thoughts we entertain while at work. There we are.

Yes, madam. (Dreamer: Not long ago, I dreamed of my grandmother. I've never dreamed about her before. She's 91 years old. *I was in a shopping mall where there were people that I knew. I knew these were people I knew but I didn't really recognize them. I was looking at different things but I didn't want anything. I saw all sorts of colored necklaces and I thought they were lovely but I didn't buy anything. Then, I joined my grandmother who was sitting on a little wooden bench and I said to her, "Do you want anything?" And she answered, "I'd really like to buy the little shoes that I see over there because they're the ones that I wore on my mother's birthday when I was four years old. But I only have two euro and they cost three." So I opened my wallet and gave her a euro so she could buy the shoes. It was a pair of little white shoes with little stripes on them.* And that's it.)

It's possible that you visited your grandmother's soul in this dream. In order to determine if this is the type of dream it is, I'm going to ask a question. Is your grandmother open to spirituality? Has she been *awakened*? (Dreamer: Yes. Definitely. She grants a lot of importance to the essence of things. When we go to the supermarket and I want to offer her something, she always says to me, "Nothing interests me anymore: now, all I want is to be happy with you." She's a woman with a big heart.) That's fine, thank you.

On the one hand, it is possible that you visited her soul. But, on the other hand, when I think about it, given the first part of the dream where you decided not to buy anything—you yourself made the decision not to buy anything and this showed your detachment—I believe the dream did not concern your grandmother herself. (Dreamer: I had money for her so that she could get something for herself and I bought nothing for myself.) That's right. So it's a dream of the first type, that is to say, where all the symbols only represent parts of you.

The scene took place in a shopping mall. A shopping mall is a place where we go to get things. In its positive aspect, the shopping mall symbolizes abundance and sharing beyond borders because there are products from all around the world on the shelves. From its negative aspect, it represents materialism and superficiality, both states of consciousness that we can feel very strongly when we go to these places. The people who spend time in shopping malls usually don't know the sacred meaning of abundance and they are only interested in satisfying their personal needs, without any awareness of the choice of products and their manner of consuming. For example, they don't ask themselves if the product is respectful of the environment, if the company that manufactured or marketed it has good values, how it distributes its profits, how it manages its resources — with or without waste — etc. I always ask myself questions when I shop. I check to see if there are animal by-products in what I wish to purchase, if it is ecological and if I truly need it.

Let's go back to your dream. You were simply looking at products; you didn't want to buy anything. This means that you've achieved a certain degree of inner satisfaction. You don't feel the need to compensate by acquiring material things. This dream denotes balance and stability with regard to matter.

You were looking at pretty necklaces. A necklace symbolizes allegiance and the same idea applies to pendants, rings and other jewelry. These objects that we wear represent an aim or an ideal and the path or philosophy that we have chosen to achieve it. I myself wear one and it represents something important for me. When we put a collar on a dog, we give it an identity to show who the dog belongs to. So it's the same idea, except that in the case of humans, it shows affiliation to a philosophy or identification to a feeling.

For example, if someone wears an object in the form of a heart, we know that love and affection are important to this person; this is his way of expressing it. If there is no particular image, as in the case of pearls or precious stones, we use the symbolism of color or the material they're made of. For example, if someone wears a pearl, we know that this person seeks emotions, purity and seeks to transform negativity.

If someone wears a pin in the shape of a deck of cards, we know that this person needs to win and would like to control his destiny. If a man wears a pendant in the shape of a boxing glove, we know that he likes to fight and that he values competition and conflict.

People who wear many pieces of jewelry all at once have all kinds of allegiances. They are captives of their attachment to matter and they lack focus and are scattered. Excess in itself signals an inner emptiness because any excess denotes a lack on a very deep level.

Let's continue to analyze the dream. You then joined your grandmother and when you asked her if she wanted something, she said that she would like the little white shoes. Your grandmother represented a part of you. The positive symbolism of our ancestors is wisdom or the search for wisdom.

Old age should be the most beautiful period in life. This is a period in life when a person should take stock of his life and transmit to the new generations the desire to evolve spiritually — ideally speaking, that is.

However, it is very often more important for our grandparents and our elderly parents to go out, watch shows and play cards. In many cases, people of these generations have experienced lacks on the material level or had too many responsibilities too young. So, later, if they have the means and resources, they start to live the youth that passed them by because they were deprived for too long. Some end up sick when they get older. But the more evolved a person is, with age, they acquire even more wisdom and because of that they are healthier.

In traditional societies, old people were the wise elders of the village. They counseled and inspired others and they helped their families and friends. This custom has been lost but it will come back. For the moment a lot of old people are dizzy with abundance and they have a tendency to dissipation and they become scattered in superficial activities. But the new children will have different values.

What is it that will truly inspire these new generations? The metaphysical. We only need to see the interest that these young people have regarding the environment. People of these generations will wish to have clean souls. They will seek to cleanse their inner earth. In a way, they will cleanse the product of their parents' experimentations. A generation always evolves on the basis of what previous generations have left them. This inheritance may seem negative but, ultimately, the inheritance is always positive because negative situations lead to awareness. Even if humanity has to go through difficult periods, these difficulties will bring about a new current, a new wave.

To go back to the dream, your grandmother represented your wise, experienced side. She wanted little white shoes. Shoes represent the way we strengthen our capacity to advance and also what we emanate as we advance, what we radiate when we act in matter. White symbolizes spirituality. This shows that you wish to advance and manifest yourself in a spiritual way.

(Dreamer: When I woke up, intrigued, I asked myself, "Why was it so important for her to have those white shoes? What was so special about her mother's birthday?")

It means that, symbolically, she wanted to *enter her mother*. The mother always represents the inner aspect. Therefore, the part of your being that wants to act in a spiritual way wanted to enter the inner side, to go within. You wanted to bring spirituality within you, into your inner world and into matter because you were in a shopping mall. Thus, the state of consciousness to which you aspire — symbolized by the shoes — will not necessarily serve to enter into concrete action but it will act on the inside and in the wisdom you develop toward your material needs.

This dream shows that you are committed to walk a truly deep, intense spiritual path. This path has become the focal point of your life. That's all for the interpretation of this dream.

Yes, madam. (Participant: I'd like to know what it means to dream of people who are deceased. I haven't dreamed of my father in 40 years and now, I've just dreamed about him. He was fine; he was in good health and he was well dressed. What does this mean?)

It is possible for us to visit deceased people except that your father has probably reincarnated by now since it has been 40 years since he died. In the dream, he represented an aspect of yourself: concrete action. Therefore, the day that you received the dream, you had a lot of vitality and energy that led you to act, to take action.

(Participant: Is it the same if it's our mother? Because I also dreamed of my mother and of my sister who is deceased.) The mother represents the inner aspect as we saw earlier.

(Participant: And the elder sister?) It depends on what she represents for you. (Participant: My elder sister died a long time ago. I adored her. I loved her very much. She was like a mother to me. She was 10 years older than me. My mother was not my mother; my sister played the role of mother for me.) Ok, I understand.

So, with a dream like that, you were taking care of your inner self; you were thinking about things. You were also comforting yourself; you weren't beating yourself over the head. That day, you felt as much comfort and consolation as if your sister had been there by your side.

You may also have visited her soul. Because the more we work with dreams, the more we receive dreams where we visit others' souls. But every time we receive a dream, we must refer the symbols back to ourselves and consider that they only represent parts of our self. And then if events show us — a few days later let's say — that we visited that person, then, and only then, do we know that the symbols did not just represent parts of us. In any case, even if we visit another person's soul, the dream is sent to us so that we will understand something about ourselves. We aren't sent into the Parallel Worlds as tourists.

If we dream of a deceased person, the idea is the same: either the person represents a part of us or we truly were in contact with his soul, and in these extraordinary moments, it still simultaneously represents a part of ourselves. This can happen normally only when the person has recently died — up to three years or less. But most of the time, when we see a deceased person many years after their passing, in actual fact it's a Guide using transfiguration; He takes on the appearance of someone we know, someone who inspires trust, in order to help us understand something. Trust makes us more receptive to the message.

Also, for deceased people to come and see us, they have to have been given permission because normally, they don't have the necessary strength to enter the Parallel Worlds close to Earth. The Earth, on the metaphysical level, is not very luminous. Our planet may be polluted on the material level, but on the metaphysical level, wow! it's more than polluted. I can assure you that the beings that live in the Parallel Worlds don't come to our planet on vacation.

When we speak of Parallel Worlds, we are referring to the worlds other than ours—outside of the earthly dimension—that are inhabited by beings, but these worlds include dimensions that are close to Earth. In the latter case, we are referring to the intentions that nourish human thought.

There is a lot of concrete, manifested violence on Earth. So imagine how much there must be on the level of human thoughts and intentions. It's far from restful to say the least. Because of the Law of Resonance—which also applies to these worlds—the more evolved a person is, the less affected he is when visiting the Parallel Worlds. Why? Because he is focused; because his spirit is not scattered all over the place trying to satisfy all kinds of needs, nor is it torn by unresolved situations.

Yes, madam. (Participant: I sometimes dream of my child. I suppose he simply represents a part of me but I imagine that we can also visit our child's soul.) We certainly can visit our child's soul. However, as I said earlier, we should develop the automatic reflex of immediately referring the dream back to ourselves and think, "He represented what I will become, he represented a certain part of me that is learning and I've got to work on that part, or, I feel all of his great qualities inside myself." Afterwards, by observing the child's behavior and what he is going through, we are able to determine if we have visited his soul or not.

When we have worked a lot on ourselves, we have done the groundwork of cleansing our conscience and so it is much easier to know what type of dream is in question. It's the same as when we hear our child crying. When an intuitive mother hears her child crying, she can say, "Now he's crying for nothing" or "He's crying because he really needs something." However, fear and insecurity can interfere with her perception. When we have our first child, we don't necessarily trust our intuition and we are on the brink of panic every time he cries. With a second child, we aren't so afraid, and so we are better able to perceive the child's true state.

The same applies to dreams. After a while, we know what type of dream we're dealing with. But, to truly proceed with wisdom, we always refer the dream back to ourselves; this prevents us from all power trips. We can never lose if we do this. Anyway, as I said earlier, even when we visit another person's soul, we are also visiting ourselves because everything in the Universe is also a part of us.

Yes, madam. (Dreamer: I have a recurring dream. It takes on different forms but each time it's more or less the same idea — at least, that's my impression. *I'm either naked or lost and surrounded by people that I don't know. I try to speak to them to ask them where I am and what direction I should take to find my way again, but they don't understand. In some of these dreams, often I can truly feel their indifference; it's as if they can't even hear me.* Of course, I wake up with a feeling of insecurity. *Sometimes, I arrive somewhere by car and later I can't find my car anymore. There's always the notion of being lost, of not speaking the same language and of not being heard or understood. As if it were another country or planet.*) I understand. Thank you.

When you have these dreams, the following day, you experience specific states of mind that correspond to the dream.

Nudity, in a dream, can be positive or negative. It can symbolize comfort with our intimacy, purity, purification, authenticity, and well-being but in order for it to be positive, it must be appropriate to the place where we find ourselves nude.

(Dreamer: But in these dreams, I don't feel good.) You don't feel good. You're in the city, is that right? (Dreamer: Yes.) To be nude in the city is negative because it is not appropriate to do this. It creates needs for love and can cause aggression. Humans are still fundamentally animals. It means you have a discrepancy between your intimate and social lives that creates an unconscious provocative, rebellious attitude caused by a profound lack of love and need for attention on others. You are also too open with others, in the sense that you reveal too much of your intimate side in order to gain attention and be recognized. But this is not the case in your dream; the person is too eccentric, it's a question of her wanting to be loved by everyone.

And indifference, in a dream, means that we are visiting memories of indifference with regard to who we truly are. The indifference in these dreams comes from memories you harbor within yourself. You're visiting parts of yourself that don't acknowledge you. You don't have enough confidence in yourself. These parts are indifferent to the change, the evolution you are going through. You may be aware of these aspects or they can manifest themselves through others. A member of your family might be indifferent toward you. You are on a spiritual path and others may not understand you; it's as if you don't speak the same language. You can feel at variance with them; you can feel a discrepancy. And the day of the dream, this feeling is amplified. So, you either experience concrete situations that relate to this theme, or these are only experienced on the inside, or both—depending on whether men or women appear in these dreams. That explains your nudity in the dream. You want too much attention from the indifferent people.

And this happens because you have engendered karma: in other lives, you gave too much importance to your work and social life, to going out, and you neglected the people that were part of your life. You may also have had a haughty attitude toward some people and this is why you see this attitude of indifference. So now, you reap what you have sown. And you see it in your dreams.

Of course, when we have dreams like these, it's very initiatic. Many people have this kind of dream at the beginning of their path. Because, when we begin to open up, we are out of phase with the rest of society, with everything else. We develop a transparency and authenticity that is out of tune with everyone around us. Authenticity is positive but if we start being very authentic in places where it isn't appropriate, it is because we have too strong a desire to be acknowledged by others.

Sometimes we want to share our best experiences but others aren't ready for that. We are like a mirror for them; we are a reflection of that part of them that wants to become better, to be transformed. We lead them to ask questions, to think, but they haven't necessarily reached the level we've reached. So they turn away from us and ignore us.

(Dreamer: In some of these dreams, *I don't even remember who I am. At least, that's how I feel. I look for clues to help me define who I am but I can't find any.*) Yes, I understand. That's what it's like.

When you have these dreams, you feel out of sync with reality. You feel a bit vague, undefined, as if you had lost your center, which is your celestial origin or your divinity. This phenomenon is common with people on a spiritual path. In the beginning, the path is more of a pastime than anything else but when the doors of the unconscious really open up, things become serious. It's normal to feel lost, to no longer know what to do or who you are in those moments.

(Dreamer: What is new for me in what you're saying is that it's a part of me that doesn't recognize my divine nature, not necessarily someone else. It is a part of me that doesn't take into account what I really am.) Exactly. In those dreams, all the characters represent parts of you. If some people are indifferent to you, it is because you are indifferent to yourself.

What we need to do when we have dreams like this is to refer all of the symbols back to ourselves. By doing this, we give ourselves the possibility of cleansing all of the memories in question and we completely change.

When you are looking for your direction in a dream, it means that you are looking for a path to follow, something that will help you find yourself. This is what this type of dream leads to. When you dream about this, you have important existential questions during the day— *Who am I? What am I doing here? What's the point in me being here? Why do we live?* These questions are just the beginning of the process because they are only questions. Gradually, as we travel along the path, we find the answers.

Yes, madam. (Dreamer: I had a dream yesterday afternoon while I was having a nap. In the first part of the dream, I was simply a witness to what was going on and I took part in the second part. In my dream, *I could see a young woman of about 22 or 23 years old who was driving to work. She stopped at a bakery to buy a croissant. In the bakery, a plump female baker greeted her. She was very smiley but wore very heavy makeup. The young woman's father came in. He was tall with graying hair and clearly a charmer. Without wasting time, he started flirting with the baker, paying her lots of compliments, etc. in order to charm her. Just then the baker went into the back of the store. And the young woman started to hit her father over the head, saying, "I've had enough of you. Stop it! Go away! What are you doing? You keep me from living, I'm fed up with this." At that moment, the baker-woman came back.* I was just there looking on; I was only a witness to the scene. *All of a sudden, I found myself outside the bakery. As of that moment, I was in the dream. There was a counter where the baker could pass food along. So, she passed me a sandwich—it was not at all a croissant—and there was a chain attached to this sandwich. I took it, really astonished to see the chain. She looked at me and asked, "Do you think your father is a reliable person?" because she had been charmed by him. Well, I felt all emotional; all of a sudden, I was filled with love and compassion for that father. I could have destroyed all that woman's hope—it would have been easy to reply, "No, not at all; he's a bastard. He hasn't done anything in his life, he lives off everybody else and he abandoned me." Instead, I said to her, "Listen, I have nothing to tell you. Live what you have to live with him and you'll see." And I felt this compassion physically in my sleep. That's all.)* Thank you for sharing this dream.

(Dreamer: I'm sorry, I just have to say that in real life, my father was the very opposite of this man: he was very dutiful—too much so even. He believed in self-sacrifice, duty, things like that, you know, whereas the man in my dream was a libertine. He didn't look like my father either. And the young woman didn't look like me. I could see her face, her hair and everything very well but I didn't recognize her.) Ok, thank you, I understand.

Through this dream, you were given a beautiful teaching. First, you were given the role of observer, then, you were integrated into the scene so that you would understand that all of the elements of the dream represented parts of you.

When we are on a spiritual path, it is normal to see scenes that are not very positive in a dream, but we must remember that we are not only what we see; we have other parts that are very beautiful. This is very important. And we mustn't be afraid of what we are shown. The study of dreams & signs leads us to truly purify our memories; we see them in dreams and daily situations and we can transform them in the course of the day.

In the beginning, the young woman was in a car. Was the car a certain color? (Dreamer: It was turquoise.)

You'll see that all the details in a dream are important. Each element adds information that helps to go deeper into the meaning of the dream.

74

That color was not there by coincidence. Turquoise is a mixture of blue and green. Blue symbolizes communication because it's the color of the throat chakra. And green is the color associated with the heart. So, by combining the meanings, we see that turquoise represents the communication of love. The turquoise car, therefore, represented the way that you communicate love when you go toward others.

The young woman wanted to buy a croissant. Food in a dream always represents what gives us vital energy. So you felt you needed energy.

Then, the father arrived and his behavior was seductive. The father usually represents the way we manifest ourselves in the concrete world. He was the young lady's father, of course, but he became your father toward the end of the dream. So, Up Above wants you to purify memories linked to seduction. When you want something you may try to use charm — consciously or not. For example, if you want a croissant, you might ask in a honeyed tone, "Could I (*sigh*) have a croissant, sir?" (*laughter*) A note of seduction may slip into your way of asking for things to speed up the process and make sure you are served more rapidly. This is the aspect of yourself that you are working on. We can see that you are already doing so, even if you are tough on yourself, because the young woman hit her father over the head and told him to stop doing that.

The baker too had a seductive side to her — not only the father — because you said that she was all smiley and wearing a lot of make-up. So, since the character in question was a woman, it's not only a question of behavior; it's also an inner attitude, and it colors your emotions, your emotional relationships.

This dream testifies to the fact that you are committed to a deep spiritual path. This is not a beginner's dream; you have entered into deep psychological frameworks.

The tendency to use seduction is something that nearly everyone has to some extent. When we have a need, we become all nice, all smiley, and then, once we've got what we wanted, we couldn't care less about the person. This is quite noticeable in stores; a person asks for information to find a product and as soon as he gets his answer, he turns on his heel and walks off. There seems to be love at the moment of asking, but there isn't really. His mind works like this, "I'll charm you a bit to bring you around so you'll give me what I need." There was some of that in the dream.

Very often, a seductive attitude produces expectations in others and this can cause problems and misunderstandings. For example, at some point, we might wonder, "How is it that so and so is in love with me? I didn't ask for this; I didn't do anything to attract this." The reason is that we had a seductive attitude with the other person — consciously or not — and the other person read a message in this; the person thought that we wished to become close to him, to become intimate. This has surely already happened to you.

Then, the baker served you a sandwich with a chain on it. This means that when you offer others resources, at the same time you hold back what you're giving. We sometimes see this in people when they're paying for a service — for example, work done at the garage — they hold onto their money while they are offering it. This doesn't show on the outside but it's in their energy. This really is something! I sometimes see these dynamics, even with our non-profit organization, when we're selling books before and after lectures. When a person is in this state of consciousness, I wait. (*laughter*) I feel the energy and I wait for the person to settle down and to feel good.

We do this in martial arts — we work with the forces that are present. We don't learn this in our societies; when someone tells us no, we seem to think that we have to convince them it's yes. But if we wait just a little and say, "Ah! I'll think about this," the other person's tension is defused. Similarly, in discussions, we say, "Ah! You have a point there. Let me think about it." At that point, the other person is a little disarmed because, in actual fact, he wanted to be right. So, he says to himself, "He's thinking about it. Mmmh… what about me, was I right in what I said?" After a while, we say: "Ah! I think we might be able to proceed in such a way." And the other is won over without losing face, "Yes, it makes sense what you're saying. I thought about that too. That's it. Yes, we can do it that way."

We can disarm very obstinate people when we have wisdom and finesse. Through gentleness we can get them to see reason. We take the time that is necessary. It's the same with a tree that isn't ready to give fruit: there's no sense in trying to push it—we wait for the right season. All we have to do is let the person's energy simmer down until he is ready to let go.

So, the chain was there to show you that sometimes you hold back when you give. And you are visiting these types of memories so as to cleanse them.

(Dreamer: At the end, the baker asked me to tell her the truth about that father, about this man who had clearly charmed her. I didn't tell her what I knew; I let them experiment for themselves. And I felt a lot of love and compassion for those two people.)

This behavior had a positive side to it. The more we evolve, the less we interfere in other people's lives. When we have access to the Metaphysical World, we receive so much information about others that if we were to use it directly—by telling them what to do—they would either stay away from us or they would lose their autonomy, their capacity to renew their life. Each person must find his way by himself. And when we speak to him about spirituality, he must be ready for this. He must be receptive to receiving Knowledge.

My wife, Christiane, and I interpret dreams and answer funda-mental questions but we never play the crystal ball game with people who come to see us. We know that such a person is going through a certain type of experimentation and that in 10 years he or she will have such and such a problem. The difficulties that people go through are karmic. So they have to learn from their experiences and choose their own path themselves. When the time is right, the person integrates his spiritual dimension. If we are more advanced, we must have the wisdom to offer the tools to people only when we feel that it is the right moment for them.

Some people say, "Oh! My sister-in-law is ill. I'd just love her to evolve spiritually! I'm invoking the Angels for her, so she'll heal." Yet, when we ask them, "Is your sister-in-law working on the spiritual level?" they answer, "Oh! Well… no, she's not at all open to it." In such instances, I say, "Then why are you trying to take her illness away from her? There is something she has to experience through this ordeal and through her being in and out of hospital."

One day, we understand that some people have to learn through the world of consequences. We understand that consulting a doctor, being on a waiting list and worrying is part of a person's program and that he will evolve through this experience. And so, we see prayer from a different perspective.

Not long ago, in Geneva, a lady came up to speak to me. Her ex-husband was very ill; he was only 57 years old and his life had been totally disorganized by this illness. He had never been spiritual—in the sense of consciously following a spiritual path—and, when he learned that his illness was serious, he implored his ex-wife to pray for him, except that he himself, of course, didn't pray and didn't believe in God.

So, she began to pray he would heal and she prayed non-stop. She was praying so much that she was exhausted—she had dark circles under her eyes. This woman is very intense. She said to me, "That's all I've been doing for five months now, but he's not getting better. He keeps going from bad to worse. Now, I'm discouraged; I'm praying and there are no results."

Then she told me that she'd read a passage in one of my books that insists on the importance of always asking for authorization before praying for someone because if we don't do this we could be disturbing the Plan God had organized for him. Well, this woman wasn't very comfortable with this idea—she wasn't happy to have read those lines. So, I told her what time had led me to understand about this subject.

Already, at a young age, I considered prayer as something sacred, not to be used all the time to ask for just anything. I was conscious of the fact that it was a force, a power that had to be respected. Then, with time, I realized that if we pray for something and it doesn't happen, it means that there is something that we haven't understood. I used to say to myself, "If God has chosen not to listen to me, it's because the people in question have to go through certain things."

So the woman said, "If someone asks you to pray for them, what do you do?"—I could feel that she wasn't happy. I said to her, "I greet the person and, right away, I speak to Up Above and say, "May Your will be done. You know better than I do what is best for this soul." She retorted, "And that's it? You have great powers, I know you have, and you don't do any Work? Oh! That's so mean!" (*laughter*)

She was visibly shaken in her beliefs. So, I said to her, "Look, you've been praying for five months. Don't you think They've heard your prayers? (*laughter*) Imagine if you had the phone number of the President of the United States and you called to ask him the same thing all the time, 60 times a day—just as you're doing to Heaven at the moment…" She interrupted me: "Oh! It's a lot more than that." (*laughter*) "…at one point, he would say to his secretary, 'Cut off that line, please!'" Up Above, it's the same thing: They've heard your prayer, you don't have to repeat it. You simply have to go within and let Them do their Work. It's as if you keep buzzing the doorbell non-stop. They're going to think you're rather tiresome!" (*laughter*)

Ah! She was thrown off balance for a minute. After a second or two, she said, "As I listen to you, I think it makes sense but I have to admit that before talking to you I was starting to get angry and to completely lose confidence in prayer."

I said to her, "It might be good for your ex-husband to continue to be ill and maybe even to die from this." Then she confided in me, "Just imagine," she said, "He asked me but he didn't even ask his new wife." (*laughter*)

We could see her emotional addiction. She no longer lived with her ex-husband but she was honored to be the person he'd asked for help. She felt valued because he'd solicited her help rather than his new wife's. It was quite clear that she was experiencing karma through this situation. Then something *clicked* for this woman. One day, we come to understand that we must remain humble in the face of God and the Divine Plan, and that we must stop hounding Destiny.

When I see a person who is ill, I know that it is good for him. I'm conscious of the fact that it's the path God has chosen to help him evolve. So, I welcome his illness, even if this is someone who is close to me. Of course I understand that doctors can help to give a second chance or a healer can be used by Heaven to give the person a divine grace. But the first true step on the healing path—even when we go to see a doctor, etc.—is to accept the illness, to study it deeply and understand that it comes from an accumulation of memories that we have created—if we don't do this, it comes back again and again, in a different form after being healed or treated. The negative isn't to be fought: it transforms itself. This is the principle of the pearl: the oyster accepts the grain of sand—it doesn't eject it—it covers it with a special substance that eventually gives it great value. Sometimes, we try to fight an illness—we would do anything to stop it—and it doesn't dawn on us that it would be wiser to encounter evil and transform it.

When we meditate, we can use the force of our spirit to heal ourselves. If a part of our body is hurting, we only need to concentrate on this area and practice self-healing. I can tell you that I've seen miracles happen with this method. Of course, if certain parts of us don't believe, the power of healing is diminished. As we experiment with our spirit, we become aware of its strength and power.

The spirit has endless powers. If illness is inscribed in our Program, one day or another, our vital energy will receive a mandate to construct illness and if we wish to cancel this program, we will have to begin very intense, powerful spiritual work. We have to understand this. Regeneration as well as illness depends on our life-plan and we can modify it by doing spiritual work.

So, if we are ill—or we have any other difficulty—it corresponds to what we are, to memories that we need to rectify. Up Above, They don't play around and have fun giving us illnesses. We mustn't get angry with Heaven and say, "You did this to me." If we do, It will answer: "You are the one who engendered your illness. In another life, you did such and such a thing. You must see these attitudes once again—live through the consequences on the concrete level—and transcend them." It's as simple as that. It is the Law of Karma and when the time comes to apply it, God does not ask for our opinion.

In our dreams, we can see which attitudes caused the illness. If we don't dream yet, we can simply analyze the problem using symbolic language. If a person has sore legs, it is because he has been advancing in a distorted way for a long time—he gives orders, he wants to be better than others, he is impatient, etc., or

80

he forces himself to act, on the surface, as though he is well. If he has brain cancer, his way of thinking is disorganized and his life is badly organized and has been so for many lives.

Symbolism is very precise and logical. Our body is a representation of our spirit. Therefore, our nose, our ears, our hair, our eyes, our mouth, etc.—all the parts of our body—have symbolic meaning. Metabolic patterns and biological processes also have their symbolism. They represent states and fields of consciousness.

Some parts of our being are sometimes so engorged with negative memories that, at a certain point, the computer crashes! And we have no choice: it's time to cleanse. It's the same as in a house. Some people live in an environment full of paintings, knick-knacks and books that release sadness, fear and anger. This is because the people who live there have these distortions on the inside. Otherwise, they would change their decor.

As we evolve, it becomes quite natural to bring changes to our environment. We lighten it up by keeping as few objects as possible so that the atmosphere will be peacefully zen and we paint it in beautiful colors. When we accumulate objects that no longer have any use, we do the same on the conscience level—our unconscious becomes heavy. At some point, we find ourselves with liver problems, difficulty going to the toilet or arthritis because we hold onto things. We hold onto our children for fear that they'll hurt themselves or that something will happen to them. We hold onto our spouse because we're afraid of living alone or we have material insecurities, etc. The problem is never merely physical.

The physical level is the last to be affected in the materialization process. Erroneous thinking, fears and distorted behavior accumulate in a *department* in our conscience and at a given moment, illness sets in. This is because the *negative* accumulates. As for the *positive*, it circulates: it knows no boundaries. It both lightens and enlightens people. Its movement is responsible for the goodness, beauty and harmony that we experience.

When God programs an illness for someone, It does so in a spirit of Love and Wisdom. The most beautiful illustration of this leads us to think about bringing up our children. When we say no to our child, do we do so because we love him or because we don't love him? We say no because we know what is right for him. If he insists on only wanting to eat cake, we need to intervene. Our conscience is more evolved than his and we know that he must eat other things to remain healthy. Of course, cakes are good — especially those made from organic products — but there must be balance. So, when faced with a child's obstinacy, we say, "Go to your room and think about this for 10 minutes." If the child does something more serious, we can deprive him of his computer for a few days.

It's in just such an educational spirit that God sometimes has to activate an illness for someone — or some other trial or ordeal — and so this trial is positive. It is beautiful. In any case, all trials lead to something positive. We need only ask people who have experienced great trials, "What do you think of what you've been through?" 98% answer, "I wouldn't be the person I am today, if I hadn't lived through this." It's the classic reply.

Of course, when we're right in the thick of it — whether it be illness, divorce or whatever difficulty — this isn't obvious. But we have to tell ourselves that evil is educational, that trials are a passage that leads to a better state of being and greater wisdom. We say to ourselves, "I am in the process of repairing, of constructing my soul and purifying my memories."

One day, we transcend a negative vision of trials; we consider them as positive. This is how we find Happiness.

This concludes today's workshop. Heartfelt thanks for welcoming me to this beautiful region of France.

WORKSHOP
Soul-States

I have a lovely story to tell you. This morning, Jean-François came to see me. Jean-François is a musician and sometimes songs pop into his head, just like that. I understand this because I too am a musician and I receive messages through songs. For example, a person can come up to me and a song will start to play in my head—sometimes it's just a few lines of the song, or even just a few of the words—and that song describes either the exact state of consciousness the person is in or the subject of the conversation we're about to have. Sometimes, the song describes my own state of consciousness. I'm being told, "Examine the way you're thinking at the moment."

This morning, Jean-François said to his wife, "I don't know why, but the song *Forever Young* is going around in my head." His spouse said, "Ah! That's happy longevity!" (*laughter*) It was lovely to see his reaction; something in him *clicked* because he realized that the song corresponded to the soul-state he felt inside.

A person who spontaneously starts singing *I Can't Live if Living Is Without You* is in a state of emotional dependency. Otherwise, there is nothing to justify why his unconscious should play this song in his head. When this happens, if we pay attention to our mood, to our soul-state, to what we are feeling, we realize that, yes, indeed, the song describes our state of consciousness well.

In the same manner, if we're thinking of someone and a song pops into our head, we know what state of mind this person is in at that particular moment. It's a form of mediumnity or ESP (extra-sensory perception) and we must use it very wisely, with a sense of sacredness. It's like the images we receive in meditation.

When Jean-François was singing *Forever Young* this morning, he emanated a certain type of energy. If he had been singing *I'm Just a Gigolo* he would have had a totally different energy. (*laughter*) His wife wouldn't have thought of happy longevity. The song he was singing represented a soul-state, an energy that emanated an essence like the perfume of a flower.

So, would someone like a dream interpreted or is there a question?

Yes, Peter. (Participant: I set off early this morning to go and get something from home and two kilometers from my house, a little bear crossed the road in front of me. He was hopping along. I had a feeling he was going to find his mother on the other side of the road. It made me think of the bear symbolism in Amerindian philosophy, introspection. This is what came to my mind at that moment.)

In order to understand the symbol of the bear, we simply need to analyze its behavior. Sometimes, it's difficult to find the positive side of an animal. In such cases, we start with the negative side: we take the negative symbolism and we reverse it. We do the same when we have difficulty finding the negative side: we take the positive behavior and reverse it.

This is how we'll proceed. When this event occurred, the bear was positive because it was gentle and there were no problems. What's more, it was a young bear.

A bear has a gluttonous aspect. This is a well-known fact. (Participant: It eats honey.) Yes, and, as a professional beekeeper, who'd know that better than you? Honey is natural sugar and sweetness. Bees make honey and the positive aspect of the bee is work. The bee works to bring sweetness, whereas the bear, it just takes. It's ready to destroy to satisfy its needs, which are very strong. When it's hungry or feels threatened, it can become very aggressive—it can even be dangerous.

I know Peter and I know that he's working intensely on his vital energy. The operation he went through lately has led him to work intensively and these days, he's been reaching high levels of consciousness. He has greatly evolved through all of this. His health problem happened for a reason. It's wonderful.

Since the bear that you saw was young, it represented youth, the energy of youth and, consequently, the activation of vital energy. Well, the first two chakras—those most directly involved in the activation of vital energy—are associated with the senses of smell and taste. And the bear is driven by these two senses. Like most animals, the bear's senses of smell and taste are very well developed and when we think of this animal we immediately think of its gluttonous, greedy side.

In us, in human beings, the sense of smell is greatly atrophied. This is a sense that should be more acute and sensitive. Up Above, They've blocked it for us because if we could smell to full capacity, we'd often have difficulty thinking. We need to have developed consciousness to a high level — to have transcended the energy of the first chakras — in order to have access to a highly developed sense of smell because, otherwise, odors would exercise very strong, too strong powers of attraction or repulsion in us. We would act like animals. A woman emitting a strong sexual odor would be pursued by men and vice versa. So, Up Above, They are obliged to block this function within us to help us think and to help us raise our energy up into our superior centers.

What is interesting is that as we evolve, our senses become available once again and we can use them as guides. How does this work? The senses open up when we need them. Our senses suddenly become very acute. For example, we may smell an odor or hear a sound when a malevolent person approaches us; it's as if the odor or sound were amplified. Clairvoyance, clairsentience and clairaudience are also senses that are sublimated, transcended and that serve people's evolution.

The more evolved a person is, the more he masters the forces that dwell within him and the more he has full access to his potential. Perception through our senses is part of a human being's capacities; it links us to materiality. If one of the senses is dysfunctional — deafness, blindness, etc. — it is because the memories linked to the sense need to be cleansed and rectified. Likewise, if a person feels unsettled by a sensation he perceives in his environment, it is because he is being made to work on memories that correspond to this sense.

To lose one of these senses has a whole meaning of its own. People who go blind, as well as those who must wear glasses, have something to learn from this loss. There is a continuum that goes from perfect eyesight to total blindness and any deviation from perfection indicates a distortion. Eyesight problems — and this applies to all of our senses — is not a punishment from God: it is a learning tool because we ourselves created our limitations.

Many people in today's societies wear glasses or contact lenses. The percentage is very high. Why? Because, when we were young, we weren't shown how to use our seeing capacity properly. Too often, we use our eyes to satisfy only our basic needs. We want so many things that our eyes are excessively solicited and not in a good way. Some people are always in front of a computer for nothing important, or read too much, or read anything. Therefore, their eyesight is poorly educated. In order to improve our eyesight, we simply close our eyes, symbolically speaking, which is to say we learn to meditate and perceive things from a metaphysical point of view — from the point of view of Creation.

Our senses are alive. Their state is an indication to us of what we need to work on within ourselves. If we do the Work, the difficulty may, one day, give way to something positive, to rediscovered potential.

During our last tour in France, a man told me about what he was experiencing with his eyes. He was very shaken because he had just been told that he would probably go blind. This man has been a therapist for 25 years. I asked him, "Have you come to see me to know what this means, symbolically?" He nodded. So, I said to him, "You have looked at others a lot but have you taken the time to look at yourself — to examine yourself?" He answered, "No. I understand what you mean…but what can I do now?"

I replied, "Sir, you are now experiencing the consequence. A consequence may take a long time to fix. For you to have reached this point, you have undoubtedly been repeating the same distorted behavior for many lives. If you've been brought to this, it's because Up Above, They want you to understand something very deep about yourself and about your need to look within. You made good use of your capacity to see others, to examine them and help them but you didn't balance this help with inner renewal. In a way, you let your battery run out of power. Now, They want to help you go within."

All blind people go within; they have no choice. Moreover, they are led to develop their other senses — touch, hearing, etc. This helps them learn to see in depth.

When faced with a physical difficulty — whatever it may be — we should analyze it symbolically in order to understand its

86

meaning—because it does have a meaning. Creation is so perfect and so simple! The mechanism of the human body is complex, but if we find the symbolism or the essence of a problem, it becomes easy to understand.

The eyes allow us to see. In terms of consciousness, they allow us to look and to discern. The ears allow us to hear, therefore to understand and obey. The nose allows us to smell what belongs to the element air, which is related to the world of thoughts—as in the expression *to sniff things out*. The tongue allows us to taste. It is therefore linked to emotions and to our way of nourishing ourselves and to experimenting—as in the expression *to have a taste for something*. Skin allows us to touch and be touched. In terms of consciousness, it is therefore linked to sensitivity and love.

There is a meaning to each sense. Therefore, if the sense no longer functions on the concrete level, we find its meaning in order to understand the reason for the problem. The same idea applies to every organ of the body. If we have stomach problems, the state of consciousness of *digestion* is in question—there are things we need to digest. If we have problems on the prostate level, we need to look at what relates to evacuation, purification and sexuality. As for the kidneys, it's the idea of filtration. The left kidney relates to the inner world; the right kidney, to the outside. The heart represents motivation, emotion, because it pumps and circulates the blood, which symbolizes vital energy.

By proceeding this way we find the deep meaning of a physical difficulty. We identify the function of the affected organ, we transpose it to the other levels and hence we avoid making an erroneous analysis. Everything in the physical state is conceived according to metaphysical functions. In fact, states of consciousness are metaphysical functions; they are great functions of creation.

Whenever we think of a company, we think of what it does. A company makes bread. It may have as many stores as it likes and a whole fleet of trucks but, essentially, it makes bread. This is its function or its reason for being. All of the rest are accessories. The same idea applies to the body. When we want to know the symbolism of an organ or a tissue, we ask, "What does it do? Why does it exist?" Its symbolic meaning is its principal function.

Another question?

Yes, madam. (Dreamer: Last night, I had a dream. *I was going back to Switzerland and I was in a vehicle with my partner. He told me, "I'm leaving you." I said to him, "Oh really! Have you met someone else?" He said he had. So I said, "Well then! I'll have to sell my house." I told him to sell the house. He called an agency to sell the house and the person at the other end said, "What are you going to do with the cupboards?" On another level, I was looking at my house from afar, thinking, "Anyway, I've never liked this house." Still in my dream, the house was sold and I left. The dream ended when I was about to plant very small, very ugly little trees at the edge of a large gray building.*) Thank you for sharing this.

I will ask you a few questions because, at first glance, there are two possible interpretations to this dream. Are you with this partner now? (Dreamer: Yes, we live together.) Are things going well with him? (Dreamer: Things are rather quiet.) Quiet...I understand. (Dreamer: I would just like to add that when I say quiet, I mean that there's a lot of respect. That's the main aspect or theme of our relationship.) Ok, fine.

Is separation a possibility? Could this happen? (Dreamer: At the moment, no, but in the near future, maybe.) All right.

So, we'll give two interpretations. First of all, we refer the entire dream back to you and consider the fact that your companion only represented a part of you.

You see that this dream truly makes you revisit memories that deal with the lack of longevity—there is no more longevity within the couple. The union is coming to an end. So this dream is intimately linked to the Work that you are doing this weekend. Your companion was used to show you a distortion with regard to happy longevity. This means that you carry the seed of separation within you. It is present in your memories.

Will you actually separate? It's possible. If the memories touched by the dream are not worked on and cleansed, they could become reality in the short run. However, this could also happen many years from now, even in another life. For example, you could spend your whole present life with your companion because everything is there—the house, the car, etc. Your relationship could remain as it is, like a sort of unwritten, unspoken convention, which, seen from the outside, would appear as the continuity of the couple. In another life, you would find yourself in a fruitless union that would not bring—no more than does this one—abundance and happy longevity. We see that you have seeds of infidelity, because he left you in the dream for another person. That is because you, yourself, are unfaithful in your memories, thoughts and emotions. You wish for another love life without trying to make this one work.

Let's analyze the symbols more deeply. Your companion, in the dream, represented a part of you, an important part of your inner man. In another life—or in many other lives—you could have been a man and abandoned your companion. You have karma relating to this because, in your dream, your companion was ready to leave you to go with someone else. If we are abandoned, it is because we harbor memories of having abandoned as well as having been abandoned—we have both aspects because each one responds to the other in order to form the distortion.

Then, you asked him to sell your house. The house symbolizes personal as well as family intimacy. Since you both live there, it represents, among other things, your intimacy as a couple. The fact that you wanted to sell it means that you wished to end your relationship as a couple in order to begin a new stage in your life.

As you said in your dream, you've never liked this house. There is certainly work to be done on this level because it isn't healthy not to like who we are on the inside. This thought also confirms that you aren't happy within the intimacy of the couple. You certainly feel frustrated in this relationship. You need to talk with your companion so that one day you will experience a happy union. Essentially, this dream deals with the emotional problems that you are experiencing within the couple.

When your companion called the real estate agency, he was asked what you were thinking of doing with the cupboards. This scene helps us to understand and allows us to delve a little deeper. What do cupboards symbolize? What is their purpose? They are used to keep objects and souvenirs that we might need at a later date. When we sell our house, we usually empty the cupboards and we get rid of everything we no longer need or that might become a burden to us. So the fact that the person on the phone asked what you wanted to do with the cupboards signifies that Heaven wants you to deal with the cleansing of your memories and anything that could clutter your life in the future. It's as if They were explaining to you, "No, you no longer want this house that you don't like, but you must think of doing a big cleanup of what you've accumulated. From union to union, from difficulty to difficulty, you've accumulated old things. It's time to think about this now."

Then, there was a change of scene in which you were shown why you need to cleanse: you were going to plant ugly trees. Planting ugly trees means to put down roots in a negative way. Rather than use the ordeal to undertake real transformation, you hang on to souvenirs—to everything negative that you've experienced. Consequently, you develop resentment for your surroundings and life on Earth and you become nasty with others. The word nasty is a bit harsh but I'm sure you understand. (Dreamer: Yes, I understand what you mean. Thank you.)

You were going to plant those trees alongside a gray building. Gray can either be positive or negative. In this dream, because of the ugliness of the trees, it was very negative. Gray is a mixture of white and black—in terms of consciousness, good and bad. So, you are sometimes negative, sometimes positive, and you don't orient yourself toward a fresh start. You are preparing to build your life in this manner. Of course, such an attitude is a hindrance to happy longevity. You will attract a man with negative energy because you perpetuate the *negative* within yourself. This is what this scene meant.

When we end something—such as when we move or sell our house—we should take stock and recycle certain energies. When things end badly, we must try to find out what we need to transform. Otherwise, we fall back into the same pattern and we attract a similar situation to the one we experienced. A sale is a form of recycling; in itself, it is therefore very positive, but when we don't take the time to clean out the cabinets, the recycling is incomplete.

In real life, it isn't necessary to move to create a fresh start in our life. We can remain in the same house and work on ourselves. However, it isn't enough to simply eliminate a few memories; we must go right down to the structure of our inner world, on all levels.

Moving habits are quite different in Europe from in Quebec. In Europe, people don't move very often. A house can stay in the family for centuries and be witness to the lives of numerous generations of the same family. That's really something! Of course, this can be very positive—there is a very positive aspect to this continuity. But there is also a negative side, that is, lack of flexibility and a certain difficulty in accepting change, and in loving and encouraging what is new.

It does us good to move. It means, in a sense, that we're changing our state of consciousness. In Quebec, we sometimes go to the other extreme: if we don't move every two years, it's as if we're not normal. (*laughter*)

I myself have moved at least 15 times. It's too much. There is an imbalance on our side as well. In many families, a sense of heritage is lacking. We have not sufficiently developed the notion of building on what has already been acquired. The *roots* aspect that heritage offers is not valued much in Quebec. At the same time, this allows for change and adaptability. Ideally, we should feel comfortable both with continuity and with change.

So, to go back to the dream, you visited memories that concerned the lack of longevity. This is the first interpretation. From this perspective, the dream doesn't announce that your companion will leave you for another; it simply signals the fact that you harbor within you the seed of separation. It also attests to the fact that you emanate this energy; it is as if you had to experience separation. And so, of course, if separation is planned in your companion's Program, it will come true.

The dream clearly shows that, based on negative experience, you have a tendency to generate even more *negativity*. Thus, if there is a separation and you don't do inner cleansing, you will inevitably feel depressed. So, it's time to cleanse the memories linked to the lack of longevity and of continuity within the couple.

What is it that contributes to happy longevity within a couple? First and foremost, trust—in the broadest sense—is the main ingredient. As for myself, I have total trust or confidence in my life with Christiane. It isn't so much in her—as a person—that I feel this trust. It is God that I totally trust. I have complete confidence that God will always bring into my life—into my lives—what is best for me and for my evolution. In fact, I received a dream that told me that Christiane was the woman of my life.

Christiane has that same trust or faith. We also have the same goal, which is to develop qualities and virtues. I know that I have to be right and so I create correct, right, just experiences. By being right, Christiane also creates experiences that are right, that are correct and just according to Divine Laws. We are aware that this orientation we both share creates a very strong union. Both of us have also established balance within our polarities—Christiane as a woman, and I as a man—and as a result, together, we can experience true complementarity. We experience extraordinary stability, understanding and communication.

I cannot remember one instance, over the years, when we've disagreed about something. We receive dreams that harmonize and are in tune with each other. Of course, as I've just said, we have evolved to the point of having such understanding and harmony. It was quite a process.

Now, our spirituality is so strong that we have total trust and confidence. If someone comes near us with distorted intentions, we see this in advance in our dreams or we receive signs. Also, if someone comes to us with pure intentions, we see this too. We know the state of consciousness of the person and so we know the type of dynamics this person can bring.

That's what Divine is—we are able to *read* Life. We're not just thinking, "Ah! The Divine is the One who will take care of everything." It goes far beyond this. We are able to see how Life is constructed, and where it's headed. Eventually, by talking and sharing, a great bond or fusion establishes itself within the couple.

The first step that aims at purifying the relationship within a couple consists in working with the Law of Resonance. We say to ourselves, "All right, I don't feel good. He—or she—was not very nice to me. Well, this is a part of myself; a part of me is not very nice." Then, we talk gently to the other person using the right words in order to de-dramatize and to try to re-establish harmony.

Sometimes, wisdom counsels, "Wait an hour or two; he'll go off for a run—or he'll knock his head on the door frame two or three times—and after that he'll be more receptive." Of course, if the other person's consciousness is not open, we don't say to him, "Hey, you! Do you know why you hit your head?" (*laughter*) If we said that, he might start roaring like an angry lion.

We speak to him with our feelings rather than with power. When we manage to speak with our feelings and to say to the other person, "You know, when you said that to me, you hurt my feelings," it's already a beginning. The other person might say, "Yes, but it was because of this." "That's true, but at the same time, try to be more gentle because I felt hurt." By proceeding this way, we've just managed to create an atmosphere that's favorable to dialogue. When we speak from the heart, things can change.

The worst thing we can do when the other person is fed up or is complaining about a difficulty outside of the relationship, is to enter into the same *ray* as him. If we listen to him and let him say what he has to say and then tell him, "Ah! Well, there's something those people need to understand"—this changes the atmosphere and allows him to see the situation in a different light.

In our society, some people are in a position to influence the state of consciousness of people—I'm thinking in particular of politicians and people who work in the media and, of course, the initiates who are able to act in the invisible worlds—but most don't have such influence. However, within our circle of family and friends, this is a possibility that is open to us. Our Work consists first and foremost in knowing and transforming ourselves. Then, as we progress along our spiritual path, we share and we express ourselves—we say what we think and feel—and our environment also changes.

If we don't communicate with those close to us, eventually, we feel a rift, a great discrepancy with the outside world. Within the couple's relationship, we need to be able to adjust things as we go along by communicating with the other person. If we've been married for 20 years and have never talked about the 152 problems that bother us, at some point, we no longer feel good in the relationship. In this case, we have to start from the beginning. With gentleness and understanding, we solve problem number one—things are a bit shaken up—then we see to number two and so on. If we proceed in this manner, we eventually get to where we're going and the relationship is regenerated, or else life leads us to change highways. When a learning experience, an apprenticeship is finished, our situation changes—this is an absolute truth.

If we leave the other person on a bitter note, if the relationship doesn't end well, we will have to continue our apprenticeship—the same one—in our next union. Of course, we try to avoid linking up with the same type of person but at some point, oops! we become aware that we've fallen into the same old pattern. We haven't closed the circle.

For some people, changing partners is like changing a roll of toilet paper. They don't take the time to analyze what happened and in no time at all they are in someone else's arms.

If we end a relationship, we must end it properly before beginning another one. We go to the bottom of things, first on our own, and if the other person is open to dialogue, we discuss it in depth with him as well. If, during this process, we are attracted to someone else, we maintain our self-command—we wait for our relationship to be over. We do things properly without skipping any steps. And Life will see to it that we meet the right person.

In any case, before getting involved in a couple-relationship, we should always ask Heaven, "Is this the right person for the evolution of my soul? Is he the right husband or life partner—or is she the right wife or life partner—for me?" We ask for a dream and if we don't receive one, we ask again the next day. We do this for many days. It's important to do this because getting involved with someone is quite something! So, before taking our clothes off, we ask. (*laughter*)

This is how the new evolved children will proceed. They won't need to behave like the generations before them and go from one partner to another. They will have a continually functioning inner GPS or SatNav; they will be guided by their dreams & signs and thus avoid many difficulties.

Spiritual work is essential to a healthy, positive relationship as a couple. I, myself, changed completely as a result of the initiatic work that I did with my dreams and my understanding of signs. In the beginning, I was completely depolarized. I was introverted and I didn't talk. I expressed myself through music but not through speech. I was very intuitive—I was ultra sensitive—but this sensitivity played against me because I felt the negative resonance that I had with people and this blocked my communication. With women, it wasn't easy: I always found myself with super dynamic, enterprising women. I found myself playing the role of the woman and they of the man.

We often see this in a couple: one talks a lot and the other not at all. Sometimes, it's the man who talks. The woman can't get a word in edgewise because her partner dominates the conversation; he's always right. When this happens, the woman must say to herself, "Wow! My inner man has a lot of nerve! He takes up a lot of space! I'm going to cleanse him. I'll do the necessary inner work. In another life, I was a domineering man. Now, I find myself with this part of me manifested in the physical form of my husband. I'll transform this force within me and I'll start talking again. I'll tell him things the right way, not in a domineering way." This is how we start to balance things and find a balanced polarity.

When we are very emissive, we attract people who have difficulty on the emissive level. Generally, people who lack emissivity are afraid to express themselves because they harbor a lot of memories of aggressiveness. Also, they have repressed their anger for many years because their partner didn't let them express themselves or intimidated them. So they don't speak anymore. They've settled into this silence and life goes on. The person has found stability with the other and ends up saying, "I'll just keep quiet. By keeping quiet, everything will be fine."

Over time, the person absorbs the opinions of the companion or spouse and begins to think like him and believe that his opinions are correct, that he's right. This is because in actual fact, she resembles him—resonance between them is very strong. The person isn't even aware of having lost her personality. This is simply the return of the pendulum for the person who, in other lives, didn't give others any room.

How do we manage to rebalance all of this? By consciously transforming ourselves. If we tend to talk too much, we consciously begin to listen to the other person and encourage him to express himself. Even if his point of view is not always right, we ask, "What's your opinion on this subject? How do you see things?" If he finds it hard to express himself, we mustn't be cross and scold him. If he has refrained from talking for 20 years, we can't expect him to defend a thesis—this would be asking too much. We give him time to reeducate himself, to manage speech and emissivity. We must remember that we have created—or at least contributed to the creation of—this situation.

The same applies to sexual relations. There are so many taboos linked to sexuality! So many memories express themselves in the intimate relationship between a man and a woman! Very often, nothing works on this level. Sometimes even, the man or the woman must think of another person in order to feel something.

We must find the essence of things—authenticity and true communication. We must begin to cultivate beautiful intentions for the other person and for the relationship and refuse, figuratively speaking, to eat fast-food everyday in our relationship. Of course, when we begin to touch upon essential points, our inner animals wake up and begin to roar, especially if they have been asleep for a long period of time. We then must take the time to reeducate them and remain in command of the liberated forces. What is so fantastic with dreams is that we can see these forces at work within us in our daily life.

If we stagnate within the couple it's because we want to. Often, we're afraid to say something that will shake up the relationship. We've built a false structure and we're under the impression that as soon as we say something that is true, everything will crumble and, above all, our soul will have to change. A relationship, a couple, must continually mutate or change in order to achieve happiness—just like a person.

The best way to improve within a couple is to become kind, gentle, and affectionate and to do for the other person what we would like him to do for us—and to do so unconditionally. In reality, we do it for ourselves. We can say to ourselves, "The other person represents a part of me. If I do this for him, I do it for myself." At a certain point, with time, the mirror becomes so positive that the other person tries to do the same; if we emanate gentleness and kindness, the other will respond by emanating the same energy.

If the other person doesn't want to change, to transform and go to the bottom of things, we continue to cleanse our memories, and at a certain point, we no longer resonate with this person. We no longer vibrate to the same frequency; we're no longer on the same wavelength. As we say, we either *make it or break it*. If we feel that it must break, we must have the courage to move on without the other. This could even be the main challenge of our life.

We have seen true miracles with couples that have worked on themselves with dreams & signs—you can't imagine. Of course, we've also seen others who had to separate.

To be right, we have to do the work within ourselves. This is what is important. Very often, people who wish to maintain the relationship without having to go within themselves end up feeling badly; they do things that cause them to feel false. They can no longer be genuine with the other person and talk about what's important. Or else it's, "You have your activities, I have mine and that's OK—that doesn't bother me." Each one does their own thing; they live parallel lives without ever really meeting, without ever fusing.

If this were a dream of the second type—where you visited your companion's soul—it would indicate that Up Above, They were preparing you for an ordeal, for a separation. But if this breakup were to occur, remember: you must not plant ugly trees. You must work on yourself because this trial could cause you to sink into a lot of *negativity*. It's probably to warn you of this that you were sent this dream because now, you're open enough. You've been shown a tendency toward negativity but you can modify this tendency.

So if you experience a separation, you'll know that it was written, that it was part of the Divine Plan and it will be easier for you to avoid sinking into *negativity*. You will be able to say to yourself, "Now, I have to move on to a new type of intimacy; to a new inner house. My life will be renewed."

When we receive a dream such as this one, we can also have a tendency to become suspicious of our partner and to hold him responsible for our woes. But it's important to try to remain neutral and to work on ourselves, on our inner man. In any case, you have this lack of longevity within you.

If a man leaves with another woman, it's because there's something missing in the relationship. It's either because one of the partners is not correct or right due to *dysfunctional* needs, or, because both have settled into indifference or coldness with regard to the other.

When I advise people to refer the dream back to themselves and do inner work, they often answer or say to themselves, "That's all well and good. I'm looking at myself. But what about him—or her— he isn't looking at himself." This is often the attitude that prevents a person from taking a step forward. If we take the first step, we give the example and we create a movement of love and kindness. When we do something for the other person, we do it with a good attitude and good intention. We try to become better. We talk to ourselves or to our inner man or inner woman. This is the way to help others transform themselves.

Yes, madam. (Dreamer: I have a dream I'd like interpreted. *I could see my sister's face. I didn't really recognize her but I knew it was my sister. Her face had shadowy parts. She said to me, "Read this book, Anna. Read it. She follows her priorities. She follows her priorities. She follows her priorities." She said it three times like that. Then she smiled—a sort of forced smile.*)

What does your sister represent for you? (Dreamer: Well, she cast me aside saying, "You and I are so different that we're better off not seeing each other anymore.") Ok. And how do you view this difference? (Dreamer: She is more conservative than I am.) I understand.

First of all, we have to remember that if we experience conflict with someone, we're responsible for this conflict. Even if the other person has a share in the responsibility, we must first of all refer the situation back to ourselves. We create conflict through lack of wisdom. We might, for example, have gone too far with someone and, at some point, this person closes up. Something slipped into the interaction—usually negative resonance—and the relationship ceased to be harmonious.

In your dream, you were visiting a part of yourself, of your feminine side. Your sister was inciting you to read a book; she repeated that you should read it. And three times she said, "She follows her priorities." So, you were visiting parts of yourself that have a tendency to insist and to impose things on others. This is not necessarily apparent — the dream shows an inner attitude rather than actual behavior because your sister is a woman. There's also something conservative about this part that imposes, which is an attitude that you perceive in your sister and that is represented by her. So, when you believe in something, you can become very focused and impose your sources of inspiration on others. For example, you might insist on recommending they read a particular book or go to a certain conference.

Your sister mentioned Anna. Does this name mean something in particular to you? Do you know someone named Anna? (Dreamer: No. It's as if it were the title of a book.) Ah! I see.

There are no coincidences; all the symbols participate in the meaning of the dream. Anna is a female name. So, it's as if you were imposing something from within on others. If the title of the book had been *James*, it would have been different: it would have indicated that you push others to do certain things and to behave in certain ways. You were being shown that you have a tendency to impose philosophies or inner ways of being.

But, you are not only that, this isn't all of you; it's very important for you to remind yourself of this. You have beautiful aspects too, except that in this dream, you were visiting a small part of you that sometimes has a tendency to impose things on others.

One side of the face was in shadows. Was it the left or right side? (Dreamer: It varied; it depended on the angle and on the way the face was set. At the same time, her entire face was in shadow as if the source of light was behind her.)

The play of shadow and light on the face represented variations in mood, in soul-states. When we see someone's face, it generally tells us what frame of mind the person is in, for example, whether this person is feeling good, sad, anxious or angry; in other words how his soul is feeling at that moment. Other parts of the body might convey certain states of mind, states of soul, but the face truly offers a concentration of expressions — especially the eyes. Through the eyes, we can truly see the soul and become aware of how the person is feeling.

Your sister forced a smile. In your soul-state described by this dream, there was therefore, the notion of a forced smile. This indicates that in your way of presenting things to others, there is something that is forced. We force ourselves to smile and we force the other person at the same time. I felt this tendency when you said *Read this* a little while ago.

You must be careful when you talk about things that you're enthusiastic about. Sometimes, you can share your sister's extra conservative side in the sense that when you believe in something, you don't see the other person's situation and you suppose that what inspires you will also inspire others. Even with *Dreams & Signs*, you might go up to someone and say, "Hey! Read this, it's good for you" meaning *Hey! Let's go! Come on! Start working!* Even if you want to help the person, even if what you propose is very good, you can be disrespectful toward the person by doing this. This is because you have a certain rigidity that stops you from seeing where this person is at and what this person's inner situation is. For example, the other person might have a spouse who is totally closed to spirituality and be afraid of his or her reactions.

We aren't right when we hold on obstinately to an idea or a way of seeing things. To be spiritual means to know how to adapt to others and be able to see them as evolving beings and to know exactly what they are able to take in when we are talking to them.

So, Up Above wanted to help you improve your way of presenting things. If your sister is conservative — as you have said — she was able to perceive this aspect within you whenever you spoke to her with conviction. You became like her and she could feel the resonance between you. She may be conservative in one area and you in another, but you both have the same tendency. You are spiritual and she may be materialistic or in an extremely religious state of mind.

So, you need to develop receptivity in your relations with others, and, before proposing a philosophy to someone, you must ask yourself, "Ok, what *country* does he live in?" and analyze his manner of dress, his behavior, the type of people he associates with, etc.

If we see a woman whose hair is saturated with hair spray, we love her the way that she is, of course, but we know that she has a somewhat rigid way of thinking. If we see another who is wearing too much makeup, hidden shall we say behind her mask, we know that she has a superficial side. With such information, we know, even before talking with them, that we won't be able to reveal to these women certain things about them. We know that we will meet with resistance. So, we go about it in a gentler, less direct way. This dream showed you that you have a tendency to be too direct. This might be all right with some people but others might simply close up. There you are. Thank you for sharing this with us.

Has anyone else a question or a dream they would like to have interpreted?

Yes, madam. (Dreamer: Is it ok if it's violent?) Of course, please feel at ease. We are listening with our heart. (Dreamer: There are two parts to this dream. It begins and at a certain point it changes. So, *I was with my uncle who was an engineer and who died about 12 years ago and a colleague of his who works in the decoration business. While I was looking at the decorator, all of a sudden, he grew old and was covered in makeup. He was wearing purple mascara. So, he became less authentic. Then the scene changed and I found myself in a concentration camp as a Nazi soldier. I was photographing the prisoners. The idea was that the prisoners who disguised themselves as Irishmen — by dressing in green with green hats, etc. — and who smiled, would not be killed. One older man was not wearing the disguise and he was protesting. I was under the impression that I was the one speaking when he protested. I knew that we were going to shoot this man and I didn't want to. I really felt bad for him but — I couldn't help myself — I told myself, "Ah! He's 80 years old, we'll just take a picture for his family" and I shot him through the heart. This man's wife appeared on his right and I shot her too. At the far end of the scene, above the people who had been shot, there was the print of a black hand.* That's all. Since then, I've had several other dreams in which the three people closest to me were being shot or died.)

The engineer — your deceased uncle — what does he represent for you? (Dreamer: He was a bit of a softie, a pushover. He was intelligent but he let his family control him. He was the last relative left on my father's side. My father died when I was very young.)

101

And the decorator, what does he represent for you? (Dreamer: He is a very competent man. He is going through deep depression, an intense burn-out at the moment.) I see.

This dream is very interesting because it has allowed you to go to the heart of your masculine polarity or your masculine side. It revealed some forces that you had within you in other lives when you were a man. You weren't necessarily a Nazi soldier or a Jewish prisoner but you experienced concrete events that led you to the states of consciousness illustrated in this dream.

Let's analyze the first symbol of the deceased uncle who was an engineer. A deceased person can visit us in a dream but not always. When this happens, it's usually immediately after the death or in the following months and he comes for a reason: he comes to give us a message, even if he or she doesn't speak at all. All the symbols surrounding the person, the way they dressed or you dressed, etc. will be part of the message you are receiving.

So this uncle, who was an engineer, represented a part of you. An engineer represents the way that we build our life. Engineering has a number of specialties — building, water canals, chemistry, computer science, etc. — and the specialty of the character we are analyzing gives us additional information to find its symbolism.

(Dreamer: My uncle was an armaments engineer during the Second World War. He worked at manufacturing bombs.)

This information is truly precious in helping us understand the dream. Your uncle represented memories that you harbor related to generating conflict. He also represented the passive or easy-going, meek side of a person that allows others to control him. These two types of memories or states of consciousness — confrontational, conflict behavior and passivity — stop you from moving forward and affirming yourself. Let's see how.

Although they may seem contradictory, these two states of consciousness are quite complementary; one is conscious and the other unconscious — passivity occurs on the conscious level and conflict hides within the unconscious. If a person is passive and afraid of affirming himself, it's because he has registered memories of abuse of power in other lives. For example, he intimidated others and in this life he is easily intimidated. He has lost his self-confidence with regard to intimidating people because his soul *remembers* the harmful consequences of conflict. So, on that day, you were revisiting memories linked to this issue.

Yesterday, we talked about your daughter — she is a very evolved, intense child. In fact, you find yourself in this very situation with her: you have difficulty exercising your authority with her. Why? Because if you exercised your authority, you'd be afraid of yourself and of your behavior. You try to compensate by being too gentle, when you should be exercising your authority.

(Dreamer: Yes, that's exactly it. I'm afraid of being aggressive when I have to intervene with Sandra. My voice changes and I become aggressive.)

This is why you are passive with her. She's only four years old and she's beginning to be very domineering at home; she controls quite a bit. She is like a child boss who decides everything. You are so afraid of being too strict when you exercise your authority that you prefer to let her do what she wants.

In your dream, the man who was with your uncle works in the decoration business. He therefore represented the way that you create ambience in your life. In the dream, his face became fully made up like a woman's. This part of you, which normally should be emissive, has the character traits of a man with feminine characteristics. There really is a problem with the polarity aspect. Your masculine polarity — inner, because you're a woman — is blocked.

You told us that this man is going through a depression. Depression occurs when the person is bogged down and stuck in very heavy memories. This stops him from moving forward on the concrete level. He is in more or less conscious contact with these forces, he feels lost and in his conscience, he's going round in circles because he doesn't know how to get himself out of this state. What is interesting is that you enter into contact with very ancient forces, which are not necessarily linked to the Nazis, but that belong to the same compartment of consciousness.

In the rest of the dream, you were shown why your daughter takes advantage of you — why you let her control you and you aren't able to intervene when you should.

(Dreamer: I don't think it's related to the Nazis—to a previous life with the Nazis—either, because the Irish people wouldn't have been there. I was given the essence.) That's right. Exactly.

It is the essence—the state of consciousness—that we are shown in dreams. Your state of consciousness was simply illustrated by one of the greatest genocides that took place on this Earth. The armaments engineer constructed war but he's a passive man. Although he is the one who prepared the striking force, he is incapable of using it. Memories are behind this.

We are in the dynamics of the aggressive victim. On seeing this engineer, we could say, "Oh! He's so sweet! He's a good, kind uncle. Why does everyone take advantage of him?" But if we could enter his unconscious, we would see memories where he took advantage of others. Sometimes we encounter people who have an inferiority complex and who, as soon as they are with someone who is weaker than they are, become nasty and scathing with them, either concretely or intellectually. They may say nasty things to a sales lady or speak to her in a hurtful tone. We're surprised when they do this—we don't recognize them.

You were visiting memories of repressed violence. This violence is, in fact, the reason why everyone must look happy, as though they're having fun. The prisoners were prepared to do almost anything: they dressed up in disguises and all sorts of things like that. These forces might manifest themselves in your family, for example; you might create zany situations simply to compensate for the lack of profound joy. You say to yourself, "Oh! We're having so much fun!" but deep down, it isn't very joyful. It isn't true joyfulness, it's artificial.

The prisoners disguised themselves in green. Green is the color of the heart chakra, of love. Since these were disguises, the love is not authentic either.

You shot at the prisoners who weren't playing the game. This meant that even if you behave like a sweet, gentle person to give the impression that all is well, as soon as things don't go your way—for example, if your husband doesn't behave as you'd like him to—you can become very scathing.

This is a very interesting dream. I'm sure many people can see themselves in it.

What happens with an inner dynamic such as this one is that your husband may be passive or even effeminate. Your masculine polarity is blocked and its outward manifestation is in your spouse's traits. It's quite a phenomenon! You have contributed to the creation of this situation. When you're ready — when the time is right — you can work at modifying these parameters that shape your relationship. You can ask for dreams that will explain to you what you need to adjust and how to do it.

You see, by working with the understandings of our dreams, you have more knowledge of the unconscious memories that stop you from exercising authority and justice.

In fact, your daughter is there to teach you to reactivate your masculine polarity the right way. You need to understand and rectify everything that this dream revealed about you; otherwise, your daughter could create unending problems for you. When our children experience difficulties, we're tortured and we experience difficult emotions. She's only four and already she's a child boss. But you and your husband still have many years to rectify the situation because she's still young. Thank you for sharing this.

Yes, sir. (Dreamer: I have a dream. It's a dream that I had this morning. *I was at the start of a car race. We had to follow a certain course that ended up at a college. I knew that at the point of arrival there was no participant list and no stopwatch. So I volunteered to bring the list and the stopwatches so we could register the arrivals. I thought I'd get there quickly because I intended to take a shortcut. So I set off. On the way, I had to cross through an experimental farm. I don't know what it was doing there; I thought I had lost my way. Anyway, I had to go through stables. As I did so, I saw that the animals had been abandoned. They looked weak and sick and there was excrement everywhere. I felt so sorry for the animals! I managed to get through the stable by walking on the left and, finally, in order to get out of there, I had to step over dead animals. Then, once I was outside, I saw a large snow-covered slope. A ski slope, in fact. I said to myself, "Ok, now I know where I am, I know my way," and I started running. It was all going well, I was running and at a given moment, I turned around and I saw that a little calf was following me. I said to myself, "I'm going to outdistance it," but I couldn't seem to get ahead: it was running as fast as I was. It was clean and looked nice. With each step, it sank into the snow but it was still strong enough to follow me. As for myself, I was floating on the snow. So, I said to myself, "I'll take him with me. He deserves to follow me since he freed himself from his situation." At the same time, I wasn't sure I should take it because I couldn't see how I would be able to put it in the car. Finally, I took it with me and I finished the race.)*

We understand why your wife teaches physical education. (*laughter*) There's a lot of strength and power there!

This dream is very interesting because it confirms that you are now in a powerful learning dynamic.

The goal of the race was the school. In a dream, a school represents learning on the conscience level. This morning, you must certainly have woken up with a desire to learn. A great thirst to know yourself is awakening within you and the dream triggered this awakening.

This dream contains a wealth of teaching because it showed you exactly what it is you have to work on. First of all, in your apprenticeship, you advance with a competitive spirit—hence the racing car and the preoccupation with stopwatches—which, of course, is a distortion. You want to go fast and know everything. Everyone has some of these racing cars in their conscience but Knowledge isn't acquired in this manner. Learning does not function through speed; our apprenticeship is not fuelled by speed. Advancing along a spiritual path is a day by day affair. We mustn't want to know everything and know it now, we mustn't want to go faster than the natural rhythm, and we must be happy with what we learn at every stage.

This type of attitude generally manifests itself at the beginning of our path. You're starting to work with Dream Study and, already, we can see beautiful openings within you. So, you need to understand that this is a process that happens gradually and give yourself time to progress step by step.

You show a great will to learn when you go toward others because, in the dream, you had a racing car to get to the school. You set challenges and goals for yourself and you want to succeed and get there as soon as possible. But we see that you force yourself to advance because a part of you no longer has any vital energy. The sick animals and the dead ones represent this part of you.

106

Animals represent instincts and other aspects of the vital energy. The animals in the dream were not well taken care of; they were dirty, some were sick and others dead. This meant that you can be very hard on your inner animals. You're learning to meditate and when you become aware of distortions or needs within yourself, you have a tendency to deny, suppress or punish them. You hit yourself over the head. You're very hard on yourself. The problem is that by doing this you are killing the vital force represented by these animals.

We often see this tendency in people who are on a spiritual path. When we see mistreated animals in dreams, we know that the person loses all of the energy that should help him advance. Because animal forces allow us to advance; they provide us with physical energy, reflexes and strength. In the beginning, of course, they serve to satisfy needs but when we are on a spiritual path, we educate these forces in order to manifest them correctly.

In order to attain this mastery quicker, some people mistreat or ignore their inner animals; they believe this will help them advance more quickly. They begin fasting for weeks. In fact, the man I mentioned earlier — the therapist who could possibly become blind — told me, "I'm going on a fast; I intend to fast for 30 days." His instincts had been so strong that he was going to the other extreme. He asked me what I thought of this. I said to him, "Fasting is an experience" and I talked to him about what I went through.

I experimented with fasting in order to dream more — my aim was to dream more. I fasted for I don't know how long and, at one point, I was told in a dream that it wasn't right — fasting would not make me dream more. (*laughter*) It was clear. And indeed, I didn't dream more. When I was receiving between 50 and 60 dreams per night, it was enough — I had enough information. Yet, I still wanted even more. I used to count my dreams and I would compete with myself. At a certain point, this type of attitude stops. We all go to extremes in the beginning — it's normal.

What is interesting in your dream is the contrast between the great power represented by the racing car and the depressed state of the animals. When you're in a group, you're very dynamic and you have a lot of power, strength and will-power but as soon as you're alone, without social stimulation, you lose your willpower and you have difficulty in getting going.

So, this was the type of memories that you were visiting in your dream—memories where you were hard on yourself. Then, you came out of the stables and you continued on your journey toward the school.

A calf was running behind you and it was a positive calf because it was healthy. Since the calf is a baby, we immediately have the notion that it is fed by its mother. Therefore, the calf refers to the idea of nourishing instincts so they grow strong and stable so that they may contribute toward maintaining the balance of energies in us. The fact that the animal was young also shows that your vital energy is in a process of regeneration.

When we have animals, we have to take care of them every day. You know this since you were raised on a farm. A farm is a place where we must take care of things on a daily basis and this is truly beautiful when it's well done. Therefore, the image of the farm takes us back to the importance of regularly seeing to the balance of our inner forces day after day, and above all not to abuse this vital force.

The fact that it was an experimental farm shows that you are experimenting on this level. You have not yet mastered and understood your vital forces. In fact, your wife—who represents an important part of your inner woman—teaches physical education. This confirms the fact that you are learning to balance this basic energy.

Through the image of the calf that managed to follow you, you were being shown that you have access to new energy and to renewed vigor. You are no longer battling two opposing forces—the vital force and the bad treatment of this force: you now have access to all of the new energy represented by this positive calf.

But we see that your competitive attitude is very strong. When we reach a point where we compete with a calf, it indicates an important problem. This distortion is prevalent in sports and physical training environments. At the gym or fitness club, we lift weights so that the cocks and hens running on the treadmills will look at us and admire us. It's classic. At the gym, it's very often all for show.

The spirit of competition weighs you down. We can see this by the fact that the calf sank into the snow at every step. Despite this, it still managed to follow you. As for you, you were floating. We see how strong your will to advance is. In its positive light, snow represents transcendence of emotional coldness. Your will to advance and make progress is so powerful that it gives you a feeling of lightness and allows you to feel good even in a cold ambience. This gives you a lot of confidence. We feel such a sensation when we practice a physical or sports activity with all of our heart. We feel like we have wings. We acquire a taste for high states of consciousness especially if we think about our dreams during training and stop wanting to win and to be the best. If we practice a sport with the purpose of inner growth, if we dedicate each effort to our evolution then, wow! We can truly reach the Summit with a capital S.

To go back to the general theme of the dream, which is, your apprenticeship, you are experiencing a great awakening of consciousness—a great opening—and when you hear this teaching, it speaks to you and lights you up. And so, you learn. However, you will have to watch your competitive spirit and your tendency to want to advance faster than at your personal rhythm. You also need to develop your autonomy and reach the point where your spiritual motivation comes from within rather than from your contact and relations with others. The spiritual path is me with me, you with you, each person with himself; we don't evolve to impress others. In the beginning, we can play at being spiritual: we meditate, we do yoga and we think we're *cool*—it's the *in thing* to do. We say, "I do yoga," and others say, "Oh Yes! Oh! Wow!" We look important but the effect quickly passes; once we've said it two or three times, it doesn't work anymore. (*laughter*)

It's the same as when we come home from a trip. When we arrive, family and friends are there and everyone is very enthusiastic, "Hello! We're so happy to see you!" It's hugs and kisses, etc. Then, a few hours later or the next day, it's as if we had never left—we've gone back to being an ordinary person. Why? Because the idea of a trip awakens a certain state of consciousness in people. They think, for example, "Oh! I'm so tired! I can't wait for my holidays!" and they listen to us talk about all of our travel experiences. And as they listen, inner needs are awakened and felt. They're impressed by our situation because they want to experience the same thing. This is why they're so open. And so, that's the meaning of this dream.

There we are, it's already over. I thank you with all my heart for your beautiful listening and sharing.

WORKSHOP

From the dictionary to the Dictionary

The title of this workshop is *From the dictionary to the Dictionary*—with a capital D. During this workshop we shall analyze in depth some symbols that can appear in both our dreams and meditations as well as in concrete reality in the form of signs. We will do this because everything in the Universe is a symbol and represents a field or state of consciousness.

From the dictionary to the Dictionary, with a capital D. I really like this title because it's a great description of what we do in our workshops: we start from the meaning of a word as it is defined in its usual context according to its usual usage and we bring out its metaphysical component.

Let's begin right away with the first word on the little list we have prepared for this evening's workshop: the word *accident*. In the dictionary the two main definitions of the word accident are: *a misfortune or mishap, esp. one causing injury or death;* and, *an unforeseen event or one without an apparent cause.*

How do we manage to find the metaphysical meaning, the meaning that applies on the conscious level, of an accident from these two definitions? First of all by examining its positive and negative symbolism, as we do with every symbol that appears in a dream.

Since the word *accident* evokes something negative, let's begin with the negative symbolism. Ok, so what are the negative aspects of an accident? The answer lies in its very definition: the aspects that are unforeseen and cause injury. Accidents cause damage, injury and sometimes even death. In a dream, if we see an accident occur—or if we hear someone talk about one—we can expect an ordeal and limitations to manifest in our life or in our interior.

And what is the positive aspect of an accident? (Participant: It stops us.) It stops us. Anything else? (Participant: It helps us to become aware and conscious of things.) Yes.

It helps us to become aware and conscious of things. That's the positive aspect and the reason why accidents happen.

If we have a very down-to-earth conscience, an ordinary conscience, and we have an accident, we simply attribute it to
coincidence or bad luck. But if we have a spiritual conscience,
we ask ourselves, "Why have I had this accident? What does this
accident mean?" We examine the symbolism of all the elements
involved and we find the deep cause, the essential or metaphysical
meaning of the accident. With such an attitude, the accident leads
us to important awareness and we become conscious—as you so
rightly said.

We always grow after an accident. We aren't necessarily conscious
or ready to admit this when we are in the middle of the ordeal,
especially if it is severe, but afterwards—and this can take several
years in some cases—we recognize that it helped us grow. An
opening was created; we may have had to change jobs, modify our
way of using money or our time, etc. After a while, people who end
up with disabilities after an accident manage to say, "I wouldn't
have become who I am today, if I hadn't had that accident. I've
learned so much!"

Guides use such events to open new horizons in a person. Thus the
positive aspect of an accident is the conscious awareness it raises.
Of course, some people never integrate the accident's inherent
teaching, because their conscience hasn't yet evolved enough.
Some people even take advantage of their difficult situation to
obtain pity and various favors.

The most direct way of understanding the deep meaning of an
accident consists in analyzing its symbolism, as if we'd experienced
it in a dream. A plane crash hasn't the same meaning as a car
crash or boating accident. A boat refers to emotions: the person
has accumulated emotional memories of a particular type and
the time has come to rectify this particular *department*. A plane
crash concerns certain ways of thinking, and a car crash, certain
ways of advancing toward others.

We can view a boating accident as an accumulation of emotional
accidents. What is an emotional accident? Let's imagine we're in
the supermarket looking for a tin of beans. If we rudely ask a sales
assistant in one of the aisles, "Where are the tinned beans?!" he'll
reply, "They're at the end of this row, on the right." We'll have
our answer but we've just committed an emotional accident. Off

we go with our tin of beans, but the sales assistant is left feeling like a worm, cast aside, trodden on. We used him: we took our information without any consideration whatsoever for the person right there in front of us.

Or yet again, our child might ask us, "Will you come and play with me?" and we reply, annoyed, "Don't you see I'm busy; I haven't got time to play!" There! We've just knocked him down; we've squashed him; we've just caused an emotional accident. Through lack of conscience and consideration for others, we create emotional accidents, and they accumulate in our soul in the form of memories, to one day materialize in our lives.

An accident that involves thought can be the simple fact of criticizing someone. Ah! This kind of accident holds the absolute record. If a mutual accident report form was sent out every time one person criticized another—oof! the printing press would run out of forms! (*laughter*) Often, we aren't aware of the influence of our thoughts, and we project negativity onto people who don't behave or who simply aren't the way we want them to be.

As we gradually evolve spiritually, we stop shooting arrows into others like this. Of course, we continue to evaluate people—to discern good from evil and true from false—we don't stop ourselves thinking, but we understand and, above all, we are aware that whatever bothers us represents distorted parts in our own conscience.

Yes, madam. (Participant: Whenever we create an emotional accident with our child, can we ask his soul for forgiveness that evening, while meditating? Or, when we realize what we've done, we can say to the child, "I'm sorry. Just now I was a bit short with you. I'm sorry.") That's exactly what we need to do.

Develop this attitude, it's the most beautiful gift we can give ourselves. If we pick up our little bags of rubbish as we create them, we can cleanse our karmas. If we only realize later on that we treated a sales assistant as less than a worm, if we only realize this when we're sitting in the car, we say, "Ah! I was caught up in my needs again; I only thought about what I wanted." Since we can't go and say this to him in words, we talk to his soul and we tell him, "I'm sorry. It was wrong of me." He's so used to being treated like this! In a way, it's part of his job and what he has to transcend.

So, we speak to his soul. We tell him, "I didn't speak nicely to you and I'm sorry. I'm going to improve; I'm going to keep improving." Automatically the soul receives the message. It's as if he's been emailed. The person receives energy. We do this in cases when we really can't speak to the other person, or if the child is too young. If the child is old enough to understand, even at the age of two or three, we say to him, "Mommy, or Daddy—because there are dads too (*laughter*)—wasn't right; I'm sorry. I didn't speak correctly to you just now. My energy wasn't very nice even though what I wanted to say was right." Ah! The child is so happy to hear this!

Some people are nicer to their friends than to their children or loved ones. They are more respectful, they find it easier to put on white gloves to talk to their friends and acquaintances. We can see this whenever we observe a fortuitous encounter in a store. The person is there with his child and he (or she, of course) chats to the person he's just met; he's all smiles and replies enthusiastically, "Oh yes! We were on holiday. Ah! It was wonderful. We had a really good time. And what about you? How are you?" The child tugs his father or mother's clothes because he feels like moving on. The parent tells him, "Stop it, you little pest! Can't you see I'm talking?" and he goes on to say to the other person, "Ah yes! Well, if you need anything, don't hesitate to call. Give me a ring. Come on over. I've got plenty of time." The child hears this and he painfully remembers that his parent never has any time for him, to play with him; he's always busy with something else, with someone else. Often people can't see what's essential.

We need to begin by looking after ourselves so as to feel good, and then we look after our family—our spouse and children. Only then do we look after others; we can enlarge the circle. If there's a problem in the close, personal or family circle, there will be repercussions in the enlarged circle. We sometimes see businessmen racing along full speed ahead to work, meetings, evening engagements, etc., and they never devote any time to their spouse and children. At one particular point, their son is into drugs, their daughter gets pregnant at the age of 13 and they wonder why; they ask themselves, "But how did this happen?"

It's simple: they didn't balance their lives and by not doing so, they created an imbalance with their children, who, let us remember, represent their works and their future. Their business is doing well, making profit, but there's nothing profitable about their family life. Eventually, their firm itself can be affected. When the son inherits it, he'll waste the money on cigarettes, drugs, alcohol, paying for rounds in bars, etc. It's typical. Children can even be impatient for their parents to die so they can pocket the inheritance. That's an extreme case, of course.

If we don't look after our works well, they turn against us. It's normal; it's the normal movement or Law of Return. It's Justice. We can see how important it is to take care of our loved ones.

So, to build our lives on solid foundations, what is most important is to know ourselves and to behave correctly, to behave right, and then to look after our close family. It's only once we've established such a base that we can work correctly in the outer, public world. Inspired by our example, our children will help others and they'll participate in creating a harmonious, healthy life that can expand and shine forth positively in society.

In our family, these principles are sacred. Every evening, we go to bed in peace and it's the same every time we leave—whether it is for an hour, a day or even a week. We settle everything as it arises. Emotional accidents, that can arise from time to time, are always repaired right then and there. We behave in the same way with people outside our close family circle. This attitude creates a lot of abundance in our lives, on all levels.

On reaching adolescence, a child who has grown up in such an environment continues to have a good relationship with his parents. In past generations, whenever parents said something, children couldn't take them up on it. Right or wrong, the parent exercised his authority and he didn't usually give any explanations to the child. Things have greatly changed. New children want to know what their parents have on the inside, what their conscious and unconscious feelings and intentions are; they can sense the hidden truth anyway.

When we don't feel good, it's good to tell our child. We aren't obliged to explain everything to him. If we had a nightmare that isn't for children's ears, we skip the details and simply say, "I had a monster in my dream and such a thing happened. Mommy (or

Daddy) doesn't feel very good; there's aggression in me. So I'll have to pay attention today. If you see my aggression emerge, please tell me."

Ah! He'll love that! (*laughter*) During the course of the day he'll tell us, "Just now, when you told me to tidy up my toys, I recognized your monster." Wow! Whenever we include our child in the dynamics of our Work, he is so moved! Because he's in touch with our inner world and with our authenticity, and he also feels he is our equal on the level of the spirit. We've always behaved like this with our daughter, Kasara. In our family, it's not the parents who decide: it's whatever is right. If Kasara's idea is right, we follow it. If it isn't, we don't, and each time we explain why. We use this moment like a teaching.

In this way, the child constantly seeks to improve himself, to suggest good ideas. But we must constantly set a good example. Whenever we realize we weren't right when we allowed the child something, we go back and we tell him, "Earlier I said yes, you could, but I've received some new information and that's why I'm saying no now." Or we can say, "Earlier I promised you we were going to do something, but there's been a change. We're going to put it off till later." And we keep our promises — because the child remembers. If we don't keep our promises and we don't bother to come back to what we said we would, it's normal that after 50 times, trust is broken. I've always behaved like this with Kasara. What has that led to over the years? Great trust, great confidence. When I promise her something, she doesn't hang around, keeping on at me to know exactly when I'll do it; she trusts my word.

In a couple's relationship, it's the same thing; mutual trust is built on proof. We need to be upright, trustworthy, because in close relationships dynamics are very strong. We can see this when one of the two is unfaithful or does something that isn't right, the other person loses confidence in him or her. Trust flies away, often forever.

So, we need to avoid creating emotional accidents as much as possible, and if we don't fully succeed, we should make repairs immediately. Hence we create harmonious relationships. When we tell our child, "I've no time now, go and watch TV!" or "Stop bothering me, go to your room!" we may think it's of no consequence. But we're mistaken. Once he's reached the age of 25 or 30, we can see the effects of our attitude; they manifest themselves in his sentimental and professional relations. If he has relationship difficulties, it's because we didn't show him the fundamentally right behavior, we didn't give him the essence. And if we didn't, because we didn't have it ourselves, we tell ourselves that that's what he has to experience — that's part of his Program.

If we've done our best, we mustn't regret anything. Whenever we awaken spiritually and we examine our past, we may tend to feel regretful and say, "Ah! On that occasion, I should have done such and such a thing." We shouldn't do this. Instead we should say, "I did my best with what I knew then. Today, my conscience is more developed." Then, with our grandchildren and those close to us, we can develop new attitudes, change our behavior, change our way of talking to others. That's what's important. The best way to repair the past — the deepest and truly the only way — is to improve, and set off in a new direction, putting our new knowledge into practice.

The past comes back to us in the form of karma: the misactions we committed lead us to experience difficult situations. But we mustn't be afraid of karma. It's normal to commit misactions; we learn from them. The only thing is, we must become aware of their consequences. Of course, the aim is to no longer have any negative thoughts or emotions and to always behave and be right, but if we develop the habit of analyzing ourselves and repairing our accidents gradually, one by one, with time, we get there. It's work we need to do daily.

Every day we get washed — we have a shower, clean our teeth, etc. It can take up to 45 minutes. Well, if we devoted 45 minutes a day to analyzing ourselves and doing some inner cleansing, oh my! how quickly we'd evolve! Because in 45 minutes, there's time to regulate a lot of things within us, time to draw great teachings from little events and accidents in our lives. That's all for the word *accident*.

Now let's analyze the word *present*. Dictionaries define it *as something we offer to someone*. Some add the idea of *giving the other person pleasure* to this definition.

Whenever we offer a present, we take a little time and energy to buy or make something to offer the other person.

The word for present or gift in French is *cadeau,* which contains the word *eau,* water, which symbolically represents emotions. And what do we transmit when we give someone a present? What remains of the present once we've offered it, apart from the object itself? (Participants: An emotion.) What remains is the emotion we transmit when giving the present. And it remains much longer than the present itself.

In English *present* can be separated into two words: *pre-sent.* In this case, it's the initial, *pre-* or prior intention that precedes the actual buying or making of the gift and it is this very intention that remains afterwards.

What is the positive aspect of a present? The pleasure felt receiving and giving, of course. Receiving a present is like being rewarded. It's as if Heaven were pleased with us and It manifests this through another person. We usually receive a present because we deserve appreciation or we've cultivated a beautiful friendly, family or other relationship.

And what is the negative symbolism of a present? There's the expression, *a poisoned gift* in French, which is usually called a *poisoned chalice* in English. A poisoned gift is a present with psychological strings attached; it's a present given with conditions and expectations or, possibly, a present given with bad intentions. Under the appearance of a gift, the present is in actual fact a request or a trap, because the person offering it wants something in return. This person subtly steals energy.

(Participant: I can give you an example of that. I have a friend who received a manicure treatment as a present. She had nails put on but then she had to go back every week at her own cost. She said it was a poisoned present; it was just too obvious for words.)

It's because often the person who offers this kind of present isn't even aware of it. If she is aware of it, then she has a serious problem! She's the village witch.

(Participant: There are also bribes.) Ah! Bribes are always poisoned gifts. (Participant: These people are aware of what they're doing.)

Yes, indeed. It's manipulation, but they've built a whole logic around it that justifies their gesture—in their thought system, bribes are correct.

(Participant: Often when speaking of a child, sometimes we will say, "He's no present!") Yes indeed. If we say this to a child, we're actually saying to him, "You know, you aren't bringing me any joy there. You aren't bringing me good things."

Such words are very hurtful for a child's soul. We should never say that to a child, even when referring to someone else. Presents are so important in their eyes! They symbolize generosity, joy, etc. Besides, children are the most beautiful gifts we can ever receive.

There are other common expressions that we should never use. For example: in Quebec there's the commonly used expression, *Tasse-toi!* Europeans don't know this expression. There are a few Swiss people here. (*laughter*) *Tasse-toi* means—(Participant: Scoot! Get out of here. On your way! Make yourself scarce!) Yes, *Get out of my way,* or even, *Beat it!* It's the equivalent of *Get lost!*

These expressions are very negative. And even if the person who uses these words doesn't include any emotional input, the expression itself bears a whole emotional charge.

Telling someone to *get out of my way* or *get lost* creates an emotional accident. Words are very powerful. As we gradually evolve, we become aware of the far-reaching, deep effect of the expressions we use and we take great care in choosing them. And what does this lead to? Better relationships with others.

When we aren't conscious of the metaphysical meaning of words, we passively integrate all sorts of expressions into our vocabulary. Hence we allow ourselves to become imbued with all of the types of distortions present in the collective unconsciousness. The fact remains that we can *read* people by analyzing the expressions they use. That's all for the word *present.*

Now let's move on to the word *chameleon.* A chameleon is a reptile that has the capacity to change color in order to camouflage itself in its environment. We use this word figuratively to refer to people who change behavior or opinion according to circumstances.

119

The negative symbolism of a chameleon is precisely this lack of constancy and stability as well as the aspect of doing anything to please others or to be like others.

As for the positive symbolism, it's the capacity to fuse with one's surroundings and to adapt to the situations presented to us. If a chameleon finds itself among green leaves, it becomes green with a leaf pattern, if it lies down on a brown stone, it turns brown and if it lies on white sand, it becomes white. Thus it symbolizes a capacity to adapt to its environment and a certain invisibility on the social level—in the sense that the person has developed modesty and receptivity to others.

If we see a chameleon in a dream, we must first situate it in the context of the scene in which it appeared, and then ask ourselves, "Was it beautiful? Was it nice and gentle? Was it calm?" We also take into consideration its color, "Was it bright, luminous, dull or violent?" And also, was it in the right place? Because when a symbol is not in its natural environment, its negative side is represented. For example, if in your dream a chameleon is in your office, it signifies that you copy others and that you try to avoid standing out, etc.

In order to analyze a dream well, we need to take into consideration all the symbols that appear—every single one of them, from the beginning to the end of the dream—and put into practice what we've just been doing for each of them.

This afternoon, a woman asked me, "Is the meaning of symbols the same for everyone?" I gave her a simple example—*a parasol*. The general idea is to find the essence of the symbol and this essence is the same, whether we're in Japan, Africa, USA or Canada. A parasol serves the same purpose for everyone: it *protects us from the sun*—just as an umbrella protects us from the rain.

Thus, a parasol is used to allow us to balance, to correctly apportion the amount of sun we are exposed to. The Sun represents God, Divine Light. It's also fire, which symbolizes our spirit, our vital energy. We all know that without the sun, there wouldn't be any life on Earth. The same goes for the spirit: without spirit, there wouldn't be any life in our body. Spirit nourishes matter the same way the Sun nourishes life on Earth. In actual fact, matter is the offspring, the child of the Spirit.

To return to the example of the parasol: from a positive point of view, it symbolizes a capacity to accurately balance the quantity of vital energy we receive from our own life-center and from other people's spirit and energy.

The negative aspect of a parasol is a constant fear of collective energies; it is avoiding others, avoiding the energy they could transfer to us, and, generally speaking, avoiding Divine Light, fleeing from or hiding from the Divine, from God.

Over the last few decades, the sunrays reaching Earth have become very powerful. This phenomenon of intensification corresponds to the fact that human beings are experiencing a much more intense inner life than previous generations. We need only think of the arrival of new children and the great numbers of people presently in initiation who have chosen to work on their vital energy. Likewise, on the concrete level, over the last few decades, human activity in all sectors has been continually intensifying.

Some people worry about exposing themselves to the sun; they're afraid. But a little exposure to the sun does us good—except that too much is like too little. There's a question of balance. It is important to learn to master and manage our vital energy well.

If we see a parasol in a dream, we analyze the scene, weighing it up to determine the positive or negative value of this symbol. If, in the dream, someone is underneath the parasol, we examine his behavior, his bearing. If he were calm or having something to eat, there'd be a notion of wisdom and balance in the parasol symbolism. If it looked as if he wanted to hide from the light and seemed afraid, that would indicate an intention—conscious or unconscious—to hide away from a particular truth or a desire for over-protection because the person has a destructive inner energy.

You see how, by ourselves, we can uncover the meaning of the symbols we receive in dreams. Symbols are pure logic in terms of consciousness. We have to respect the order in which the various elements appear and analyze each one to then come to a synthesis. Needless to say, the exercise as a whole can prove to be complex. Imagine *I was walking in a forest and there was a parrot in a tree and I saw my brother-in-law coming toward me.* We analyze the path, the forest, the parrot, the brother-in-law and the general atmosphere, taking care to determine if the symbolism for each was positive or negative and then we combine their meanings. In doing so, the meaning of the dream emerges—we understand its message.

Yes? (Participant: Can one's personal perception make a difference? For instance, I like parrots but someone else might not like them at all. So the symbolism would be different for him.) Absolutely. It would have an influence on the positive or negative value of the symbol. (Participant: Ok.)

However, we mustn't only rely on the sole fact of liking or not liking a symbol. For example, a tree on first sight is positive—everyone likes trees—but a tree could be negative in a dream, it could be a mean tree. Likewise, as much as we may love parrots, if we see one in a dream that behaves aggressively, its symbolism would be negative.

One day, we love all animals, characters and objects that exist, because we know they are part of Creation and they have their rightful place and, most of all, because we no longer have any negative resonance with them. However the positive and negative values remain and we need to measure them and determine the aspect of each and every symbol so as to be able to correctly interpret dreams.

If we saw a sweet, gentle parrot in a dream, it would represent a positive state of conscience. The parrot could even prove to be very intelligent and knowledgeable: it could teach what it had discovered by itself rather than simply repeating everything we'd taught it to say or, like a child, it could repeat and learn through imitation. Everything's possible in a dream. But if it repeated silly nonsense or naughty things, we'd have to consider the notion of unconsciousness or incapacity to think for oneself. Sometimes, parrots aren't very restful; some have been trained to insult people, and lots of people find that funny. And yet, there's nothing funny about it. It's like when we use expressions without understanding their deep, metaphysical meaning.

Whenever we see people behaving like this, we can smile politely, but we avoid reinforcing their distortion. Because if we start laughing in complicity with something that isn't right, we encourage the person to begin again, to repeat what was said.

122

Sometimes a child spills his juice or throws something down on the floor on purpose and the parent says, "Oh, don't do that," with a great big smile or a burst of laughter. How do we expect the child not to repeat that action? He has registered, "Go on! Do it again! You're on the *Tonight Show*! Show us another of your tricks. We'll have a good laugh with you." He'll feel like showing off and, rest assured, he will, even when he's a grown adult, he won't change his attitude. Attention-seeking clownery as well as attention-seeking misbehavior stems from early childhood behavioral patterns—at least this is generally the case.

We must be careful not to encourage the distortion in a child; otherwise, we help him to multiply it. A child experiments with the use of words, gestures and soul-states and we need to guide him, to point out lovingly to him, "No, that's not right," Or "Yes, that's correct."

We need to avoid a repressive attitude. We can tell him 'no' in a way that is both beautiful and firm. When the 'no' isn't clear enough, the child captures our duality even if it's unconscious—and he'll test our limits again and again. The first thing a child notices—even before he can talk—is our intention. He knows the difference between a weak 'no,' a medium 'no' and a solid, resolute 'no.' He can distinguish all the nuances of 'yes' and 'no.' If the 'no' isn't solid and he still gets punished, over time, the child stops trusting his feelings. He starts granting more credibility to his rational mind, which then becomes his principal guidance.

We should teach children metaphysics from a very young age, and continue this teaching at school, just like math and grammar. It should be an educational priority. If a child can integrate the concepts of metaphysics, he will understand that what he feels is real and that it is validated by adults. He can constitute markers for himself and, from these, he can construct and edify his inner world. The parent plays an important role in this apprenticeship, for example, when he shares his own attitudes and reactions and when he talks about his feelings.

Sometimes we're surprised by a child's behavior when other people look after him. When he's at home, he gets all angry and upset and even aggressive for the slightest reason and as soon as he's elsewhere he's nice and well-behaved. That's because he's used to our yeses and nos. With people he doesn't know, he has none of his usual markers, but it only takes a few visits to learn what he can or cannot do in that *country*, and you can be sure he'll use this information.

If our intentions aren't clear, it's because unconscious memories intervene. If a mother has unconscious memories linked to needs and finds herself in a situation where she must refuse to buy her child an ice cream, her unconscious energy will convey the message, "I told you 'no' for the ice cream but I could eat 50,000 of them myself! Oh! How I'd love to go off and lie on the beach at Cancun!" The child captures these unconscious messages and the emotional charge linked to them. The mother says 'no,' but there's a great big 'yes' crying out behind it. So the child is all mixed up, because what he has perceived on a subtle level doesn't correspond to what he's been told. Whenever the message is clear, the child becomes calm once again.

I often experience these dynamics with my sister's children—my niece, Ariel and her little brother, Gabriel. My sister is experiencing a beautiful evolution, she's come along an extraordinary path, but she has memories concerning needs that prevent her from giving clear messages to her children when the time comes to say no. And her children are so advanced that she has no other choice but to work on herself.

When I arrive in their house and the children misbehave, I only have to say, "Ariel, that's enough," and she stops. Just like that. I even had to tell my sister not to compete with me, because the children listen to me, they do so completely naturally, as if it were the only thing to do. I have already accomplished great inner work with regard to needs. So the children react to a different energy than their mother's. When I say 'no,' it's a real 'no' and the child feels the power behind my words. It's not like I'm only addressing his thoughts or his behavior: I speak to his entire being. His soul hears and he calms down.

Yes? (Participant: I can identify with the ice cream story and I agree. But if I'm aware that I'd like to go to Cancun and eat 10,000 ice cream cones and half an hour before dinner my son asks for one, what do I do?)

It's all a question of authenticity, which I mentioned earlier. Whenever you say no to your child, you can also say, "Mommy isn't perfect. Maybe my 'no' isn't solid enough. I need you to understand my 'no'." If you speak to him like this, you'll see, it'll make all the difference. Because children seek authenticity and they see beyond what ordinary senses can perceive.

Of course if the child is very young, we can't say that; he wouldn't understand. So, before saying 'no,' we focus, take a deep breath and go within ourselves to find an authentic 'no,' so that when the time comes to speak to our child, a soul-to-soul contact can be established.

Let's go on now with another word: *baldness*. Baldness naturally evokes something negative. So let's begin with the negative symbolism.

By definition, *baldness is the total or partial absence of hair*. It manifests itself more frequently and more intensely in men than in women—and that's no coincidence. Generally speaking, women are much more emotional than men, and men are more cerebral than women. Men rely on logic and rational thinking whereas women use their emotional force, which is powerful. That's part of the masculine and feminine polarities.

Everyone who has baldness has a very active intellectual side. We often see intellectuals who are bald or have almost no hair at all. Their overactive mental faculties create a split—a discrepancy or imbalance—between the intellect and the emotions which prevents the hair roots from being properly nourished. Plants need water to grow. (*laughter*) From this perspective, baldness symbolizes a form of deficiency on the emotional level and the person who loses his hair has something to understand related to this discrepancy, this imbalance.

We can analyze any physical phenomenon symbolically and find its metaphysical component. This is because our physical body corresponds to ways of thinking, loving and acting that we have developed over the course of our lives.

Of course baldness depends on hereditary factors, but genes aren't the only cause. To try and understand why they're losing their hair, some people examine their family's past— "My grandfather was bald, my mother's hair became really thin, etc." It's good to do this—these influences are real—but *soul genes* are much more influential than physical genes, in the sense that these are what determine our physical structure. Besides, why is it that a child inherits the genes of his father, who began losing his hair at a young age, rather than those of his mother whose whole family has really thick hair?

If we are bald, we need to grant a greater place to emotions in our life, we need to develop our emotional potential, including communication and exchange of feelings. That's all for the negative aspect of baldness.

As for the positive aspect, it's the transcendence of this imbalance between thoughts and emotions. Because initially baldness isn't positive, it's not something we'd offer as a wedding gift. (*laughter*)

Men who are bald or balding can develop a lot of complexes. They can be afraid of losing or of having lost their virility—a false idea, of course—and this can undermine their self-confidence. Women too can suffer in their physical esteem when their hair becomes so thin as to appear balding in parts. So the positive or transcended aspect of baldness is also acceptance of oneself and one's physical appearance.

Often we think beauty is physical but it isn't. An initiate who sees a person who emanates beautiful energy will find him beautiful, even if he's obese or deformed. And vice versa: someone whose soul is weighed down with distortions won't seem beautiful to him, even if people in ordinary consciousness consider him to be really good-looking. Because an initiate sees beyond the form—he sees a person's soul.

Moreover, when we are in the presence of someone who's had beautiful dreams, we can feel his inner beauty. His spirit radiates so much beauty that, in a way, his body disappears.

If we have physical disadvantages, we analyze them symbolically, we meditate on them, and, with time, we manage to establish links and cleanse the corresponding memories. Because each physical feature is the result of memories that have accumulated over multiple experimentations, just like sediments on the seabed. Whenever we have reached the point when we have to experience a consequence, it's because it's time. Difficulties don't come just from this life; they also come from other lives.

Now let's analyze the word *corpse*. According to the dictionary —with a small *d*—a corpse is defined as *the body of a dead person or animal.*

Let's see the metaphysical dimension of this symbol. What is the negative aspect of a corpse? Naturally we don't often use this word to describe a dead person. For example, we don't say, "My grandmother's corpse is in the coffin." We're more likely to say *my grandmother's body.* We use the word when it's a question of a violent death due to an aggression. This word refers to something violent, and, in terms of consciousness, to memories of aggression.

Now let's have a look at the positive symbolism of a corpse. Of course, at the sight of a corpse, compassion can be awakened—we can feel compassion for the person or animal that suffered a violent death, but the positive meaning comes from the negative meaning, from its transcendence, from having transcended the negative aspect.

How would the transcended aspect of violent death be expressed? If a person dreamed of a corpse…

Yes, Kasara? (Kasara: A positive corpse could be a bright, luminous corpse.) Yes, that's right, and that would indicate that the person is beginning to understand something related to memories of violent deaths. Something would be in the process of being sorted out and settled related to that.

The transcendence of a corpse could also be expressed in a scene where we'd see—or maybe walk among—lots of corpses and we'd feel absolutely fine; we'd be filled with serenity, love and compassion for the deceased. Such a scene, of course, could also be one of our worst nightmares—just imagine all the suffering it represents—but the positive state of conscience felt during the dream would make all the difference concerning the symbolic value.

A corpse in a dream is comparable to an icon on a computer screen. We click on it and a whole file—or folder with lots of related files each containing several sub-files—opens up. Thousands of

127

memories are awakened all at the same time. The person feels attacked, his children, his parents die before his very eyes, his house is on fire, etc., or else he finds himself in the role of an aggressor.

If ever you dream of corpses, you'll have a strong feeling of death that day; you'll be permeated by it. However, this kind of dream is quite rare; we must be very evolved spiritually to have transcended such memories. Usually, Up Above has us go through various stages before leading us to do such Work. However, the more we evolve, the better we are able to enter the reservoirs of collective memories. These are initiations which strengthen us.

We don't need to dream about corpses to be able to feel a *corpse* state of conscience. All we need to do is watch TV or war films. Whenever we see bodies and cars torn to bits, we can feel really bad. But if we've transcended this state of conscience, if we've cleansed our *corpse* memories, we feel fine. We feel strong and stable. We feel solid. We understand the Law of Karma and the Law of Reincarnation, and we know those people are going through a stage.

Of course, I'm not talking about indifference or insensitivity here. I'm not referring to people who have absolutely no social conscience, and who watch scenes showing genocide on their screen, while calmly eating their supper — you know as well as I do that there are many people who do this. These people are disconnected and feel above other people's suffering. All we'd need to do would be to deprive them of their material abundance and, in no time at all, we'd see forces emerge from their unconscious and great chaos would manifest in their lives.

Yes? (Participant: How do we transcend that?) We can do inner work while watching TV.

At the beginning of my spiritual path, I was a bit puritanical, like most people who choose such a path. I didn't want to watch TV; I no longer read the newspaper. I didn't want to be contaminated by all the distortions shown by the media. Then, after a while, I realized I had no friends anymore, that I didn't see anyone any more. It was all fine and well for me to be on a spiritual path, but I'd practically become a hermit. I had cut myself off from so many sources! When I realized this, I was deeply committed spiritually, I had already done major inner work and I was ready to get in touch with the outside, social world once again. So I behaved a little like a child discovering the world. Click! I turned on the TV and I began to watch what was going on.

However I was often captivated by what I saw: this led me into all sorts of soul-states. And I was very conscious of what was happening since I'd developed my capacity to interiorize. So when this happened—when I felt bothered or disturbed by what I saw—I'd push the Mute button and I'd start to meditate to understand my resonance with what I had just seen. Whenever I felt better, I'd open my eyes and turn up the volume again.

It's amazing how much that allowed me to discover about myself, about my memories. I used to do the same thing with DVDs. I'd push the Pause button and I'd meditate when I felt bothered or put out. In addition to this, I started to analyze symbolically everything I saw on the screen. When I couldn't understand—because there are so many symbols and it's very fast-moving—I'd push Pause or Mute once again.

In order to cleanse my memories, I worked at this so much that now I'm no longer afraid of being contaminated by anyone or anything. Sometimes when someone comes up to me to have a dream interpreted and he starts coughing, I don't take a step back or say inwardly, "Ooh! Hey! Keep away from me. You're going to give me the flu and I'll pass it on to my family." No, I tell myself, if I catch the virus, I'll manage to transform it, and if not, then there's something in this for me to understand. So, I accompany the person—I enter into his field of energy so as to help him—and I love him as if he were my own child. I don't keep a distance from him.

Well, we need to adopt the same attitude with the images we see on TV. When we watch the news, we analyze the soul-states these images awaken in us and we seek the causes. And while we study ourselves, we tell ourselves that the people we see or hear about have something to understand.

Yes? (Participant: Let's say we're watching TV… well actually, it happened just recently; there was a bomb and we could see lots of corpses lying there. I said to myself, "Well, actually, I'd really rather not watch this." Except transcendence isn't avoidance, is it?)

Transcendence, among other things, is studying the reason why it happened. The people who found themselves in the scene you saw have already planted bombs themselves. They were blown up by their own inner bombs. They had a lot of aggression on the inside; they were former aggressors. No one can be treated aggressively if he himself hasn't already been aggressive with other people, because God and His Divine Justice is absolute.

The collective unconscious is loaded with all sorts of violence, and certain forms of violence that existed in the past aren't generally considered as such. People find the castles in France beautiful; they *ooh* and *aah* in front of them. Personally, the first time I took my daughter, Kasara to one of these castles, I told her, "You see, the men and women who lived in these castles were not nice. They made all the people around them suffer and they used up all of the village's resources." There was no democracy then. If we could go back in time, we'd realize that violence and aggression were daily occurrences.

The earth symbolizes the unconscious, the sea too. When there are earthquakes and landslides, people are captured in the rubble and their goods are destroyed. The same thing happens when there are tidal waves, hurricanes and other storms: people and goods are swept away, destroyed, engulfed. These natural catastrophes are the consequence of acts where we greedily, selfishly grabbed and seized material goods and where we destroyed emotional relationships. Let me give you one example of such karmic causes. In certain eras, kings and militia chiefs assumed the right to break up families and entire villages and they stole all their goods. Often they killed the men and captured the women and children to make them concubines and slaves. So, in another life, these people will lose their children, their relatives and their possessions in earthquakes or tidal waves. It's the Law of Karma.

The more we evolve spiritually, the more conscious we are that we mustn't play with life or death, that they are sacred. We need only think of what awaits those who've committed suicide when they reach the other world. Of course, that person's soul continues its evolution—it will reincarnate and will be able to cleanse itself over time—and like every other soul, it will attain the Light one day. But, in committing suicide, a person sets himself on a difficult path. In another life, his father could commit suicide, and consequently he'd experience the abandonment and pain that he caused others to suffer.

Yes? (Participant: When it comes down to it, all a soul wants is to evolve. It could live for thousands of years or I don't know how many lives so as to approach and merge with the Light of God. Anyway, that's what I believe. There's an image that keeps coming into my mind since you spoke about old souls yesterday. It's Mother Teresa. She must have been an old soul because, with the life she led, she must be close to the Light now. But how far have I, Marcella, how far have I got control of what can happen to my soul? It seems a bit complicated to me. Basically, my question is who and what am I evolving for?)

It's for the sake of evolution itself. Whatever we do for others, in actual fact, we do for ourselves. Because life is like a dream: other people represent parts of ourselves. If we are kind to someone, that person will be kind to us — the energy comes back to us. We are always in relation with ourselves. Because we are a whole, complete universe in ourselves, we possess a masculine and a feminine polarity, we contain planets inside us, and we also have all the animals, elements and kingdoms within. We are all gods.

Basically, the aim is to install harmony and balance in and among all the parts of our being, of our divinity. Then, the aim is to create a world around us that reflects this harmony. We are constantly creating: we make decisions, we decorate our interiors, we create atmospheres, we create children, a family, etc. We are all angels — with or without wings — we are all parts of God.

And the ultimate aim is Enlightenment, that State where the Light is constantly present, where happiness and harmony reign all the time, at each and every moment. In this State, everything is in order, everything is in its place and existential questions have been answered.

When we've attained this stage, we transmit the Light to others and we help them, just as the Guides in the Parallel Worlds do. Guides are highly evolved, and that's exactly what They do to continue to evolve and improve. Each person evolves at his own rhythm and some souls are older and more experienced than others.

131

Yes? (Participant: You mention old souls and souls that aren't so old, etcetera. But how does a soul begin?)

Imagine we take a tiny particle of the Sun and we entrust it to someone. That energy, that little Sun, forms a soul. We could call the soul memory. The soul is like computer memory, and the spirit — or vital energy — is like the electricity that the computer runs on. This energy creates a memory by experimenting. It begins — it incarnates — then it stumbles and falls and gets up again. This is how it learns.

In Africa, for example, there are a lot of new, young souls, compared with other continents. That's why Africans find it difficult to manage their economy and their present-day political forces — to mention only these two sectors. They behave a little like children who aren't yet aware of the consequences of their actions. They are given resources and, some of them — not all of them, of course — once they've eaten, don't think about going to work to ensure that there will be food on the table the next day. It's like a child: we give him food, then he goes off to play and he's happy. At some point, he's hungry — "Oh! I've got to find something to eat!" This example is a good illustration of the attitude new souls have toward responsibilities, toward materialization.

The evolution of conscience is intimately related to general evolution; it's a reflection of it. Everything that occurs in the outside world reflects what happens in our conscience. By taking on responsibilities, we discover our strengths and this helps us evolve, on all levels. Countries that have organizational difficulties on the material level are, in a way, the children of the great human family. And our countries, rich in ideas, intelligence and supposed maturity on the concrete level, exploit those countries, which, very often, constitute the cradle of our past lives. A country experiences the prosperity its inhabitants create and this prosperity depends on the souls that incarnate there.

As for old souls — that, generally speaking, incarnate in developed countries — even if they have lives and lives of experimentation behind them, they haven't necessarily acquired wisdom. Very often they experience great distortions, sometimes even greater than new souls', because of the material abundance in which they evolve. All the shining glory and ease this abundance offers makes them lose sight of what's essential. Blinded by matter, sated by the abundance that surrounds them, sometimes filled with a feeling of superiority when compared with people who are less privileged on the material level, many of these souls deny the very existence of the spirit or simply set spirituality aside and concentrate on the development of their material lives. It's a stage in the evolutionary process.

When we haven't got many resources, we do little, and when we have more, we can do more. It's the same on the conscience level. Here's an example to illustrate this. By the way, it also describes the attitude of many people who work with dreams & signs.

Imagine a soul who's lived most of its life in a monastery, who has attained high levels of wisdom and plenitude and who's reborn in our time. Of course, the fundamentals this person has established —i.e. the beautiful stability acquired through meditation—are turned upside down. He's tense and stressed. He finds material life complicated, etc. This soul will have to reincarnate several times before he'll manage to master his spirit in matter, i.e. neither to flee it nor try to control it. This stage—the perfect marriage of spirit and matter—is the most difficult stage a person encounters on his evolutionary path. It's easy to be spiritual when we have few or no responsibilities in the concrete world. And this is often the case of people on a spiritual path. To be both spiritual and committed in matter, and to live these two dimensions beautifully balanced and responsibly on both sides, is a very difficult thing to do. Everything depends on this balance, in the sense that karma is engendered on this level.

Often people who live through great difficulties—poverty, war, natural disasters—seem spiritual, but as soon as material abundance arrives, they are like little children receiving new toys and immediately becoming absorbed by them. They set their spirituality aside and cease praying until the time comes when matter no longer holds any interest for them. Then, feeling totally jaded and in search of new sensations, they either take to all sorts of abuses and disorganize society, or, they take their first steps toward transcending matter. A country can take several centuries, going from one extreme to the other, before discovering Divine Materialization, i.e. the capacity to experience matter while remaining spiritual. This idea also applies to the individual, to the soul. A country is like a person with its own character, with a

133

whole potential, and, as I mentioned earlier, its degree of evolution reflects that of its inhabitants.

To conclude the question of a soul's age in relation to the country of incarnation, I'd like to add that a soul can incarnate in any country whatsoever. It will incarnate in whatever place and whatever era that will best allow it to learn what it needs to learn. In actual fact, souls that have incarnated on Earth are relatively young compared with those that inhabit other worlds and help us to develop. The souls that populate the other dimensions have also been through long, intense, difficult, deeply moving stages of material experimentation, all those stages that prepare a person to succeed in creating correctly, divinely.

We should remember that one world is always contained in another, bigger, more evolved world. Inhabitants of the bigger, more evolved worlds help the others to rise toward the Light, just as in a family where parents help the children learn and advance.

Often, spirituality is opposed to matter and it is believed that the world of the spirit has no structure, whereas in fact, it's quite the contrary. It's in the world of the spirit that there's the most structure. Beauty, wisdom and all the other aspects of structure that can be found on Earth are only pale reflections of what can be found in the Metaphysical Worlds.

There we are. That's all for this wonderful workshop. I'm off to join Kasara to help her with her math homework. That child is a gift from Heaven for me. Her upbringing is one of the greatest responsibilities God has entrusted me with in this life.

I wish you happy continuation on your path, and may dreams, signs & the Dictionary of Life inspire all your acts.

WORKSHOP
Flashback

Yes, madam. (Dreamer: It's a dream I had last night. *I was walking alone on a gravel road and I knew it was the road where I grew up, because I recognized the houses. Today, in concrete reality, it's an asphalt road. I was walking on the left and I was wearing high-heeled shoes. One of the heels had broken — I had it in my hand. Then I arrived at a place where there was a party going on. On the road, I felt lonely, and when I arrived at the party, I felt relieved to be with other people.*)

Was it during the day or at night? (Dreamer: It was during the day.) Were you dressed in a particular way? (Dreamer: I don't know.) OK. If we don't have certain details, it's ok; we use what is presented to us and what we remember.

Were there any other symbols? Little details? (Dreamer: I was aware that some of the people who lived in those houses when I was young were no longer there. As I was going past the houses, I said to myself, "Ah! So and so is dead. So and so is dead.") Were they dead in your dream? (Dreamer: I only saw their houses and I made the connection: "Ah! Those people are dead.") Ok, I understand.

Did you notice what color your shoes were? (Dreamer: They were dark blue.) Ok, fine.

First of all, all the elements in this dream represented parts of you. And it's very important to understand that you are not only that; you have other parts that are very beautiful. This is only a collection of memories you've been shown so you can become aware of them and work on them.

You were walking on the left. The left represents the inner world and inner action, and the right, the exterior environment and action in the outer world.

The left is also related to the feminine principle, to receptivity, whereas the right is related to the masculine principle, to emissivity. Whether we are a man or a woman, we have both principles—masculine and feminine. A woman has the masculine principle on the inside and a man has the feminine principle within him.

As you were walking on the left, the dynamics described in this dream are to be found on the inside of your being; they don't necessarily manifest themselves on the outside.

You had a feeling of solitude as you walked along. Solitude can be positive but in this dream it was negative. It weighed on you since you felt relieved when you arrived at the party. Today, you probably felt lonely and a little sad until you arrived here and found yourself surrounded by people. And even though you may be surrounded by people—as you are this evening—you might still feel this loneliness tonight. We can be surrounded by people and still feel lonely. You are experiencing this on the inside only, because, in your dream, you were walking on the left. Today, you were immersed in this feeling of loneliness and you've been feeling a little sad. You have a tendency to seek out people's company when you feel like that instead of facing it and encountering the memories that causes this inner state.

What does walking mean? Usually, we walk in order to advance, to go forward. In terms of consciousness, walking means that we are walking, journeying along our Life Path, that we are advancing toward our destiny. So it's related to our spiritual path, to the way we advance in life.

You are on a spiritual path, you feel lonely and this loneliness weighs on you–this is what is happening today. Tomorrow, you may feel happy but today, it's a feeling of loneliness that's dominant.

It was your childhood road. So you're visiting old memories and it is not the first time you've felt like this in your life. Whenever we dream of scenes referring to our childhood, it shows that we are truly visiting memories of our past, and even sometimes from our past lives. So, in your childhood, and way beyond that probably, you experienced moments of great sadness and you're being led to reflect on this, to meditate on such moments.

Gravel. Whenever we walk on a gravel path, we are less stable than on asphalt. The road surface is coarser and less finished. So, your journey toward healing and your path to cleansing and transcending your past isn't finished yet. You need to return to these sectors of your conscience and reconstruct them, complete the *road-building*, so to speak.

High-heeled shoes. Shoes represent the way we advance socially, what we emanate when we are active. They were dark blue. Blue is the color of the throat chakra; it's related to communication. And the dark aspect leads us to include the symbolism of black, which is the hidden aspect of things. Therefore, the dark blue color of your shoes refers to the hidden aspect of communication, to what isn't perceived by our ordinary senses.

They were high-heels. It's a well-known fact that high heels aren't comfortable. They're a very distorted invention when we really think about it. Wearing them can even be dangerous. Lots of women wear high heels because it makes them taller and slimmer and being slim is considered a social value in our society. What do high heels symbolize? High heels raise the body from the ground; they create an elevation, but it's an artificial elevation. They symbolize a feeling of superiority, because the wearer is trying to appear taller than she, or he, really is. So, you need to work on this attitude.

The heel was broken. That's interesting. It's as if, up until now, we felt confident about life, everything was going well — we even felt above our tasks — and, all of a sudden, things don't work anymore. The old force that helped us advance and artificially raised us up is now broken. We find ourselves deflated, back on the ground, and we are obliged to eliminate the superficial elements in our lives. This is what is happening in your life. You are on a spiritual path and you're experiencing profound, major changes. Hence certain attitudes and activities you had up to now have become superfluous; there's no need for them in your life anymore.

Up Above wants to help you go further. We can see this in your dream with the presence of the houses of the deceased people you knew when you were a child. The fact that these people were dead shows once again that you have deep memories concerning the notion of having used others to elevate yourself and now these forces are not in you anymore. Positively, death symbolizes renaissance and renewal; but negatively, it is linked to some potential that we do not have anymore, a lack of something.

Then you arrived at a party and you felt relieved to be among people. Here we see the compensatory aspect of parties and social activities. This scene shows that you still have some difficulties with the *solitude* aspect of your path. You feel like being with others. When you don't feel great, when you need attention or compliments from others, you might start calling up friends so as to have some positive action in your life. The simple fact that being among people relieved you denotes a form of dependency, a need that hasn't yet been transcended. Because if we only feel well when we're surrounded by people, it means we have problems with solitude and introspection. You need to go through this stage where you learn to come to terms with solitude and with your inner work. You need to learn to live well on your own, to be happy when alone.

This reminds me of the story about natural potato chips that Kasara tells in her book *The Spiritual Diary of a Nine-Year-Old Child*. We were on a lecture tour in Europe and she'd had some potato chips — natural potato chips — that day. There were some left and she felt like having some more. I said to her, "You could wait another two days before you have some more. You've had enough today." She accepted this well — she's a marvelous child. Well, two days later, she was allowed to have some but she didn't have any. So I asked her, "How come you aren't eating any potato chips? It's ok, go on, you can have some if you like." She told me, "No, I realized I want them far too much. I'm going to wait until I don't. I'll have some when I've calmed down." (*laughter*)

Wow! That's really something at nine years old. She said to herself, "Those potato chips bother me too much. I'm certainly not going to let chips lead me by the nose!" So she waited until her need for chips had gone away. It's wonderful! This is how we train ourselves. She ends her story saying, "That's how we develop mastery." She's often heard that. Since she was very young, she's heard me talk about self-command and mastery and, for her, it's become natural. She learned the words *conscience* and *mastery* long before other words. She was born into it.

In your dream, there's this idea of need. So, you were being shown that you need to learn to *tame* solitude, to work on it so it becomes positive.

(Dreamer: Does holding the broken heel in my hand mean anything?) Yes, it does. The hand symbolizes giving, receiving, manifestation and making, creating, manufacturing things. It's as if you were trying to create your life and manifest in the old way, wanting to continue the same way including, among other things, the feeling of superiority you developed so as to feel important.

For example, you could get up in the morning and say, "Maybe I'll do such and such today. Ah yes! I'll go see that film—No, I don't really feel like it. Ah! I'll go have a coffee in that new coffee bar. Oh no! It'll be far too noisy." You try to find something that will raise you up, elevate your conscience, but the old method doesn't work anymore; it's broken. So you feel lonely and down; you feel a bit depressed. This is very common at the beginning of a spiritual path. Previously, we did all sorts of activities, we went out and we didn't question any of this. We just went wherever we felt like going and generally speaking, we were content; those activities satisfied us. But now we've lost the taste for doing such things. Why? Because we've changed; we no longer live in an ordinary conscience. And if we force ourselves to do these things that don't do anything for us any more, we don't feel well. When we have Knowledge, we understand this process and that takes the drama out of it.

(Dreamer: I didn't feel like going to work today.) I understand. Most people feel important when they go to work, and work provides them with motivation—sometimes it's their only motivation. But when we change on the inside, at some point, these forces are de-activated. When this happens, we need to reprogram the way we work so as to be able to go on enjoying it. We need to tell ourselves, "When I work, it's not for the money. Of course, I'll have a salary, but my main reason for working is to develop qualities and virtues." We are conscientious and we try to do things well. If we work with the public, when we speak to people we try to consider them as parts of ourselves. We try to be nice to everyone.

We don't do this for the benefit of the company or firm, nor for the boss or the client or customer; we do it for ourselves. This may seem rather selfish and egotistical but it isn't. If we work well for ourselves, we feel good and the people around us feel good too.

Similarly, when we look after our spouse or our children, we are actually looking after ourselves. When I take care of my wife, in actual fact I'm taking care of my inner wife, who materialized in the form of Christiane. From such a perspective, we no longer compare what we give and what we receive. We stop calculating and worrying whether we've given too much or not. And we don't expect anything back; we don't do things for what we'll get in return. What happens when we integrate this attitude? The other person is moved and feels like giving too.

There we are, that's all for this dream. (Dreamer: Thank you.) You're welcome.

Yes, sir? (Dreamer: I've got a dream I'd like to tell you. I had it six years ago. In my dream, *I was at home, in my bedroom, and it was dark because it was during the night. I saw my body lying on my bed, but I was standing up beside it. And in my wardrobe, there was a silhouette of a figure with a beautiful blue aura all around it, blue light shining as if it were an Angel. On the wall, I could see a violin play, but we couldn't hear the music. Then the Blue Angel, or the blue light, threw me a luminous ball. I felt it in my hands as I played with it. Then I looked over to the left and through the window overlooking the balcony, I saw a woman floating in the air. Her dress was transparent and I could see her head. In fact, it was as though there was no body underneath the dress; I could only see her head and the transparent dress floating out there. Like the Angel in the wardrobe, there was a light all around her too.*) Thank you for sharing this dream with us.

In this dream, you had an out-of-body experience. You left your physical body and you could see it. It's similar to what happens when we die: we enter another dimension, except that when we die, we don't come back into our body.

The bedroom represents your personal intimacy.

A wardrobe is a place where we keep our clothes. And clothes symbolize the aura, what emanates from our being. We wear clothes to keep warm or to feel confident that we're suitably dressed when we go out socially. Well, the clothes we choose to wear actually depend on our soul-state at that moment, whether we are aware of it or not; that's why they represent our aura. Consequently, as a symbol, or in terms of conscience, a wardrobe contains our usual soul-states, the ones that we experience regularly.

As for the Angel, He symbolizes high levels of conscience. You were experiencing a very intense, very powerful spiritual awakening. And it was principally manifested on the communication level, because of the color blue. So, six years ago, there was a great opening in you regarding spiritual communication, with the idea of your beginning, your being able to talk about it, to share at that level.

A violin was playing all by itself on the wall. Like all musical instruments, a violin represents a capacity to create atmosphere and ambience, to share our inner world, and this particular instrument has a certain affinity with feelings. Musical strings are called cords in French and call to mind our vocal cords. Once again, we are brought back to the idea of communication. As for the wall, it serves as a loudspeaker. Thus the violin playing on your bedroom wall represented sentimental communication in your personal intimacy—easy, magical, spirit communication because it was playing all by itself.

Then the Angel threw a luminous ball into your hands. Throwing a ball evokes a children's game. In terms of conscience, you were taking part in the game of learning to share your energies, like children, because when children play with a ball, in actual fact, they are learning to share all sorts of energies and behavior with others. And the fact that the ball was luminous meant that, in your sharing with others, you were experiencing Divine Energy in a manifest way, because you caught it in your hands; hands symbolize manifestation, forces that can create and manifest.

Essentially, light represents understanding and clarity, but, since it was night in your dream, understanding was deferred; you were experiencing an awakening of conscience which would later lead to understanding in your daily life. Once you had the luminous ball in your hands, you turned to the window and saw the woman floating in the air outside. Consequently, your awakening of conscience would not only lead you to understand yourself and your personal intimacy, but also the outside world, from a spiritual point of view, as the woman was floating in the air. It's as if the fact of understanding yourself was going to lead you to understand

141

the outside world. If you hadn't seen the woman outside, the awakening of conscience would have only applied to your inner world. You would have begun to believe with more conviction in spiritual worlds and have more mystical experiences and spiritual thoughts, but that wouldn't necessarily have led you to a better understanding of the outside, social world, the environment in which you lived. Do you follow me? (Dreamer: Yes.)

The fact that this took place near your reclining body meant that the Forces of Light were being infused right down into your physical body. And the fact that you were asleep in the dream indicated that this infusion of the Forces of Light wasn't going to be conscious, at least not at first. It's very interesting. If your body hadn't been asleep in your dream, you'd have been convinced that what you experienced on the metaphysical level was real, as real as what you experience on the physical level.

So, when you received this dream, you experienced a great spiritual opening. Your spiritual potential was very intensely activated. Following this dream, great inner seeking was probably set off and you received lots of other dreams. Because the fact that you were thrown a blue ball meant that Up Above was initiating your apprenticeship, like a child, to communicate information that would allow you to manifest and, essentially, create your life through communication. But, initially, it would be limited to your inner life, because you were sleeping. When we see ourselves sleeping in a dream, it means that we aren't yet completely aware of what we experience in the totality of our dimensions. Thank you for sharing this dream with us.

Yes, madam? (Dreamer: I dreamed that *I was with other people in a meditation guided by your wife, Christiane. She told us to sit down, back straight, well supported, and to relax. Then she began the guided meditation. At the end of the meditation there was only music; Christiane had stopped talking. Then she told us to lie down and listen. So, I lay down and at one point, I saw three babies. Christiane got up to take care of her baby — one of the babies was hers — but he was right at the edge of a bed and he started to slide off. I quickly got up to try and catch him but he rolled off the bed before I could catch him. I told Christiane, "He didn't hurt himself; he just rolled gently onto the floor." I too had one of the three babies — a girl. She was tiny and she walked over to me all by herself, with no help at all. So*

I told her, "Wow! You are getting strong!" Then, Christiane said to me, "You're not to go back to your meditation now." But I went back to it all the same. The dream ended like that.) Ah! That's a really meaningful dream for you!

My wife Christiane represented a part of you, of course. She represented your inner principle regarding your spirituality. You are working intensely with Dream Study and we can see this in your dream. Indeed, that's why you dream about Christiane. You have affinities with her.

The fact that you were meditating in the dream shows that meditation has become more important in your life. And when we say meditation, we mean inner study, because when we meditate, we reflect on our life with the aim of becoming better. When we think about something that bothers us and we refer back to ourselves, when we say to ourselves, 'That's a part of me,' we study ourselves and we reflect spiritually. When we do meditation, it is like a dream; the same meaning applies. We can do it with our eyes open or closed. We can do it while walking, driving, doing the washing-up, etc. It becomes active meditation.

There were three babies. These babies represented new parts of you, parts that are beginning to develop. As for the number 3, it's a symbol related to construction, to development, because 2 is mom and dad, and 3 represents the arrival of a child, a project, an expansion of the self. Therefore, you are in the process of constructing your soul.

When there's a young child in a dream and there is no negative element present, then it's a really beautiful dream; it's as if we were beginning a new life. We undertake new apprenticeships, new learning experiences, we do new research, we develop new concepts. Given the other elements in the dream, it's clearly a question of spiritual apprenticeships and concepts—especially because Christiane is there. And our child always represents both our works and our future.

The fact that Christiane's baby rolled onto the floor shows that this new spiritual project, this spiritual future, is still unstable and your 'inner Christiane' lacks presence: She's too *up in the air*; she doesn't sense that her baby needs help. So, for the moment, meditation generates discrepancy and dualities: you are either too anchored in matter or too airy. This often happens at the beginning of spiritual apprenticeships.

Your little girl walked all by herself. This shows that your apprenticeship has become strong, that you've already uncovered some truths and are advancing in your discoveries. And you are aware of this, because you told your daughter she was strong now.

The fact that Christiane advised you not to return to the meditation means that you have now reached a stage where you need to face responsibilities in material life. These responsibilities were represented by the fact of having a child. Sometimes, at the beginning of our spiritual path, we tend to be more introverted, we meditate a lot and we are mostly in a receptive state. In the dream, your spiritual part was telling you, "You have three babies now. It's time to look after them. You need to stop floating up in the air on ideas and concepts; you need to look after your future, to be more concrete." It's a really beautiful dream to learn to marry spirit and matter, thank you for sharing it with us.

Yes? (Participant: I've been doing meditation for over a year now and sometimes my behavior surprises me. It's often distorted. One morning I was aggressive with everyone and I didn't understand why. If anyone said a word to me, I'd retort fiercely. It's happened two or three times. It's so intense, so powerful!)

It's completely normal to have this kind of reaction. Meditation, especially at the beginning, has very powerful effects. Whenever we work with dreams, signs and meditation all together at one and the same time, we are led to experience great variations of mood, of soul-states: when we are in touch with our distorted memories, we feel bad and when we cleanse them, we feel liberated; we feel good again.

The distortion that dwelled in you that day didn't come from the meditation; it came from you. (Participant: Yes, of course.) It's important to understand that. A meditation does not have any distortions, but it awakens distorted memories. Often when we meditate intensely on a particular quality we'd like to develop — patience, for example — our inner reservoir of impatience can surface and erupt! This intense experience occurs

144

in order to help us work on our impatience so that one day we can incarnate beautiful patience. When we meditate, it's as if we shine a powerful spotlight on our imperfections or distortions.

The word *distortion*, to talk about our weaknesses, is perfect for what it describes. We take something pure, something right and we distort it. Thus a State of Divine Conscience, a quality, can become a fault. We take a quality, we twist, deform and distort it and it becomes a fault. The energy behind a distortion is the same as the quality. What a beautiful principle!

When we do meditation and praying, we call on a Powerful Energy, a Divine Force, and when It manifests, we experience very powerful effects. We mustn't be afraid of these effects. Up Above, They know what is good for us and They administer exactly the right dosage. Sometimes people who have just begun working with dreams and meditation start to feel afraid. They shouldn't; they are in a process of rebirth and birth requires intense effort and courage.

We need to develop humility when we explore our unconscious because we are obliged to see our faults, not just our potential. It's in understanding our faults, our weaknesses that, one day, we can look upon others with love. Whenever we see others behaving in a distorted way, we'll remember, 'A couple of years ago, I behaved just like them.' One day, we look on others as a doctor does. A doctor doesn't look at a patient and think, 'Oh! Look at him with those yellow eyes!' No, he thinks, 'Ah! He's got such a symptom. That means he's got such a problem.' And he exercises his talent to understand the illness and he tries to find a solution to be able to help the person. When we develop the habit of always referring back to ourselves, when we study our conscience with humility, love and compassion for ourselves, we develop compassion for others. And we develop mastery of our thoughts. Whenever we are put out, it's as though we are throwing knives at the other person. Of course, the police won't arrest us for having negative thoughts about someone—they don't see them. But there is a police force Up Above and they see everything.

When we say to ourselves, each time we are put out, 'That's a part of me,' that isn't narcissistic or self-centered. On the contrary! A selfish, egotistical person only wants the icing on the cake, whereas when we constantly refer everything back to ourselves, positive as well as negative, then we are in a process of evolution: we don't flee and we don't sit up in a tower trying to convince ourselves we've reached the top. This is how we live when we refer to our reality as if it were a dream experience. We analyze in symbols and we see the beauty, the source of creation.

The moment we transcend a distortion, we are aware of it because we feel a sort of *click* within ourselves. It's so beautiful! We manage to see beauty in what's negative. I'd even say more than beauty: we understand Divine Organization, that Great Intelligence, and we feel the Immense Kindness, the Infinite Love It manifests in allowing us to experiment.

The more structured our meditation is, the clearer the answers we receive and the easier they are to interpret. Why? Because they correspond to structure. Usually, when a person becomes spiritual, he tends to reject structure because he associates it with rigidity, heaviness and complexity. But the Universe is very structured. It has a right, rigorous structure. However this great structure also has the enthusiasm of a child; it hasn't got the negative aspect associated with rigidity. Rigor and discipline are great qualities and to turn our back on them is to be content to float along on our ideals, to uproot ourselves and lose our anchorage in matter.

Personally, I write down all my dreams. I have done so for years. It's very important to write down our dreams because it allows us to free up our conscience so it can receive more. With time and meditation, we become capable of waking up after every five or six dreams and of remembering each of them. We become aware of their importance and we start to love dreaming more and more. Our memory develops and expands and we can then remember many dreams.

Last night, in one of my dreams, I saw a child I know who is very evolved. I was shown what responsibilities he will have later on, when he grows up. My dream allowed me to see his mission. With time, when we have done a lot of work on ourselves, we are allowed to know other people's Programs. Sometimes I'm told, "Yes, it's good to associate with so and so, but you'll need to watch out for a particular attitude in him; be vigilant."

That's what is so wonderful with dreams. Above all, we benefit from the greatest spiritual autonomy that exists—because our answers and guidance come to us directly from Up Above.

I did a lot of experimenting with asking questions and receiving answers with little things, before going on to plan my own life and my family's life in this way. I was like a scientist who needed proof and I had a lot of doubt. I didn't doubt God. Ah! No, not Him! I doubted myself. I always asked myself if my answer came from Up Above or if it came from my ego, from my needs. I doubted my clear-mindedness. And this kind of doubt is healthy. Because our ego has a lot of needs and it speaks out very loudly. If it feels like doing something and, during meditation, we ask, 'Should I do that?' we may hear a 'Yes, yes, yes!' that is so persistent that we end up saying, 'Ah! ok, permission granted! I've just been told I can go ahead and do it.' But then, when we act on this decision, things go wrong; it doesn't work.

At one point, I understood; I understood with Christiane. Together we came to understand that the true radar is within ourselves. It's our spirit that understands things, and when negative resonance or needs create interference, it can't see clearly. Whenever we have difficulties or when our projects don't work out, we need to work on our spirit; we need to reprogram it and we need to cleanse our memories. But we mustn't expect things to be rectified rapidly. Sometimes it's true that it can be very fast, but that's not always the case; it usually takes time. With this teaching, with the understanding of dreams & signs, we've seen miracles, extraordinary transformations—all sorts of healings take place on all levels. You can read about them in the true stories told in our books. Up Above can grant us grace. But, fundamentally, it's really all about Work that is accomplished gradually over time.

When we meditate intensely on our dreams to understand them, we obtain results. Usually our spirit is scattered over all sorts of memories, moving from one to the other according to the events—big or small—that occur in our lives. But when we meditate on our dreams & signs, it's as if we called everyone back home and concentrated our forces. Whenever we enter a dream—which is a state of conscience in its intense form—and because there are no borders between the worlds that exist, using a symbolic approach, the concentrated focus opens up the parallel

147

dimensions for us and provides us with access to the Knowledge of the dream. And then, we can understand more dreams and signs. I remember a dream I received once. I was meditating intensively to understand a symbol — it was the meaning of the horse. I was thinking about it, over and over in my head. I read up about it on the Internet to find out more about its behavior, etc. The following night I dreamed that *I was in classroom and there was a teacher. He said, "Today, we are going to talk about the symbol of the horse" and he drew one on the board with his chalk and gave a summary of its meaning.* Wow! I woke up all amazed by this meaning. It was so precise that I started to do that over and over again. I understood that it was the intensity of my intention that had led to such a precise answer. By repeating my question like a mantra, I was transporting myself during the night into dreams that were furthering my spiritual education. It was a true revelation. Qualities and distortions manifest themselves through my requests and demands to the Universe. We can receive proof like that, every day and every night. And it works like this for everyone — not just for me — whether you're 10, 50 or 90 years old. All we have to do to verify this is to ask intensely, really intensely with respect and love, for some time. We ask our question before going to sleep and throughout the day whenever we can.

Sometimes, when our thoughts aren't required at work — when driving, walking, having a bath, etc. — our mind is busy thinking all sorts of things that we do not necessarily need to think about. Well, if we use these moments to ask for more Knowledge, for signs to understand what we need to do to be just and right, our mind and spirit become clear and answers come to us quite naturally.

However, work with dreams & signs isn't for everyone, because it takes us very far and not everyone is ready to re-assess and transform so deeply. In the beginning, before receiving our answers precisely, during the de-structuring phase, we experience great anxiety; we have real nightmares. The Work is so deep that sometimes we no longer know who we are and we feel as though there's only great emptiness beneath our feet. We feel dizzy and lost.

Whenever we ask for dreams & signs, we activate such a pure Force or Powerful Energy within ourselves to change, to transform ourselves—it's not just a push button, *question & answer*—it is normal that when we ask, we also receive nightmares to express what we experience, what we're going through that's led to our question; sometimes, distortions have no other choice than to manifest themselves, one after the other, through nightmares. We have to be courageous, to know that at first, dreams are there to help us improve ourselves. So we keep working and asking for guidance and gradually, one step at a time, the distortions give way to Light and we regain our spiritual powers. And we dream more, of course, because we ask to. And often in our dreams we are given an apprenticeship. It's as if we were following a course, being given a lesson. We can learn great things in a short period of time. Einstein woke up one morning with his famous equation $E = mc^2$, which constituted the grounds for a whole new perception of the world we live in.

This is how I learned. At night, I found myself back in various schools, where I was taught the workings of the Universe, the nature of dreams and the meaning of symbols. In some dreams, I saw information go by at phenomenal speed; sometimes it was so fast, I couldn't see or distinguish anything. I was like a computer being uploaded with a new program. The following day, I had new questions, new aspirations, I felt a great thirst to head toward something that could provide me with answers and the keys that I hadn't yet acquired. And I had new perceptions—new levels of perception—were being opened in me. I'd say to myself, 'Ah! So this means this and that means that.'

I see some of you smile because you know what I mean. At one point, we have to re-learn how to manage all this information. In the beginning, we don't know what to do with everything we perceive, but over time, we integrate symbolic language. It's like learning to drive a car. In the beginning, it's frightening having to handle such a big machine. We wonder how we'll ever manage. We see cars, vans, trucks, pedestrians, traffic lights, highways and AAAH! Everything goes so fast. After a while, we sit calmly in our car and drive along, and all that is completely normal. We can think about other things, even meditate, as we drive.

When the Metaphysical World opens to us, we have to learn to *drive* our spiritual *vehicle*, to gradually get used to handling it. We need to give ourselves time to learn and integrate the processes

149

involved in this veritable mutation of our conscience. In this wonderful adventure, there's really only one thing to know and that is: *Know yourself and you will know the Universe.* It's by knowing ourselves that we know the outside world, because everyone we know, everyone we encounter and every situation we experience, all represent parts of ourselves. The unconscious is not only abstract and inside of us. It is there; it is also the outside world. Everything we don't know, every character and way of thinking is our unconscious. Living with dreams & signs gives us this perspective, this true vision that the physical and metaphysical worlds are the same: they are connected and co-work together all the time.

And that's it for this evening. Thank you for your lovely listening and sharing. I wish you a safe journey home and a happy Path. Sweet dreams and sweet nightmares!

WORKSHOP
Inner Beauty

Yes, madam? (Dreamer: I had a dream. *I saw a house, and above it, the sea. In fact, it was just decor, like in the theatre. At the same time, it all seemed real because I could see and hear the waves. The house had no front facade and I could see inside. Part of the decor was a kitchen. Then there was a flowing waterfall; then a sitting-room and another waterfall, and there were lots of tropical plants. It was beautiful. I was wearing a pink bikini with yellow daisies and other colors on it. Then I heard a voice say, 'Come and swim in the sea.' So I tried to climb up the first waterfall to get to the sea. And it was a real waterfall because I could feel the heat of the water on my skin. At first, I couldn't get up, then, at one point, I managed to climb up. And as I was climbing I had a funny feeling: I was supposed to be barefoot but, given the funny feeling of the water on my feet, I realized I was wearing pantyhose. When I reached the top, the sea was real sea; it was no longer just decor. It was vast. At the edge of the sea, there was a toilet and I went in to take off my pantyhose. The toilet door was huge and I couldn't close it. Then I woke up.*)

In this dream, you were being shown memories you need to purify. I say that because of the toilet.

As you were wearing a swimming costume and, given the presence of the sea and the waterfalls, this dream concerns your emotional world. Was the swimming costume you were wearing a two-piece? (Dreamer: Yes, it was a bikini.) Was it sexy or just ordinary? (Dreamer: Not particularly sexy. No, that idea wasn't present.) Ok.

This is an important detail. If the bikini had been an overly sexy one—because sexy clothes can be ok when not excessively so, especially in public circumstances—it would have expressed seduction and memories of promiscuity or loose morals. However, given the color pink along with a flowery pattern and other elements in the scene, it was more a symbol of affection, tenderness and gentleness.

Let's see. At the start, it was just decor. What does decor symbolize? It's something that serves only to give an appearance of something—it wasn't a real house, it wasn't a real sea; it was only the appearance of a house and a sea.

But a house in a dream always symbolizes intimacy, our private self. The fact that the rooms in the house were social, communal rooms—the sitting-room and the kitchen are rooms where people tend to gather—shows that you really have no refuge, no intimate, private world. You live more on the outside than on the inside; you mostly live for other people's attention and what they think of you. You haven't got the intimate life you'd like to have. True, real emotions are missing in your personal life because, first of all, you have created a world with a facade saying "everything is going pretty well." We can have a family, a husband and friends and still feel there's no appropriate place or no one we can share our intimate world with; there's no one who appreciates the lovely things we have to offer. This situation is loaded with emotions, which is why there were waterfalls in the house. Therefore, you feel a deep lack on the emotional level and, because of this, you may tend to seek people's attention too much—hence the pink bikini which, in this context, expressed a quest for love and affection—and to offer others a false image of yourself, a facade, symbolized by the decor.

Then, you climbed up the waterfall. In terms of conscience, going up signifies rising toward the Causal world—heading back up the river of Creation, so to speak—so as to elevate our level of conscience. Then you reached the real sea, which represents your real emotional unconscious. The sea is vast and deep and in it, symbolically, we find wrecks, symbols of old memories buried in the depths of our being. The sea represents all the emotions we have experienced, the positive as well as the negative. You were visiting your ancient and present emotional memories. But at the same time, you are beginning to be more connected with yourself. Less fake, less a facade, so to speak. You're becoming more authentic, more truthful. This is very important for your evolution. Emotionally speaking, you are changing deeply, elevating your soul, your life, to the next level of evolution. You are discovering more and more what real emotions are instead of experiencing them in an ordinary conscience.

There was a toilet. And you noticed you were wearing pantyhose. (Dreamer: It was while I was climbing up the waterfall that I realized that. My feet felt funny. I said to myself, 'My goodness, how come I don't feel the water as I usually would?' Because I couldn't see my pantyhose, they were transparent.) Ok, I understand.

So this scene refers to purification directly related to the symbolism of pantyhose. What do pantyhose represent? We have to look for the negative symbolism because in the dream, the pantyhose weren't in the right place: when we go swimming, we don't usually wear pantyhose, do we? Pantyhose are worn on our legs, and legs represent the way we advance. Hence the negative symbolism is dissimulating faults we have in the way we advance. This recalls the idea of a decor, of an artificial setting or image. So the pantyhose referred to your need to hide faults in order to please, so as to be loved.

Sometimes we lack self-confidence and self-esteem, and we think we have to mask reality so as to give others the impression we are beautiful and that everything is fine. Therefore this is the issue related to the pantyhose in the dream.

Some women have stretch marks or varicose veins and they feel ill-at-ease in a swimsuit. It's very common. They think, very often unconsciously, that exterior beauty is more important than inner beauty. Of course, the best is to have both, but we should be able to feel beautiful whatever the body shape we have. The reason why some women or men don't accept their body sometimes is that they feel a lack of love within themselves and have developed a dependency on others. Hence they exaggerate their seduction to dissimulate a lack of confidence and the fact they need to be loved so much. So they hide, or sometimes show too much of their body, thereby losing a certain form or degree of authenticity. Everything that is too much is linked to a lack within. We naturally overdo things to compensate. It's a well-known fact in psychology. And in dreams, we can see when we have these sorts of problems through different types of symbols.

It's not our body that makes us beautiful; it's our soul.

A happy, luminous, spiritual soul is beautiful, no matter the form, shape or size of our body. When our spirit is serene, the people around us feel so good they don't even notice our appearance; they feel good and that's enough for them. And when we feel good in ourselves, this is reflected on the outside and we look good too. At these moments, we often receive compliments as people respond to our inner beauty, our spirit's well-being, our soul's happiness.

Of course, our body remains a representation of what we are and what we have been in previous lives. Because it's our spirit that creates our body: it creates a vehicle for experimenting that corresponds to its strengths and weaknesses. And all physical features, right down to the slightest detail, have a particular, symbolic meaning.

Let me give you an example. Someone with an ear problem would have something to understand in relation to what the ear represents. The ear is the organ of receptivity. Hence, an ear problem is directly related to a difficulty with receptivity, with the way we listen to others. We can be over-saturated with an accumulation of things we've heard as well as with things we don't understand or that we don't want to hear. This manifests itself through this physical feature. We see this very often with children who suffer repeatedly from ear infections. Sometimes, when they are very young, children become saturated with all these different, new experimentations they have to learn through the sense of hearing; it feels like it's too much for them and that's why they develop ear problems. When this happens to our child, we should automatically ask ourselves, 'What is it that he doesn't want to hear, or has problems with? Have we, as parents, said something not quite right for a child?' As parents it is very interesting to listen in symbols, to read the sign as if it were a dream. We have no idea how much we can assist in the development of our child in this way.

The symbolism of our body parts is very precise. There is a reason, a cause, for every exception to the norm, for every disproportion. Hence, if we have a physical deformity, we should say to ourselves, 'This represents a part of me and it's up to me to transform it through my inner work.' Of course, as the distortion has already condensed in our body, it probably won't change—at least not in this life. But learning to live with it is already wonderful and really evolutive for us.

154

Because if we don't like our big nose and we have it changed surgically, we still have a big nose on the inside; it hasn't changed on the metaphysical level. A lot of people who resort to cosmetic surgery don't recognize themselves afterwards. Some of them even develop personality problems. This is because the surgery creates a discrepancy, a disparity, between what they really are and the image they see in the mirror. They don't recognize the essence of their being.

Our body moulds itself on the qualities and distortions that dwell in our soul. So if we inherit physically manifested distortions, we should simply accept them and consider them as prime raw material to work on and not as something dreadful. Our society is too materialistic; it does not place enough value on the metaphysical components of reality. A spiritual person who only thinks in terms of Qualities and Virtues, ceases to compare himself to others. He likes and appreciates himself as he is, because he knows that God loves him *warts and all*, i.e. with all his faults and weaknesses. With such an approach, every intention to improve our appearance—going on a diet, surgery or any other method—can be OK if we do it the right way and, with deep spiritual work, our intention to improve our appearance can find itself purified, freed from the burden of the desire to please. The drama is taken out of the whole issue, and we undertake steps to change without encountering frustration or disappointment because when we are spiritual, it's our inner change, not the outer one, that counts most.

To go back to your dream, you are in the process of purifying memories relating to this acceptance. Once you have completely accepted your body, you'll regain your authenticity and you'll no longer feel the need to resort to artifice.

(Dreamer: At the beginning, I didn't know I was wearing pantyhose.) Yes, that's right. You were discovering these parts of yourself. Sometimes we think we accept our body, but the slightest offensive remark sets off an inner storm. Similarly, people who live alone or who haven't felt appreciated for some time, feel de-stabilized whenever someone takes an interest in them. They start to examine themselves from every angle—almost obsessively sometimes—because uncomfortable memories about their appearance have been awakened. Such situations provide us with an opportunity to realize that, in actual fact, we don't fully accept ourselves.

To be capable of emanating love, we must love our own body; that's an absolute fact. Otherwise, it's as though we had children we didn't love. If one of our children has a more difficult character than the others, we love him all the same, but we keep a closer eye on him and accompany him a bit more; we help him learn to transform himself. It's the same for our body. Our body is a vehicle that we have to learn to see as a reflection of our soul.

Then you saw a toilet and you went in. A toilet symbolizes purification. You began to remove the artifice that, up until now, allowed you to—(Dreamer: I didn't have time to take off my pantyhose because I couldn't close the door properly. It was a huge door and it kept on opening.) That's interesting.

You see, once again, this indicates a problem with intimacy. Memories have opened the door to be loved, to have attention, too wide, too often. This is why the door keeps opening all the time. You are also the door in the dream. It represents a part of you that doesn't have enough intimacy. And this was caused by a need for attention that has created a preoccupation with appearance, with appearing well in the eyes of others.

Sometimes when we do inner work, we purify ourselves, but we don't want others to know. Of course if we are in a public place and we deliberately leave the toilet door open, that's distorted behavior. But if we are at home and we feel blocked because our child or spouse opens the door, then we've got a problem. It means we retain, we repress and hide things; in a way, we hide ourselves. Otherwise, we feel at ease in these moments of purification and we can continue. It's OK if our child comes into the bathroom. We can simply, calmly and serenely, ask him to leave us alone for a moment.

Sometimes men cannot use urinals when there are other people around. They only feel comfortable if no one is looking, so they can only urinate in the toilet with the door closed. In such a case, we need to work on ourselves. I was like that once. I found it difficult to urinate in public urinals because there were all sorts of energies around. I lacked self-confidence; I hadn't fully integrated my masculinity. I was very receptive; I could feel other people's energies and that blocked me. I didn't have enough focus and confidence in myself. When we want everyone to be happy all the time, when we want to please others, this sort of problem arises. So I worked on this; I used these situations to transcend my blockages.

In your dream, the fact that you couldn't take off your pantyhose because the door kept on opening indicates that you are committed to a purification process but you are encountering resistance: parts of you do not want to change, to purify. It is easier not to change than to change, that's for sure. That's absolutely normal. As you gradually transcend the memories you have related to resistance, you'll become more authentic—first of all with yourself, and then with others. It will be easier for you to identify and accept your distortions.

At first, when our unconscious opens, we may tend to hide our less than beautiful aspects from ourselves and then comes a time when we move on to another stage.

We have to develop a lot of humility to follow our dreams & signs, to undertake a spiritual journey and walk a spiritual path. Often spirituality is presented as being only luminous, as though on such a path we only encounter beautiful states of conscience. Of course, we do manage to enjoy and be immersed in beautiful atmospheres and, as we continue, for longer and longer periods of time. However, we must do some deep cleansing along the way and the memories we encounter are not all beautiful or easy to accept.

When our distorted memories turn up in our dreams, it is time to cleanse them, because our conscience is in touch with them. When we notice something isn't quite right within ourselves, we have to have the humility to recognize it and, then, the willpower to transform it.

It's the same idea on the physical, concrete level, in our house. When we begin to feel less happy in our home, when, for example, those khaki green walls in the sitting-room start to bother us, we need to be capable of changing them. When we first painted the walls that color, we thought it was lovely, but now we find ourselves saying, 'It makes everything dark. It's not bright and luminous. I've changed and that color doesn't suit me anymore.'

Budget restrictions, a lack of time or simple laziness can make us put off re-painting until later, or we may say to ourselves, 'I only rent this place, it isn't mine.' However, we should really say, 'This color influences me and my near and dear ones every day; it affects our mood, our soul-states. Well, I'm now going to create a new living space. I'm changing on the inside. So I'm going to materialize my change right down onto the physical level. A few liters of paint and a few hours of work won't ruin us. Afterwards the whole family will feel better in this home of ours.'

Similarly we often accumulate things and we constantly put off tidying up and clearing things out. Oof! It's really something, you know. By constantly postponing this sort of thing, we clutter our mind and burden our spirit. Everything is symbolic, and everything we surround ourselves with affects our states of conscience either positively or negatively.

Just think of all the cassettes and CDs that we've accumulated beside our stereo system. If we analyze the contents of these recordings, we very often realize that we are keeping songs that are not very inspiring for our mind and spirit. Some people have an almost exclusive collection of songs about emotional dependence — *AH! Don't leave me! I Love you, I'm cold when you aren't near me, etc. (laughter)*

Some people buy paintings that aren't beautiful symbolically-speaking and they hang them all over the house — in the sitting-room, in the children's bedroom, etc. They think these paintings are valuable works of art because they paid a lot of money for them, whereas they actually end up bringing illness and ill-being into the home. This is because they emit a distorted vibration.

When an artist paints a picture, he paints himself. If the painting isn't beautiful, it means that a part of the artist isn't beautiful. Some paintings are estimated at being worth two or three million dollars, or more, and yet they emanate such sadness or aggression that it makes them ugly.

When we think of this, we are reminded of how society vibrates at such a weak level of conscience. Often it's rich businessmen who buy distorted paintings. These people are so stuck in the grip or vise of social convention — having to follow certain codes of behavior, being obliged to turn up at certain meetings in a suit and tie, to look respectable, etc. — that it consoles them to have a representation of delinquency under their eyes. They envy the artist's bohemian lifestyle and part of them identifies with him.

Yes, madam? (Dreamer: I'd like an interpretation of a dream I had recently. *I was in a room in the middle of a group of people, and a travel agent was preparing a trip for us. At one point, I asked him where we were going, what our destination was. He replied, "Our destination is happiness." Then the question of age was raised. I don't know if it only concerned my age or if it also included the others but, in any case, I was 13, 14 or 15 years old. Then the travel agent told the group, "Sunglasses are forbidden." And I asked him, "How long will we be gone for?" He replied, "We're going for seven years." And so I started to cry, because I've got a son and I didn't want to leave him for such a long time. As I cried, I said, "I don't want to abandon my son; I don't want to go." Then there was a change of scene and I saw myself sitting down, and on my back there was a puppet with a big, red, spotty face. The puppet wasn't heavy or cumbersome.*) Ah! What a beautiful dream!

The travel agent was a Spiritual Guide announcing your imminent departure on an exploratory trip down memory lane! Because journeys represent the exploration of the unconscious, the Guide was informing you that you are about to undertake great exploration of your memories. When we change countries, we change cultures, and our state of conscience changes too.

The fact that you were a teenager shows that, in terms of conscience, you are preparing to enter adulthood and that you will be more aware of the needs of others, not just your own. The other people in the group also represent parts of you, of your social behavior. Their presence indicated that the conscience-trip being prepared for you will influence your social life and relationship with others.

When you asked about your destination, the Guide told you that your destination was happiness. This dream announces a serious change in your life, a real spiritual path, because the process of self-exploration leads to happiness.

The Guide told you sunglasses were forbidden. This is very positive: it means you will no longer be able to hide your soul-states or your thoughts because the eyes are the mirror of the soul. The positive aspect of sunglasses is discretion and protection of our capacity to see, and also of our soul perception, because the eyes are connected to the soul and we can absorb all sorts of energies from our environment and from others. The sun is the symbol representing global energy in a very large way. The negative aspect of sunglasses is hiding or playing the role of a star who doesn't want to be recognized. It also represents being overprotective and a difficulty to manage other people's energy, to be open to the Light, to God.

Then you started to cry because you didn't want to abandon your son. The Guide didn't ask you to abandon your son; he didn't make any such suggestion. You yourself made the association between abandoning your son and your departure for happiness. This scene revealed negative memories related to the abandonment of a child for self-transformation and spiritual reasons.

Many people who become priests, monks or nuns are one day confronted with having to choose between entering a religious order or getting married along with the responsibility of bringing up a child. Over the centuries, many people have created important karma by abandoning their family for the sake of a spiritual quest.

God doesn't abandon His creations. He continues to take care of us all. Guides do so too; they don't abandon us to continue with their own evolution. On the contrary, their evolution is related to the responsibilities they take on regarding God's creations. An infallible way to proceed when we have to make an important decision is to ask ourselves, 'Would God do such a thing? Would I do this if God were here in front of me?' I can assure you that this repositions our thoughts, and I know this because I've been practicing this method for many years.

To go back to your dream, we see that you are experiencing this duality concerning your spiritual path. In another life, you were very probably a monk or a nun, and you abandoned your child.

The reaction you had in your dream, based on the belief that you had to choose between a spiritual life and responsibility for a child, indicates that you need to rectify this concept. We aren't obliged to abandon our children when we choose a spiritual path.

160

It's the complete opposite in fact: we should transmit the fruits of our research to them so they can go further.

Then, in the scene that followed, you were shown the deep cause of your difficulty, of your sadness: the puppet. You had a red-faced puppet on your back. First of all, the back and what's behind us represent the past, where we've come from. You were being shown an attitude you had in one or several other lives.

What does a puppet represent? A puppet cannot move by itself. People who are manipulated by others are often referred to as puppets. Hence, in terms of conscience, a puppet represents a tendency to let ourselves be manipulated, to give up our power and our autonomy. In the context of your dream, we think of someone who blindly follows a religious doctrine, who never calls himself into question to check whether what he advocates is right. This also applies to a social trend or to a fashion. At times, everyone harbors little puppets within. You were shown that it's not solely your spiritual power that directs and guides your life, that you haven't really integrated your spiritual autonomy.

The puppet was red. Well, red represents action in matter. Hence this scene showed that, for a long time, you let yourself be manipulated by a materialistic view of things and that is what is at the root of your present distress.

It is important to understand that this dream has nothing whatsoever to do with your son as a person. It's the adolescence of your conscience that is being referred to here, which includes an attachment to false pleasures and everything that prevents you from actually applying spiritual concepts in your daily life.

We mustn't confuse love and attachment. The attachment we feel for our near and dear ones is nothing other than a desire to possess them—this is the case for those people in an ordinary conscience. This attitude has nothing to do with unconditional love and compassion.

One day we need to be able to detach ourselves from the people we love. This is one of the positive aspects of monastic life; it leads us to develop unconditional love and detachment. However we can develop these qualities outside monasteries and convents. In no way does being detached from our children prevent us from loving them and being constantly available for them. Being detached means trusting their evolution program and accepting the experiences they go through, their hardships, trials and ordeals as well as their victories. It also means giving them freedom while continuing to guide their steps and not taking credit for what they become. Very few people have acquired the level of love and wisdom that real detachment requires. Indeed, very few people understand this concept.

This reminds me of the great step my sister took in this regard. One evening, she and her husband, my wife, Christiane, and I went to see the film, *The Passion of the Christ*. My sister was really moved, especially by the scenes where Jesus shows his mother how, in the very depths of his being, he has understood the sacred sense of suffering. While he is being whipped and while he is carrying the cross, Jesus is bleeding and his whole body is suffering, and yet the look on his face, in his eyes, testifies to a state of complete transcendence — we can see he is enlightened by God. He looks at Mary and his eyes say, 'Oh Mother, see how wonderful it is to go through this for my evolution and for all mankind.' Mary is totally overwhelmed by his look and by the message she perceives. These are the most powerful scenes regarding transcendence of suffering and self sacrifice that I've ever seen. Just telling you about them gives me the shivers because my soul resonates so strongly with this mystical dimension of sacrifice. In another scene, as Mary draws close to him in the crowd, Jesus, referring to what he's going through, says, "See Mother, I make all things new." The reason for suffering is renewal, purification of our conscience.

Well, my sister was really moved by this film and she was able to understand the sacred aspect of suffering. She is someone who is working intensely on herself — she's been on a spiritual path for many years now — and she has two young children. Every time her little Gabriel cried, she wanted to meet his needs immediately. (It was the same with her daughter Ariel when she was a baby.) It was so difficult for her to hear the baby cry! Of course, the baby felt his mother's distress and, among other things, he also felt her duality. For example, he was only eight or nine months old and already he had begun to manipulate her by crying so that she would take him into her arms. All children are very quick to find ways to manipulate. Especially very young children — they've got such intelligence! Their intelligence is multi-dimensional.

When my sister saw the film, she became aware of the fact that we shouldn't seek to alleviate our child's suffering at all costs. When we've done everything necessary for him to feel good—we've fed and bathed him, changed his diaper and tucked him into bed—if we then feel a little whim or caprice in his energy, we tell ourselves, 'Ok, fine, let him transform his energy.' Before this film and her new awareness, my sister tended to give in to her child's every whim. Now she is better at discerning what the matter is—if he's in pain, sick or simply wants to be taken into her arms. And now, instead of trying to alleviate his suffering, she leaves him to work on himself, saying, "Ah! There's something you need to understand, my boy. Mommy has done all she can; it's in your hands and in God's hands now." Even if she hasn't completely integrated this change yet, even if she sometimes falls back into her old ways, she has begun to change her attitude and that is helping change the family spirit. She's evolving at her own pace and that's wonderful.

So, in this dream, you were being shown that you need to work on detachment; you need to develop this attitude. Your son is here this evening and he's nearly an adult. Of course it's still your responsibility to accompany him well, but Up Above, They wanted to help you overcome your fear that something might happen to him.

In a way, you were also being invited to completely transform yourself, to grow up and to die within, except that you immediately objected, saying, "Oh no! I can't do it!" It's as though you were saying—remember the red-faced puppet—"I want my little pleasures. I want to watch my TV series on Mondays, Tuesdays and Wednesdays, and play cards the rest of the week." That's what was expressed by your crying and protesting.

A popular expression says, *Death comes like a thief in the night.* I'd improve on this saying. I would say: *When the time is right, Death comes like a Sage, with Wisdom and Love.*

In actual fact, death, as most people conceive it, does not exist. One day, during an out-of-body experience, I found myself in a Parallel World. *I was swimming in the water with a spiritual Guide and he was teaching me things. I said, "Wow! It's amazing; it's just like real water. It's the same water as on Earth. I can feel it. It's the same temperature, the same consistency, etc." At one point I stopped swimming and I realized I could remain afloat but I didn't sink even though I was still in the water.* On Earth, we normally have to move our arms and legs to remain afloat.

I asked the Guide, "Can we die, can we drown here?" He replied, "Well yes, you can drown. But what's drowning? We continue to live afterwards. You might be scared, you'll choke and leave your body, but afterwards you'll keep on living because death doesn't exist as Humans perceive it. We only transform ourselves."

Needless to say, the idea isn't to deliberately die; we mustn't commit suicide. But, let's say we're far out at sea and our boat capsizes, and we swim and swim and swim until we have no strength any more and we simply cannot manage one more stroke. Well, then we should take a deep breath and say, "Dear God, may Your will be done." A person in a terminal phase should think like this. He should say to himself, 'My time has come. I accept that and I let myself go, I abandon myself to death like a child drops off to sleep in his mother's arms. I detach myself from my physical envelope. I'm going to move on into another world, just as if I were in a dream except this time, I won't come back into this body." It is as simple as that.

We need to understand that when we die in the physical world, things don't stop there: we continue to live. We don't find ourselves floating in the dark between two stars, nor sitting on a cloud waiting to see where we'll reincarnate next. We pass through to the other side, where there exist very structured worlds, whole societies — some of which are thousands of times more evolved than ours. One day we can visit these Worlds. We can also enter into contact with deceased people who can describe these worlds and tell us about their experiences there.

So, through this dream, you were being invited to change your point of view and, in particular, to rid yourself of your teenaged, spotty-faced puppet attitude, whereby you tend to undermine yourself by comparing yourself to others who aren't correct and who are in ordinary experimentations, without conscience or Knowledge. You were being invited to make an effort to develop detachment so as to be able to move on to a new stage, with happiness as your destination.

That's it for this evening. Heartfelt thanks for your beautiful sharing. As you can see, these workshops take place in all simplicity and you can see how your sharing can greatly help others. Thank you very much everyone. I wish you all a safe journey home and may your dreams & signs consciously light up your lives!

WORKSHOP
Awakening of Vital Energy

Yes, sir? (Participant: I had a dream. *I was looking at a beautiful painting; I was looking at it intensely. Then I found myself in it, as if it were real. It was really beautiful.* It's already happened that I've looked at a photo during the day, while awake, and then dreamed about things related to the photo during the night.)

This dream is a good illustration of what the metaphysical aspect of reality is. If you are able to enter a picture or a photo in a dream, you can also do so in concrete reality. Your work with dreams & signs has led you to develop your spiritual capacities, your powers of extra-sensorial perception. The more you progress on your path, the more you'll be able to receive subtle information about people and other things that are imperceptible via the ordinary senses. For example, if you see a person making a joke or being amusing but who actually feels sad, you'll perceive his sadness. You'll also find you can pick up the vibrations of objects more and more.

Objects also have a form of memory. It has previously happened when I have been in a store and concentrated on a pair of trousers because I was wondering whether or not I should buy them and, during the night, *I found myself in the very factory that manufactures them.* We can also have this kind of information on the spot — and it's very useful — because if we know that in such a factory the workers are well treated by their bosses, we encourage them by buying their goods. And if we know they don't treat their workers well, then we don't buy from them.

I use these Powers a lot now. In my dreams, I find myself visiting printers and attending meetings with representatives of various distributors we do business with for our organization's publishing house. I can follow the whole process and make an appropriate decision. We all have these Powers. Work with dreams & signs can quite naturally lead us to activate these powers and, one day, we can live our lives with great depths of perception.

To go back to your question, yes, indeed, by concentrating on a photo, we can feel what the person is experiencing, even if it's an old photo. We contact the essence, the person's spirit. I do this regularly with my daughter, without any photo. I close my eyes, I think about her and images come to me. Through these symbols, I can know what she's going through, how she feels, and it's absolutely concrete.

It's also possible to do this with correspondence. We receive a lot of emails from all over the world about the organization of the workshops and lectures and for various other reasons, of course, so I very often write emails and text messages. I usually sign off with *Angelically yours* or *Angelic thoughts*. However, if, for example, I'm writing to a hotel to rent a room, I go within and I know exactly how the person I'm writing to will react inwardly to this formula. If I feel the slightest stiffness or awkwardness, I'll write *Best wishes* or *Yours sincerely* because I'm aware that a direct reference to Angels won't do; it would awaken all sorts of unwelcome feelings.

For me an Angel is the perfect symbol for our capacity to dream, to elevate our conscience and to enter the Parallel Worlds to learn about ourselves, our Program and Life. But for many people the term awakens memories of overbearing religious indoctrination or airy-fairy unreal, irresponsible spirituality as well as personal spiritual distortions. Indeed, until I myself had analyzed and understood the perfection of this symbol, I too found it difficult. It is very important to respect people, wholly and completely, and never to impose our Knowledge. Taking those few minutes to go within and check the most appropriate expression to use ensures harmonious, respectful communication on a deep level. Our relationships are improved and our whole life is enhanced.

And, yes indeed, we can do that with photos and paintings.

Yes, madam? (Participant: I have two symbols I'd like interpreted: the ocean and ocean liners.) Ok. Fine.

An ocean is made up of water. We had this symbol in a previous lecture recently. So right from the start we know it's related to the emotional world. The ocean is different from a glass of water: it is vast and contains a lot of water, most of which is situated down in the depths. So we can refer to emotional memories. The ocean is full of fish, invertebrates, coral reefs, etc. There's a whole intense life in the sea; there are also memories that have accumulated in its sediment over hundreds of years. Treasure and wrecks can be found on the ocean bed. The ocean has also covered over ancient ground where man once lived. Since so much information is contained in the sea, it symbolizes the emotional unconscious with its reservoir of deep memories and all the force of life that is associated with it.

As for big boats, given that they sail on water, they too relate to the emotional world. Like a car or truck, a boat allows us to move around and to transport things; hence it symbolizes the way we advance with our emotions. Are we stable or do we easily flare up and lose our temper? Do we tend to provoke emotional accidents, to hurt others? The boat's movement will tell us. Various characteristics of the boat will inform us about our emotional stability and our emotional life in general. For instance, the bigger the boat, the greater and more powerful the emotional force present in our way of advancing. A cargo ship allows us to transport merchandise. Hence there's a connotation of resources — affective, emotional resources.

As for an ocean liner or a cruise ship, it allows people to travel from one country to another by sea and, therefore, represents a capacity, on a collective level, to change our state of conscience by means of our emotions. The positive symbolism of a cruise ship is relaxation, enjoying life and pleasure, and its negative symbolism is an intense need for a superficial social life. A cruise can be very positive. It's all in the intention. A person who sees a negative image of an ocean liner in his dream clearly feels a lack on the affective, emotional level, which he tries to fulfill by going out and by getting involved in all sorts of social activities.

Yes, madam? (Participant: I'd like to know what the point of awakening the kundalini is. Because I've had dreams about this. I'd also like to know what we feel, physically, when the kundalini awakens.)

For those of you who don't know what the kundalini is, I'd like to give an explanation. The word kundalini refers to the activation of the vital energy that keeps us alive and which enables us to move, create, have emotions, thoughts and intentions. It's also the energy of our spirit that lives in our physical body and that can be concentrated, at first, in our sacred zone. Some people consider the kundalini solely as our sexual energy, but it is not only that. It's principally the vital energy that we use in our body. For the majority of us, this energy is not developed and it is mainly confined to the base of the spine. Why there? Because this part of the body is the seat of the first chakra, the survival chakra, and because the energy of people who are in a conscience of intense needs and various negative desires makes it somewhat like an animal's energy, it is completely oriented toward the satisfaction of their needs.

Needless to say, this energy rises and descends from one chakra to another in a whole network of what are called energy meridians, but its intensity is usually rather weak. Whenever the kundalini awakens, this powerful force is activated and our capacities are multiplied on all levels: we have more physical energy, deeper feelings, livelier intelligence and stronger willpower. The sole act of awakening vital energy amplifies charisma on all levels as well as the sharpness of ordinary senses and the feeling of need. The aim of this amplification is to lead us to master the intensity caused by our needs and to allow our vital energy to vibrate on a higher wavelength, thereby increasing extra-sensorial perception and to remain right, calm and gentle even if our senses and spiritual powers are activated.

In actual fact, vital energy is the creative energy of our spirit incarnated in our body, and its power is truly limitless. Whenever we do yoga breathing exercises or engage in intense prayer and mantra recitation, we activate vital energy, and it tends to rise up along the spine to open the superior centers of conscience, including the third eye (the sixth sense).

This is where the distorted memories that have yet to be cleansed intervene. These distortions intermingle and combine with the awakened Powers and Forces, and the negative force thus engendered can manifest itself in the form of various physical and mental problems, including serious ego problems. That's why it is so important to work on purity of conscience as we gradually develop our spiritual powers.

Various practices, including some belonging to yoga, are oriented toward awakening the kundalini, but they don't take into sufficient account the fact that the purification of our memories is essential.

The aim of these practices is to develop spiritual powers. Well, what happens when the kundalini awakens is, as I mentioned before, that our needs, if we have dormant ones, become very insistent. We are obliged to constantly work on mastering this force, and it creates great discrepancies with concrete reality and can lead to extremism if there are false spiritual concepts within us. We've all seen films or pictures of monks or members of various religions flagellate or mortify themselves each time they have a sexual thought or negative desire. They become so sensitive about their memories in their unconscious that they very easily tend to become religious fanatics or extremists.

We can also think, positively or negatively, of people with great charisma who, through their conviction, have a natural opening of the kundalini, for example salesmen, politicians and spiritual leaders, or people with great willpower and determination. Some of them shine forth and are ever so inspiring, while others strive to satisfy their personal needs. Many people unknowingly create karma. For them, the kundalini, to a certain degree, has been awakened but they haven't got knowledge, so they can *bite* people and continually compete with others. That's why the kundalini is usually represented in the form of a snake—the word is originally from Sanskrit and literally means *snake*. We find this association in the Hindu and Buddhist traditions. Unlike other animal species, a snake is cold-blooded. It attacks in cold blood, without any emotion, so to speak. This is why it is related to the power of needs. In order to effectively use great resources without hurting others, a great amount of wisdom is required.

The wonderful thing about work with dreams, signs & symbolic language is that it is oriented toward the integration of Qualities and Virtues, thereby sparing us from creating supplementary discrepancies and karma. In this work, the acquisition of Powers comes naturally; it isn't purposefully sought after, and we can *read* or understand through the symbols presented what sort of experimentation we are undergoing. Dream teachings lead us to this and so, very gradually, they grant us Powers and they teach us how to use them correctly, in the right manner.

Yes, madam? (Dreamer: I've had dreams with snakes in them. In one of my dreams, *I was in my car and there was a snake down my back. It was really small. I took it away and another snake arrived and it was a bit longer and a bit fatter. As with the first one, I removed it. Then another even bigger one arrived and I felt it in my back.* I woke up at that moment. I still had my eyes closed and I could really feel it intensely, as though it really were in my back. I wondered, 'Why have I got this?' and I fell asleep again. More recently, just last week in fact, I had a dream where I was simply told to invoke an Angel and Jesus.)

In the first dream, you actually experienced an awakening of the kundalini, of your vital energy, and because of the car, this awakening was destined to manifest itself in the way you behave and the way you conduct yourself socially. That dream announced that at first you'd try to stop this force, but it's growing in you; more and more intense needs are coming into your life which is why you took the snake away twice. It is related to your needs for a social life and activities. They're getting stronger in you. This is why the snake appears in the dream.

We shouldn't be frightened of this force because it's potentially positive. But of course it's normal to react fearfully because this force makes us advance with so much more intensity than usual! Simultaneously, this symbolic gesture indicated that you were advancing with a non-transcended animal energy, that you were still led by needs and selfish, cold motivations. As I mentioned earlier, for this force to manifest itself positively, we have to transcend our needs, our instincts. And, please, everyone should remember this: to know if a symbol is right, it has to be in the right place in a dream. It is so important to know this when interpreting dreams and signs. A snake in a car is unusual—and not very relaxing, to say the least—and therefore it is negative because of that, even if the snake is not aggressive. It represents a force that is too strong in our consciousness. We see that you are really working on yourself, on your instinctual needs. That's a sign of a spiritual opening. And that's the reason why you were invited to invoke an Angel and Jesus in your more recent dream. You are leading a very evolved life. Like Jesus, you have to transcend all the evil forces in your soul.

An Angel, like Jesus—like all the great initiates that came to Earth to help Humanity—is one of the Highest symbols we can see in a dream. An Angel is the representation—symbolically speaking—of human evolution toward the transcendence of all forms of limitation of the human spirit. It is not a being with wings. That's only a metaphor. An Angel is, in fact, the most powerful symbol to represent a person who has the capacity to travel in dream-worlds and develop the highest level of awareness and Knowledge of the Universe. It's Angel Energy that gives us intelligence, that creates intensity of vision and intensity of intention. People whose vital energy is practically asleep have great difficulty manifesting themselves or having dreams. Their intelligence is limited to rational reasoning, and their love is often self-interested and lacks intensity. All this creates a heavy energy that has difficulty dreaming, difficulty connecting to Higher levels and difficulty interpreting signs, symbols and dreams. As I've said in other lectures, we all have the potential to dream. Some people don't dream, or don't yet remember their dreams, because they are too emissive; they're not receptive enough. Prayers, meditation and self-development are beneficial in activating our receptivity and our dreams. We only need to take an interest in dreams, to think about them, to believe in them and the doors will open.

To return to discussion of the snake, it certainly represents a great force but, as long as it hasn't been educated or elevated above its instincts, then the person won't do things for love. He'll attack, either directly or subtly, without any thought for others. He'll play competitive, controlling, manipulative games to get what he wants. He'll also use his sexual energy for selfish motives because the snake is also a phallic symbol since it shares the form of the male sex organ. So, you see, we need to learn to master and educate this powerful force, and not avoid it like some spiritual people do. The sexual act, if performed between two partners, in fidelity, with love and respect, is a beautiful fusion of the two principles, of our masculine and feminine aspects.

(Dreamer: I was like that before—before I started to cleanse my conscience. Today, I find myself visiting all sorts of facets of myself.) Yes, I understand.

In any case, your dream is very constructive, because the snake was gentle; it wasn't aggressive as you have probably seen in other previous dream experiences. It means that you have greatly evolved toward mastering your force. However, if a snake is aggressive in a dream, we shouldn't be afraid either. I've had snakes of all shapes and sizes and colors in my dreams. It takes a long time to master

173

this force—especially for men. I had quite a lot of work to do! It took quite some time before I started seeing them in gold and white. It's really very powerful when we undertake this process to educate and elevate our vital energy.

This is what we mean by transcending our sexual and vital energy. The word *transcend* means *to be or go beyond the range or limits of, to terminate a cycle, to settle something.* Regarding conscience, it's a synonym for elevation. In the expression *transcendental meditation*, the term *transcendental* indicates that the meditation leads to higher states of conscience.

The awakening of the kundalini allows for such an elevation. Whenever we pray or meditate, we can circulate this energy and feel heat, or sometimes a burning sensation, in certain parts of the body, especially the back. People who suffer from fibromyalgia aren't usually aware of the fact that these difficulties are caused by an awakening of their vital energy. The awakening of the kundalini is considered to be the exclusive domain of fakirs.

In the beginning, when the energy awakens strongly, we can— (Participant: We can feel pain in our lower back, at the base of our spine.) Yes, that's right. (Participant: There's also a pressure of sorts that can lead to a kind of vibration effect.) Exactly.

Yes, sir? (Another participant: I had a little experience with that once. I was lying in bed, half asleep, but aware of what was going on in the room. At one point, I felt a vibration at the base of my back and it rose up along my spine. After that, I couldn't move— I tried but I couldn't. Then it went down again. I wanted to say 'Ouch!' to my wife, but I couldn't.) (Participant's wife: When he came out of the shower, he told me the bed had moved, but I didn't think so.) (*laughter*)

Ah yes! I understand you. I know it moved in your conscience, because I've had experiences like this many times. Sometimes, during intense prayer and meditation, people who've meditated for a long time—one or two hours, for example—may start to shake. When we do the Angelica yoga exercise* where we arch backwards, we can sometimes hold our breath for a few

* *Angelica Yoga Introduction: The Backward Arch (p.122)–cf. back of book for publication details.*

minutes, and, at one point, our body starts to tremble, to shake. Subsequently, we can also shake or tremble that same night. This happens because of out-of-body experiences and blockages. It's normal. We shouldn't fear these manifestations.

When this happens, it's actually our spirit collecting all its energy to be able to exit the body. Up Above, they let us feel this transfer of energy because it provides us with an experience. We are confronted with our fear. At other times we don't feel anything—They anesthetize us, so to speak.

Often, in the beginning, we cannot leave or exit our body by ourselves; we haven't yet developed this capacity. It's the Program that does it to give us a taste of these experiences. Sometimes people say to me, "In the beginning, I had lots of signs and dreams; it was amazing. But now there seem to be fewer." I tell them, "In the beginning, we are a bit like babies, spoon-fed and taken care of by our parents. Everything is beautiful; we have only to enjoy ourselves. And then comes the time when our parents tell us, "Now, you have to make your bed, tidy your room and help with the washing-up." So we have to start working. It's the same thing on the level of our conscience: we have to work to be able to re-live the same quality of experience, to rediscover the mystical states we were given a taste of previously. Up Above stops spoon-feeding us. Only by working deeply on ourselves can we develop true autonomy.

That's also why sometimes people tell us marvelous dreams but, at the same time, we can sense that they have a long way to go. They are elated because they think they are almost at the summit. But they're deluded. We listen to them with lots of love and without contradicting them too much. Sometimes they don't really want to hear what we have to say; they only want to show us they are good. So we listen. Six months later, we see them come along, all pale, and they want to tell us of their misadventures. At that point, they are ready to listen. This is when I tell them, "You see, when you told me you had marvelous dreams, yes indeed it's true, that was very powerful, but now, you're going to have to become what you saw then."

It's as if we had tasted the best apple pie in the whole world, and to taste another, we have to go from A to Z. We have to plant an apple tree, wait for the fruit to grow and ripen. We know we'll have to

175

give it all the time and love that's necessary. Likewise, as we advance on our spiritual path, we integrate High States of Conscience and one day, we will experience Mystical States night and day.

So, in the beginning, we are sometimes shown wonderful spectacles, superb firework displays, but these wonders don't come from within ourselves—at least not yet. This what I call dream, or spiritual, tourism. People are brought to wonderful countries, except that those who are not very evolved have to stay on the bus and can only get out at certain stops. They can't travel around as they'd like in the Parallel Worlds and visit other people's souls.

This is because the power we can have when in an out-of-body experience is so great! If an angry or negative person visited the Parallel Worlds just because he felt like it, after an out-of-body experience he could wake up completely paralyzed, no longer able to move. It could go as far as that. In the Parallel Worlds, there are borders or frontiers that God has installed, which are a sort of natural protection for the beings that live there. It's the principle by which the negative cannot alter the Light. If a person traveling in these worlds manages to affect another being in a negative way, it is because the other being did the same thing in one of his lives. It's just like here on Earth. So, if we have karma that has not been cleansed and we venture into the Parallel Worlds, we can come back quite destabilized because we will visit our negativity and our anger; we will see what it is made of and if we are not ready to know ourselves, this can be a very difficult experience that can completely destabilize our facade-personality.

(Participant: That's because we attract the negative through our own resonances, isn't it?) Yes, that's right. Because otherwise we are totally protected.

Let me give you an example to illustrate the idea of our Program taking over to protect us. When I'm driving, sometimes I start meditating and for two or three minutes, I no longer see the road at all. Needless to say I do not advise you to do this just to test it out for the fun of it. In any case, I don't do it voluntarily, in that I'm not sitting there saying, 'I'm a spiritual person, my car will deliver me to my destination safely on its own.' No, not at all. I don't try to put the Program to the test because otherwise God would see to it that I was taught a lesson. Whenever I do this, it's simply natural. At some point, I find myself saying, 'Ah! We're already this far. I didn't even know we'd passed such and such a place.' It's special. It's as if I black out on the level of material reality but all my antennas remain open. I do my meditation and I watch the road, but I don't really see it. And yet I'm present all the same. I remain in that state and when my attention is required for one reason or another, I come back at the right moment. I've meditated so much that, even in states like this, I unconsciously maintain an overall view of my surroundings. My conscience doesn't need to be completely present.

These are the kinds of experiences we can have after a while, when we have worked on our fears and lack of confidence in God. One day, our confidence in the Universe is so great, that we are, once again, like trusting children. It's like when we talk to someone and we say something but we have no idea why we said it and afterwards, we are told, "Ah! It's incredible how your words moved me! That was exactly the answer to my question." This often happens to me. I simply say what comes into my head. Of course, I don't just say anything; my words make sense and there's meaning to them. If there weren't, I'd stop the process. I'd feel the discrepancy: the other person wouldn't understand what I was telling them. But often I mention the exact example that they will understand, sometimes the exact same situation they're going through. The right ideas just pop into my mind because I'm wholly receptive and I listen and I'm open to receiving what is right and useful for this person, for their Program.

One day we fuse with everything. We no longer have needs that limit our perception of people and things. That's what God or the Universal Conscience is. We are in a global conscience that allows us to manifest, to experience ourselves simply as a spiritual being, as a spirit.

It's as if we were on automatic pilot. Here is another example: we find ourselves thinking about someone as we walk along the street and, even though we hadn't planned to go into a particular store, in we go and the first person we encounter is the one we've just been thinking about. We say, "Ah! How extraordinary! I was just thinking about you and here you are! Wow! We haven't seen each other for at least three years." What actually happened in this case is that Universal Conscience led us to that person because he was part of our Program; we had to meet him. So, we didn't plan or think about contacting him: the Program made us move and act as we did. And it has the right to do so, because it always acts for our good. It influences us like this all day long, without our being aware of it. It is active in real time, 24 hours a day.

If something dangerous arises and it isn't meant to affect us—if it isn't inscribed in our Program—we are warned. Universal Conscience acts.

It's wonderful when we understand this. Because then we are always confident. I've really integrated this concept of Celestial Insurance. I feel insured by Heaven. I'm 100% covered by Up Above! Whatever happens, I tell myself, "It had to happen; I accept the situation." I don't dramatize anything any more. It was meant to be.

Sometimes in spiritual circles, when people mention an accident they had, we often hear people tell them, "Ah! You were tired; you didn't protect yourself enough. You forgot to create your protective bubble." Or others say, "Ah! I've put a bubble of light around my car. I'll be safe; nothing will happen to me."

If we gathered statistics on the numbers of accidents that people who protected their car like this had, the idea of a protective bubble wouldn't hold up at all. It would never be validated. The same goes for theft. We often hear people say, "If they'd placed an invisible wall of light around their possessions, nothing would have been stolen." Come on! Intelligent people who hear such remarks simply laugh and keep away from anything remotely related to dreams, signs and spirituality.

In actual fact, we are always protected. A person who has an accident, even a serious one, is protected because his accident has a deep metaphysical meaning that he can use as a lesson, as a learning experience. This person had to be subjected to limitations, because those limitations would allow him to take a step forward, and it was written in his Program that he would take a step at that particular moment.

Let me tell you quite a special true story related to this idea. During our last lecture tour in Europe, a woman came up to tell us about an experience that had led her to a great spiritual awakening.

Before this experience she wasn't spiritual and she didn't dream. She told us, "One day I dozed off and I heard a voice say, *'You're going to have an accident.'* Well, I thought my mind was playing tricks on me. A few hours later, I heard *'Your accident will be in two days' time.'* 'Oh!' I said to myself, 'I won't go out. I won't take the car.'"

Well, two days later she and her husband had to go to a family gathering that had been planned for quite some time. That day, she heard a voice say, *'Tonight. The accident will be tonight.'* She said to herself, 'This doesn't make sense but what should I do? We shouldn't go.' At the same time, she didn't want her husband to think she was crazy. Moreover the whole family would laugh at her. No, she felt she had no excuse for not going to the family gathering. So off she went with her husband as planned. She asked him to be careful on the road. She didn't want to worry him by telling him what she'd heard for fear of increasing the risk of an accident.

On the way home at about two o'clock in the morning, she dozed off a little while her husband was driving and, as she half-dozed, she heard the voice say, *'Take off your glasses and put them in the glove compartment.'* Nervously, she took off her glasses, opened the glove compartment and put them there. The Angel voice said, *'Unlock the door.'* Her heart was thumping. The voice insisted, *'Unlock the door.'* She unlocked her door. Thirty seconds went by and then a car came towards them and WHAM! their car ended up on its roof and the only door that could be opened was the one she'd just unlocked. Their car was a complete wreck. Ultimately, both she and her husband got out of it, uninjured. If she'd been wearing her glasses, she could have lost her eyesight.

Since this accident, this woman has become spiritual. It created a whole opening in her. When I heard her tell her story, it really stirred me; it pulled on my heart and soul strings and I felt myself vibrate. I said to myself, "One day the whole world will know this story," and I knew that I was going to tell it. I felt that this experience was meant to serve the community, to help mankind. And indeed, this woman tells it to everyone she meets and it makes a lot of people think and meditate on it.

What's the point of having such an experience? What purpose does it serve? The person experiences a great spiritual awakening and he or she then becomes a beacon in the night for all those who doubt. It's a bit like those people who have been declared clinically dead and then come back to life changed by what they experienced in the other world. These experiences are so powerful, so intense, that the people have great radiance. Those who hear their account add their own proof to it and use it to help construct their own spirituality.

Is there another question?

Yes, madam? (Participant: Is it true that a child born with the palms of his hands very creased is an old soul?)

It is certain that the palm of our hand is full of codes. That's true for all parts of the body but the palm of our hand is particularly rich in information.

There's no such thing as coincidence; it's no coincidence we have such and such a crease or fold in our skin. So, undoubtedly creased palms have a meaning. Is it a positive sign? Not necessarily. Personally I am not skilled in palmistry, it's not my field, but I do know that very precise information about a person's soul and Program is to be found in the palm of their hand.

But it does not matter how many courses or years of lessons in palmistry a person may have taken, it will not suffice in rendering them capable of reading palms correctly, deeply. A person on a spiritual path, however, could carry out intense, deep study into the lines of the hand, physiognomy or the characteristics of the iris and, via his dreams, could go and seek very precise and much more valuable information there than any available via theories taught here on Earth.

This is what will happen in the future with the therapists of future generations. They will have more metaphysical knowledge. Because we cannot understand a field in depth by trusting only what ordinary senses can perceive. It's essentially through dreams, out-of-body experiences and meditation, through deep thoughts on our life, that we can have access to people's Programs.

Hence, therapists and people who teach in fields that touch the soul should always do deep work on themselves before intervening with others and before offering advice, help or giving lectures or workshops.

The idea of teaching didn't come from me; it wasn't my idea or plan. Neither was it Christiane's. We were placed in this role, so to speak; it came about naturally. Christiane and I received dreams in which we were given our mission and these were followed by several other signs which confirmed that. If I hadn't concretely received my mission through my dreams, I wouldn't have felt strong enough, I wouldn't have felt confident enough and I wouldn't have started teaching. I needed a Higher Reference than myself.

(Participant: It's important to go and seek this information within ourselves.) Exactly. That's what spiritual autonomy is. Because often people project onto others what they'd like to do themselves but don't dare to; with our own dreams, it is not someone outside ourselves telling us what to do, it is our dreams telling us. We just need to learn to interpret them. Very often we ask for signs to corroborate the dream message to be entirely sure. Once we are sure — we've received it on the inside via our dream, and it's been confirmed in the outside world via several clear signs — then we proceed with complete confidence and no matter what happens, no matter how things turn out, we know it was right for us to make this particular decision or choice and to have taken whatever steps we took.

We can also be told that we have a particular mission but that it will take some time before things work out on the material level for it to materialize. Some years ago, I was working intensely on myself, praying and meditating virtually 24 hours a day. I didn't envisage teaching at all; it wasn't part of my plan. And then, one night I received a dream telling me a great Mission awaited me but that nothing concrete would materialize for three years. And indeed, nothing concrete happened in the next three years so I continued my inner work.

Other people receive dreams like this. Dr. François Bouchard and Denise Fredette, who teach with us, received their Mission in a dream, and Christiane and I received dreams informing us that it was right to help them promote their teaching. Following our dreams to orient ourselves and associate with others is a wonderful way to live. Teachers of the future will proceed like this.

Personally if people offer to associate with our organization with a particular project in mind, I always ask Heaven, "Is it right to do this?" Because if I'm told, "Yes, it's right," then I'm sure it's part of the Plan and I'm willing to go ahead and work with them.

There we are. This completes our wonderful workshop this evening. Heartfelt thanks for your attention and beautiful sharing. My wife and I wish you a happy continuation and we'd like to thank all the volunteers who help spread this teaching.

WORKSHOP
Repressed Memories

Yes, Marie? (Dreamer: *I was at the seaside and everything was pink, light beige, very light grey. And the sky, the water and the sand were all the same color. It was really soft and very beautiful. And I saw a young woman arrive; she'd been swimming in this water and she came out of it. She was wearing a wonderful white dress and she had long black hair–she was really beautiful. But she wasn't wet. Next I saw a long, very narrow, wood-colored boat arrive. And I knew her husband was coming for her. But I didn't see the husband. I just knew it was him. She saw him arrive too. So she went back into the water to go and get into his boat. It was very beautiful.*) Ok, thank you.

That's a very beautiful dream. That day you must have felt really good on the emotional level; you must have felt complete.

First of all, the water represents the emotions and feelings you had that day. The landscape was pink. Pink represents love, tenderness, gentleness and femininity.

Then you saw a woman with long black hair who swam up to the shore and got out of the water. A woman represents the feminine polarity and the inner world. Was she young? (Dreamer: Yes.) So she also symbolized youth, the vigor of youth.

She was very beautiful and all dressed in white. White represents the spiritual aspect and clothes represent the aura, what we emanate. So, that particular day, you emanated beautiful spiritual energy. You were truly in a beautiful soul-state; you felt profound well-being of a spiritual nature. You were full of life and youthfulness; it was as if you had no age, as if time didn't exist. (Dreamer: The fragrance is still with me; I still feel that harmony. It was really amazing.) Yes, I can imagine.

Furthermore, the woman wasn't wet even though she came out of the water. That indicates emotional transcendence. It really is a beautiful dream! It testifies to great emotional mastery and a very elevated state of conscience in terms of spiritual love.

Then you noticed a long, very narrow boat. All boats represent the way we conduct our sentimental, emotional life and our level of emotional, sentimental mastery. The length and narrowness of a boat automatically means fragile balance. Handling a long, narrow boat requires agility and dexterity, and, in terms of conscience, great emotional mastery. We simply apply logic; we say to ourselves, 'With a very long, very narrow boat, we need to be dexterous, agile and have good knowledge of the winds and currents because we can very easily capsize.' Hence, you had great emotional mastery, great command of your emotions. I understand why this dream should move you so much: it truly announced a great elevation in love.

The man came towards the woman and she went to join him. In dreams, whenever there is beautiful harmony between a man and a woman, then the dreamer automatically feels accomplished, fulfilled. Sometimes we read texts about the masculine and feminine principles, or about masculine and feminine polarities, and we don't really understand what they are; it seems very abstract to us. Well, the day you received this dream, you truly experienced something related to these concepts. That beautiful harmony, you experienced it within yourself. That's why you didn't see the man. If you had, that would have announced an outer manifestation, because a man represents manifestation and action.

So, that day, you were in a state of beatitude, of completeness. You didn't need love on the outside to feel this state of union, unlike other days when you can feel a lack on the emotional, sentimental level. You were given a great gift, the gift of a direct experience of love, of well-balanced polarities within yourself.

Through this dream, Up Above wanted to reassure you, to show you that you'll always have access to love since it dwells within you. Maybe you had an emotional, affective difficulty the evening before — only you can know this — but, on the day of the dream, you were sent this message: "There will always be a boat for you. You have access to this emotional stability and to beautiful spiritual sentiments of beauty, gentleness and completeness. You have this potential within you."

Love is a state of conscience. We sometimes believe it has to come from another person, but true love dwells within us. One day, we become complete, we no longer long for the other person; we no longer feel emotional, sentimental, affective lacks. We simply feel and emanate love all the time.

We can see that everyone can attain High States of Conscience. We have great sages within us. The only thing is that we have to work to stabilize these States, to continually dwell in Love and Completeness, which leads to a great feeling of beatitude.

You were given an experience of these States so that you can get to know yourself and to inscribe within you High ideals regarding Love. That's where Up Above wanted to lead you. (Dreamer: Thank you.) You're welcome.

Yes, Madam? (Dreamer: I dreamed *I was on a station platform. I seemed to be returning from a trip with two other women that I saw going off along the platform. I was holding my suitcase and it burst open. All my clothes fell out onto the ground. I crouched down to pick them up and I noticed that I wasn't wearing any pants. I said to myself, 'I must go and put on a pair of pants.' At that very moment, I saw a man dressed in black grab my handbag. I said to him, "At least give me back my cards," and I was sobbing my heart out.* I woke up with this dream.) That's certainly an initiatic dream you had there!

First of all, the station. A station represents an important change regarding our conscience. Trains symbolize changes in orientation, direction, so returning from a train journey indicates that change in orientation was coming to completion. It also indicates that — regarding what occurs in the dream — you need to work on this from now on. You will have all sorts of difficulties cleansing the memories regarding what you are going through in the dream. You may say: "I'm regressing…I'm not evolving toward Good with a dream like that, am I?" I can answer, "We never regress — what you are going through is what you need to understand before you reach your next destination."

As for the idea of traveling in the dream, it testifies to the fact that you are in a process of exploring your conscience concretely, because the train is related to the earth element, namely, to the world of concrete actions. The two women going off along the platform represented parts of you, inner parts that are traveling within your consciousness.

185

Your suitcase burst open and your clothes fell out onto the platform. We can easily imagine how a person would feel if that actually happened to them. They'd feel embarrassed about people seeing their intimate things, their underwear, etc. They'd feel disorganized, their clothes would get dirty, all that. Hence, that day, you felt this kind of soul-state. You are being shown that because you have memories that are too open to others; you expose yourself too much by wanting everyone to know what you are doing. This is why your suitcase burst open. Too many memories like 'I want to tell you this and this or show you this and this.'

Then you noticed you weren't wearing any pants. In terms of conscience, pants represent the masculine polarity and emissivity. Whenever we use the expression, *He or she wears the pants*, we mean that person makes the decisions, that they have authority. Pants are worn on the legs, which symbolize action and a capacity to advance. So, not having any pants on indicates a feeling of vulnerability or impotency and you no longer have the capacity to decide for yourself. You open up so much to others to have their approval and to be loved that you can't decide anymore what your destination is. We can all imagine how we'd feel with no clothes on the lower half of our body in a public place. We'd feel embarrassed; we'd have difficulty manifesting ourselves, making decisions, etc. because everyone would be looking at us.

Then a man dressed in black took your handbag. Generally speaking, black represents the hidden aspect of things and matter, because, in a way, the spirit is hidden in matter. Needless to say, it's the negative symbolism that applies here — it wasn't right of the man to take your bag. Consequently, he represented a part of you that, in the past, took or stole other people's resources and identities with the intention of using them. Generally speaking, this character symbolized memories where you took advantage of others and because of that, there is so much accumulation of these kinds of behaviors that you have to experience the opposite of what you have created in order to learn from it; that man is you. If you do not work on the memories that you see in this dream, you will have to go through some difficult situations in your day-to-day life. I can assure you of that. You will no longer

186

be able to make decisions and, simultaneously, people will steal your resources, your social identity, and your capacity to manifest yourself.

The idea of having one's handbag stolen reminds us of the feeling of vulnerability and impotency or helplessness. In a handbag, we keep our wallet and our identity cards, and, if we lose them, of course we feel de-structured and helpless on a personal and social level. Hence, you were visiting memories marked by these feelings. That day you felt really de-structured, as though you'd lost your identity. It's a typical dream to have during initiations. Such dreams allow us to cleanse karmas, and when they occur, we are dispensed from having to experience them in concrete reality.

I had a lot of dreams like this at the beginning of my spiritual path; I understand very well how we can feel on such a day. We don't feel well no matter where we go, we are disorganized and we haven't the energy, the resources to advance—even if we have money, if everything is OK on that side of our life. We are in a transition zone, a zone of change with no landmarks for the Self, for our central personality; it's as if our usual signposts or markers had disappeared. The energy of change can also manifest itself on the outside. In this case, we go through concrete events that can really de-stabilize us. You are the only one who can know how the change manifests itself, but one thing is certain: you are undergoing profound transformation. In reality, you are visiting memories that are causing you to relive certain blockages, and it's normal that you should feel all mixed up. The man in the dream represented part of your inner man, so old behavioral patterns are presently creating difficulties in your life—a lack of self-confidence, a feeling of helplessness, the fact of your excessive desire to expose yourself to others, etc.

It describes the soul-state you were immersed in that day. The next day, you might feel fine. When we are on a spiritual path, we receive a lot of dreams like this. This is because we are re-visiting our blockages, all our distorted zones. These memories must be re-educated. If nothing in particular happens on the material, concrete level, the disorganization will still be experienced, but on the inside. It's as if we can no longer see beauty anywhere. Otherwise, the de-structuring manifests itself on the physical level, we find ourselves in the same soul-states, because the concrete situations reflect the de-structuring we are experiencing on the metaphysical level.

(Dreamer: That's exactly what happens; sometimes I no longer recognize myself — I no longer know who I am. And so I try to hang on to what I was before, except that it no longer works.) That's right. That's exactly what happens. We are changing identity and we haven't yet got our new one. So we can feel quite lost regarding our self-definition.

And this phenomenon of de-structuring occurs not only on the conceptual level, but also on the spiritual level. We forged ourselves a certain way of thinking, being and acting socially. Our parents taught us to act in a certain way, and we did so for quite some time, but now it doesn't work anymore. We always greeted our mother in a particular way — a way that lacked depth — and now we don't feel right doing it like this. Or let's say that up until now our parents' attempts to control us didn't particularly bother or annoy us, but, all of a sudden, from one day to the next, suddenly this really bothers and infuriates us.

In such situations, we need to refer back to the spirit because it is our spirit that is upset. Hence we can cleanse the memories that have been activated.

Sometimes we hear about great sages meditating all day long. Materialists wonder, 'What on earth can they possibly do with their meditation; what use can it be?' This is because they don't understand. In their other lives, these sages were like the materialists, now they have reached the stage where the time has come for them to think about and reflect on how they materialized.

It is generally thought that meditation is emptying one's mind. But it's not that at all. I've tried what is called transcendental meditation but I couldn't do it. Everything — thoughts and images whirled too fast in my head, it was like a real Internet. So there came a point when I said to myself, 'Ok, this is my meditation; I need to meditate on what pops into my mind.' When images related to insecurity or fears popped up, or when I was obsessed with someone's faults, or by a particular situation, I'd say to myself,

'This is the symbol that has just popped up. It's just as if I were in a dream so I'm going to reflect on this. Why this image now? Why does this person bother me? What does it mean?' And from then on, I developed and applied a different concept of meditation.

It's amazing how we advance when we analyze the images and feelings that arise during a meditation — it's like going into our personal archives and studying one *file* after another, and, little by little, our soul is set free. When we have sufficiently analyzed a file, it doesn't come back any more. It's like when we are at work: we don't need to re-open a file we've thoroughly analyzed; we know what it contains. We've settled the question and we move on to another file.

Meditating is marvelous. We repeat a question for a while — one or two minutes or longer — and we stop, we pause…and images pop into our mind. It's like with dreams: invoking a question intensifies the imagery process; it leads to more frequent and more intense images. We can then work on the information these images reveal. Or if we have a decision to make, we ask a question — *What should I do in this situation?* An image appears, let's say a bird with a letter. Ah! A bird: thoughts. A letter: a message. *I should send a message. OK. Is it a good idea to phone this person right now?* And we wait for the reply. Sometimes we receive a flash image of the person and we see he's busy doing something so we know it's better to wait until later. Other times we receive a symbolic image that we need to analyze. There are many ways, many symbols that can be used to explain what we have to do.

It's a language; the same language as dreams. Little by little, very gradually with practice and time, we manage to integrate it and can rapidly understand the messages we receive.

These dimensions are accessible to all of us. What's more we can see the representation of this in concrete reality. We only need to think of how a search engine functions on the Internet: we ask a question using a key word and information almost immediately appears on our screen.

Young people who play video games move a little guy forward in their virtual world and they find out where the wall is because

189

their guy bumps into it. This is like when we ask in meditation whether we should opt for such and such a choice and we see where it'll lead us.

In some video games, the players discover doors behind the image of virtual objects, and when they open these doors, they discover other worlds. By playing these games, young people develop similar capacities on the conscience level. Why do these games exist? Because the young are ready for multi-dimensional levels and such games nourish this aspect of their being. In other words, they have access to the Metaphysical Worlds within themselves. They don't yet use this access consciously or voluntarily because they don't know how to, but it's only a matter of time. Of course, when it comes to conscience, it's no longer just a game linked to feeling or experimentation, it's for real.

But, in a way, even games are for real. Hence the importance of not allowing young people to play just any game. Sometimes we visit spiritual people who are all calm and serene and we see guns and tanks and all sorts of symbolically violent things among their children's toys.

For me, these toys are real weapons. Just imagine a four-year-old and his friends pointing a gun at us, saying, "BANG! BANG! You're dead!" He's training for violence, to dominate other people's energy; that's the field of conscience he's exploring and integrating. If we want to become an economist, we study the economy, obtain a diploma or a degree in economics and find a job in this field. If we want a child to become violent, we let him play violent games for a few years and maybe he won't stop at a Master's degree but go on to do a doctorate! (*laughter*) In any case, he'll become aggressive and strongly inclined to competition.

We often wonder why teenagers can be so difficult nowadays. Take away their video games — not the good ones, not the ones that are all right, of course — and you'll see. By dint of being immersed in states of aggression, we become aggressive. By dint of being gentle, acting and speaking gently, we develop gentleness. The entourage of a child, his friends, his choice of movies, etc., all of that has a strong influence on the development of the child. If we encourage our children to play Monopoly throughout their childhood, they'll end up wanting to buy and sell properties. And if we encourage our children to play humanistic, humane games, they'll become humanists. Because the more a child is immersed in the field of conscience induced by the game, the more it rubs off on him, until it is eventually absorbed and becomes an integral part of his conscience and will be exteriorized one way or another.

Personally, I don't allow my daughter to play just any game. I'm always attentive to what she watches, listens to and plays. I keep my eyes open and I observe what she's absorbing. Because I know she'll come back to me with that. She'll materialize through her behavior whatever it is she picks up and I'm the one who will have to live with it. It is very important to guide our children well. When they are 25, they're free to lead their own lives, but when they're young, we need to be there to give them good guidance. If we nourish them well physically, they'll be healthy. If we nourish them well emotionally, they'll have good hearts, lots of love for themselves and others. Likewise, if we nourish them well intellectually, if we stimulate their minds, give them good books, games that are appropriate, etc., they'll integrate a right, just vision of the world and this will be reflected in their attitude and behavior.

Why do more and more young people reject school? Because the majority of teachers lack dimension and depth. Young people often manifest more interest in searching on the Internet than listening to their teachers.

Take the play *Romeo and Juliet* for example, that is presented to the young as a marvelous, admirable work. Well of course it's a masterpiece from a literary point of view, but try applying Romeo and Juliet's attitudes to your own life and you'll soon see they won't lead to happiness within a couple. (*laughter*) Books like this nourish affective, emotional dependency in young people and adults don't warn them. The teacher just comes along with the play and tells them they are going to spend the next six months studying it. Just imagine the concepts of love such a book can install in their minds! The young person plunges into distorted fields of conscience and no one helps him understand that these concepts are false, the very opposite of what is right, of what will lead to true, lasting happiness.

These teenage students are going through an intense period of development on all levels. They're beginning to feel new emotions and their reading material immerses them in feelings, thoughts and reactions such as, 'I love him… my heart is breaking… I'll die if they don't let us be together… I'm going to run away in secret with him…' and, of course, they think this is love. Then they play out the same roles, 'Ah! I love him. Should I write to him or not? I'll climb up to his balcony. I'll go out the window so my father doesn't see me.' And we wonder why young people run away from home. (*laughter*) The answer's easy. They learned it from *Romeo and Juliet*! (*laughter*)

We nourish passionate, languorous attitudes, wants and needs and the like. It is the last book we should give our children to read unless we help them read it in an initiatic way. That's what we do with our daughter, Kasara. Whenever she has to read a book for school, and we find false concepts in it, we explain them to her. Regarding *Romeo and Juliet* for example, we'd say to her, "Look, Romeo was emotionally dependent and Juliet was depressed." Or, if we decide to go further to include the idea of reincarnation, "You see, in another life, Romeo and Juliet were parents who prevented their son or daughter from seeing the person they loved." So, of course, the child finds this analysis, these interpretations, very interesting because they help him understand phenomena in the world around him and he no longer considers passionate love as an ideal to be attained in his life. Of course, older students reading Shakespeare's tragedies are indeed taught to study human flaws, weaknesses and distortions. Such analysis stimulates them to think more deeply about the ravages flaws, such as jealousy and over-ambition for example, can lead to.

The idea is not to be puritanical and forbid our children all films, books and games. Not at all. The idea is to be aware of what they are absorbing, to offer them healthy nourishment and whenever they find themselves facing a distorted work, with the discernment Knowledge provides, we help them and allow them to apply Knowledge themselves to see where the book is situated from a conscience point of view — whether it is on the side of qualities or distortions. Hence, our child can gradually learn to read from a metaphysical perspective and he finds it so interesting! Later he may even go on to write a metaphysical thesis on *Romeo and Juliet* for his Master's degree! (*laughter*)

192

We've done this with Kasara since she was very young. When she watched a cartoon with aggressive scenes in it, I'd explain it to her, saying, "Look, the lion is roaring, that's the little boy's inner feelings and attitude. The lion is part of him, just like in a dream." This is how she now perceives what she watches.

I'll always remember the time when she was five years old. One morning, we were still in bed and she was watching TV. I could hear it and I knew it was something very ordinary that she was watching. So I asked, "Kasara, what are you watching?" She replied, "I'm studying evil, Daddy." (*laughter*) Just imagine! Five years old! "Ah!" I said, "That's perfect. You can tell me what you understand when you've finished." And, of course, I wasn't going to forget to ask her what she'd seen and understood because it was important for her. So at breakfast, she gave me her analysis and, in her own way, explained to me the symbolism behind the story. I listened very carefully—it was as important for me as for her. If I had just brushed over these exchanges, paying them no particular attention, if I hadn't listened deeply, she'd have switched off because on sensing my lack of interest, she'd have lost interest herself.

We must remember that children's motivation comes from parents', or stand-in parents', love. Today, Kasara always analyzes things symbolically. And it's wonderful to see how much progress she's made, how advanced she is! She can listen to a singer — in any language, he could be singing in Russian — and she can describe his soul-state. If he sings "*Mi Amor*", for example, solely from the intonation of his voice, she can say, "Oh! He's a great emotional dependent. He's a bit snakelike, isn't he? He'd do anything to be loved." (*laughter*)

The first time she made a comment like this, it was so funny! She was only seven. One of Jacques Brel's songs was being played on the radio. It was "*Ne me quitte pas*." It's a classic, very popular melodramatic French love song where the singer is begging the other person not to leave him. And when she heard him sing, "*I will be your dog's shadow (je serai l'ombre de ton chien)*", she laughed and laughed! She kept saying, "But that doesn't make any sense!" Once the song was over, she turned to me and, full of compassion, she said, "Oh Daddy! That man's not well, is he,

Daddy? He's sick, isn't he? That song's dangerous. It can make people sick, can't it?" "You're absolutely right, Kasara."

If we were to measure the influence of this song on suicides and crimes of passion, we'd be very surprised to see the effect it could have had on people. This is how I taught her to develop discernment. Always with love and compassion, of course, and understanding that although something is negative, it is useful because it serves experimentation.

It's very important to make sure our children assimilate quality nourishment on all levels. You're careful about what they eat. And you're more advanced than some parents because some people feed their children things that really aren't good, physically. But you should see the emotional level! When the physical level isn't good, the emotional level is worse. And the intellectual level is worse again! As for the spiritual level, ah! it's abysmal; it's simply non-existent. Many parents live like animals do, and that's what they transmit to their children. They work to earn money so as to be able to eat. They are like animals except they have a little conscience all the same. It's just that their main concern is really just basic, physical survival, satisfaction of their most basic needs.

When we watch films such as *Kundun*—the story of the Dalai Lama when he was a child—we can imagine the deep levels of understanding children will have in the future. At the beginning of the film, when the lamas visit Kundun to see if he is indeed the person who should succeed the previous Dalai Lama, they speak to his soul. After showing him some objects that include belongings of the former religious chief of Tibet, they observe the child's reaction—what objects he picks up, how he looks at them, etc.—and indeed, the child selects precisely what belonged to the former Dalai Lama. There are truly magical moments in this film. The way that the child was spoken to really moved me. It was as if I were reactivating memories of this.

I learned to do likewise with my daughter—to speak to her soul—and, later, I continued to do this with all children. When I look at children, I speak to them in my head. I converse with them. They tell me things—for example, they say, "Agh! The boat's sinking!"—this seems to have nothing whatsoever to do

194

with reality, but there's a whole meaning behind it! The child is talking to me in symbols and I can know all sorts of things like this. It's wonderful.

When I arrive in a home where a child has strong spirituality,— I see it. I can see it in the Light in his eyes. And if I ask him—in my head, of course—"Is spirituality important to you?" the child will go and find a white building block or something similar and give it to me. He's still tiny, not even two years old! And I say, "Good! That's good!" At that moment, I know he's an evolved soul because he went to find a spiritual symbol in answer to my question. I do this with very young children. Some of them come to speak to me in my dreams. Like my young nephew, Gabriel. He's really amazing! If you could see the intensity he has in his eyes, the way he looks at everything, at everyone! Recently I encountered him in a dream. *He was all smiles, happy and joyful with his almond-shaped eyes. And I had blanched almonds in my hands. I knew these almonds represented nourishment for the spirit. They were like very concentrated vitamins. I wondered, 'Can he have some?' because it was as if Gabriel were eating my almonds. He ate and ate. He was really happy. Still in my dream, I said to myself, 'He already knows what he needs. In his life, he'll know exactly what he really needs.'"* It was so powerful! I saw him the next day and, in my head, I said to him, 'We saw each other last night, you know. It was a lovely visit. I know who you are.' And he smiled at me. I often say that to him and he smiles at me. He's so happy when I acknowledge his soul! Sometimes I take him in my arms, I look deep into his eyes and I tell him a story. I've often told him the story of a film I love, *Joseph, King of Dreams*. It's the story of a young boy who tries to understand dreams. It's actually the Bible story of Joseph who interpreted the Pharaoh's dreams.

The boy, Joseph, goes through different ordeals, which symbolically, depict the various stages of an initiatic path very well. If you ever feel like renting this film, it's located in the children's section, as is *The Prince of Egypt*. Both of these cartoons were produced by Dreamworks; they are truly initiatic films. In *The Prince of Egypt*, we see Moses who dreams that although he believes he's a true Egyptian, he's actually a Jew. This dream destabilizes his whole conscience. He goes to see his father, the Pharaoh, and asks, "Father, am I really a Jew?" It's amazing! These films are really magnificent.

So when Gabriel was really young, I used to tell him this kind of story. I also used to imagine stories and I'd describe them in images. I'd say to him in my thoughts, 'Look how beautiful the kite is!' And I'd see a beautiful kite in my head. I'd see a little boy, running, and then he'd go up a mountain. And there he'd see an eagle. Gabriel would follow the story as if he saw everything–he could read my thoughts. Sometimes, when I see a baby, I stand still in front of him and I put blue light all around me and I say, "Blue." And he looks intensely at me. Sometimes I don't need to say anything, the baby just perceives it.

When we create images in our mind, the other person can capture them. New children have this capacity to see — it's what we call clairvoyance. This faculty is much more developed in them than in previous generations.

Ok, has anyone a question or a dream to be interpreted?

Yes, madam? (Participant: It seems so easy when you interpret dreams! I've been working on trying to understand them for a year and a half now and sometimes I get tired of analyzing all of these symbols.)

Yes, but with time, it will become more and more natural. When we learn to interpret dreams, it's like learning a foreign language. Think of all of the years spent studying whatever language we chose to learn and still we need a refresher course to perfect it, whether it be Mandarin, English, French, German or Spanish. We did not become fluent overnight, did we? It's the same with any new skill: Math, information technology, driving, whatever. It is the same with dream language. We keep trying to translate, work out, and make sense of our dreams, dream language and dream equations, and, at some point, we understand; we obtain access to the depth, to the code behind an image. It's a little like being on the computer: we click on icons and multiple dimensions open up. In concrete reality, we see an object, but, simultaneously, we see something else: we perceive the metaphysical, symbolic dimension of what we are observing. We all have these life-giving, multi-dimensional aspects within us. Poets use this language because they speak to us of states of conscience.

Yes, madam? (Participant: What can we do if we don't dream?)

First of all, when we pray and meditate and are on a path that seeks to uncover the true meaning of life, then we become more open to the symbolic meaning of all things. Desiring the knowledge of how to interpret dreams is a first step in preparing the terrain, so to speak. Then we have to learn to be more receptive to life and people and to be less emissive. It is a lack of receptivity that stops us from dreaming. This is why meditation can be so helpful; furthermore, meditation is not difficult. We just have to close our eyes, inhale and exhale deep breaths and, simultaneously, think about something, not to nourish worries, but to find a solution, to ask God to help us to understand our life. This is what I call meditation. It is accessible to anyone and we sometimes do it without even realizing we are doing it. Especially when we have a life problem, then we naturally go deeper; we enter our ancient memories by going to the root of our recollection of how this problem started. That is certainly something that you can do to start dreaming. Then, each night, have at your disposal a dream book and a pen and wish or pray with all your heart to dream. Pray intensively and ask Up Above to reveal and open your unconscious. Another piece of advice is to sleep well, because your body needs to be rested, not exhausted. If you sleep three or four hours per night, it is difficult to remember your dreams because your body is never sufficiently recharged. A good eight to ten hours' sleep is required, especially to dream. Also, it is helpful to remain in bed for a while upon waking. Take your time. Do not transfer too fast from the sleep stage to the awake stage. You can set your alarm clock 10-15 minutes before your children wake up or before it is time to go to work and use this time to meditate and to do breathing exercises while your eyes are still closed.

This particular period is very important for the dreamer because, often, it is easier in the morning to remember your dreams. One day, whether it is the morning or the evening, it will be the same. But in the beginning it will be easier to remember your dreams in the morning. It is a question of will power also. If you really want to dream and pray for it, you will, I can assure you that. Our intention is the key. First we want with all our heart and soul. And then the doors open. But be ready for that. It is not easy to dream: yes, the unconscious is certainly full of treasures but, also, of dust and old memories of lack and difficulties. We have to be brave to enter our own universe. Our intention must be pure and just. If you only want the power to dream to win the lotto, yes, you can open the door, but all of your ambitions and distortions will haunt you. The world of dreams is not a game. A lot of people are in psychiatric hospitals because they are too open on the level of their unconscious; they have opened the door too soon, before having the Knowledge to deal with it. If we do it by praying, and asking God for guidance, then it is much safer. One should ask to dream in order to receive and to develop qualities, to become a better person — this should be our true and only intention at first. Then, with time, we use dreams to learn to manifest well, to receive guidance for the material aspect of our decisions. But in the beginning, it is to improve ourselves. By thinking like that, we embark on a beautiful, safe journey.

And what's wonderful is that while we don't have dreams, or only very few, we still have signs. All we have to do is consider our concrete life metaphysically, symbolically, as if all the little events we go through were parts of a dream. We say to ourselves, 'Ok, such and such a thing happened. What am I to understand here?'

Let me give you an example — a little event that occurred this week. We are in the middle of preparing the schedule of our lecture tour in Europe this fall. So, as the dates for different towns are confirmed, I take note of them. Well, several times this week, as I was tidying my notes into my briefcase, I said to myself, 'A lot of people have access to this bag and I've got so much information in my notes! I've got a feeling something's going to happen to them. I ought to put them in another bag.' But I didn't. I kept on putting them into the tour briefcase.

I usually listen to these feelings and I take heed, but this time, Up Above created a blockage. On Saturday evening, I was in a volunteer worker's home; he'd offered to organize a two-day workshop in his town and we had to find a date that would suit everyone. So I went to get the rough draft of the schedule in the tour briefcase but I couldn't find it. I asked myself, 'Why can't I find it now? There's a reason.' I still continued discussing the workshop plan with the volunteer but we had difficulty finding a date. So I meditated and after a while I heard an inner voice say, 'No 2-day workshop.' I had my answer. Regarding my notes, I immediately realized I'd left them in Christiane's son's apartment when we visited him last week.

So that evening, I explained to the volunteer that there wouldn't be a 2-day workshop. I'd already agreed to one some time ago, and he'd already been in touch with a few people about it, but I had to override his hopes. I like him, he's very nice and we have a good relationship, but I had to say no to his idea of the workshop because that's what Up Above had decided.

Information from the Metaphysical Worlds doesn't only come to us via dreams. Reality is like a dream and information is transmitted to us all the time. So if we don't have dreams yet, we can begin by reading daily signs.

We can also read our feelings. During the course of the day, we meet people, exchange with our family, friends and colleagues and we feel, we sense all sorts of things in their presence. If we work with the Law of Resonance — if we develop the habit of saying to ourselves as soon as we're put out, bothered, annoyed or disturbed, 'I'm feeling put out here, so this is me, this is a part of me.' It's wonderful because by doing this, we acknowledge that concrete reality shows us parts of ourselves just as dreams do. And also, it helps us to understand that what we perceive from others can help us to decide what is appropriate to do. Especially when we reach the point where we no longer feel disturbed by the resonance we perceive.

Yes, madam? (Participant: What if we don't remember our dreams? Does that mean anything special? Because sometimes I know I've had a dream but I can't remember it. It's as though the curtain drops when I wake up.) Exactly.

This happens — as I explained earlier about the concept of being too emissive — when our spirit is too busy in matter. For example, we may be feeling insecure — financially or otherwise — and we may have a lot of responsibilities on our shoulders. Well, in many cases, an overload of responsibilities awakens our willpower, which means that, as soon as we wake up, we immediately go over the list of all we have to do that day and our dreams fly away like feathers in the wind.

What happens in these cases is that the first chakras are very much in demand and so the spirit is pulled downward to these lower regions, so to speak. Actually these two questions — what can we do to have dreams and what can we do to remember them —

go hand in hand. In both cases, the solution is to maintain as much contact as possible with the Metaphysical Worlds. If we are preoccupied with matter from morning until night, it's normal that our spirit remains on this level during the night. However, if we take time to meditate during the day, if we read signs and work on our resonances, we maintain a level of energy that favors dreaming and learning symbolic language.

(Participant: We should work more at meditating, that's what you mean, isn't it? It's our intellect that works too much, isn't it?) Yes, that's right.

The intellect tries to maintain control, because it isn't open to other dimensions. Sometimes we see people who have been doing Tai Chi or Qi Gong for 20 years and who don't dream. This is because they have great willpower and their intellect works in such a way that it prevents this opening.

Imagine a ball of very concentrated energy inside you and, in order to dream, this ball has to rise up into the higher levels of conscience — in particular to the 6th chakra (located in the centre of the forehead, one inch above and between the eyebrows) and 7th chakra (located on the top of the head) — which are directly related to dreaming. When our conscience is constantly busy being active but without sufficient confidence or relaxation, then this energy ball cannot rise into the higher, superior centers. Most of this energy is devoted to action and basic needs.

On the other hand, the aim of meditation is to help that energy rise and develop in the medulla oblongata — a region of our brain situated at the base of the back of our head — which is a key center for awareness and spiritual development. If it's difficult to sit still and meditate or if we don't have time — we may not have half an hour free to ourselves every day when we have children — we can simply meditate while active — walking, driving the car, waiting in line at the checkout, doing the washing up, etc. Active meditation is so powerful! It develops great intensity, comparable to the intensity we can observe in children. Whenever a young child has a drink of water, he is so present in what he's doing! Whenever he does a drawing, he is totally involved in his drawing, he doesn't think about other things. Adults are usually dispersed; they've lost the capacity to

200

concentrate their energy in one and the same place. Meditation allows us rediscover this intensity.

It is also important to have a healthy lifestyle, including healthy food. Vegetarian food also plays an important role in the physical balance that allows us to dream, because it favors meditation and a spiritual opening in general. It's easy to understand: vegetables require less time and energy to be digested than meat. Normally meat takes 48 hours to go through the digestive system, and if we eat a lot of meat, we are nearly always busy digesting. Thus the energy used to digest isn't available for use elsewhere. We all know that when we have eaten a large meal, we feel heavy and often our energy is so busy digesting, we don't even feel like going for a walk. With vegetarian food, usually after two or three hours, our stomach has completed its cycle, and even immediately after a vegetarian meal, we feel light. Moreover, whenever we eat meat, we don't only eat the animal's flesh, we also assimilate the animal's character and energy. This is important for our society where animals are generally mistreated and die in a state of fear.

At the same time, we mustn't overdramatize; it's not necessarily a serious problem if we eat meat. I myself ate meat for years; I only became a vegetarian when I felt the time was right for me to do so. When my daughter Kasara was very young and was with her mother — my first wife — she ate meat. I've never said, "Oh! How awful!" No, I've always respected her mother's lifestyle and I simply told myself that Kasara would decide for herself when she was older. I didn't have a fanatical attitude and, at 13, she chose, by herself, to become a vegetarian and now, at 18 years of age, she is still a vegetarian.

Everything has been done very easily because I didn't impose my lifestyle on her and her mother. With time, her mother realized it was her own choice and she respected that. I think it was the intention I kept in my mind during all these years that created a good environment between her mother and me for Kasara. I've always told myself, as a separated parent, 'I am responsible for Kasara when she is with me. When she is with her mother, she's under her responsibility, not mine.' And I knew Kasara had received both parents for a reason. She needed to learn all the qualities of both her mother and her father.

The more we evolve on the spiritual level, the more conscious we become of the power of our true intention, our spirit, and the more we sense that our elevation potential increases when we respect other people's choices.

To come back to our subject, a healthy lifestyle is a key that helps us provide ourselves with the best possible conditions for spiritual evolution, dreaming and remembering our dreams. It's as if we were preparing for a journey. Before going to bed, we put a glass of water, some paper and a pen or pencil on our bedside table. We get ready for bed. Then, before falling asleep, we meditate and we ask for a dream. We know that when we dream, it's God speaking to us and so we pay attention to it. It's as simple as that.

The idea is to establish a balance in our life between the energy we devote to matter and the energy we devote to our spirit. To do so, we need to bear in mind the true role of matter in our evolution; we need to remind ourselves that matter merely provides grounds for experimentation; its sole purpose is educational. We use the situations we go through every day in order to evolve, to develop our spirituality. Indeed, this is the aim of meditation, which teaches us to marry spirit and matter.

Does anyone else have a question or a dream?

Yes, madam? (Participant: Some people talk about waking dreams, do they exist?) Yes indeed. When I mentioned earlier that I'd heard a voice saying, "No 2-day workshop," that was a waking dream. Whenever we meditate and we see images or hear voices that come to us from the inside, we are having a waking dream.

(Participant: That happened to me once a few years ago. It was in the morning and I was still between two zones — not fully asleep and not quite awake either — and a voice said to me, "*There will always be a boat for you.*" The evening before I had felt a lot of compassion for someone. It was actually then that I understood what true compassion is.) I understand. That's exactly it.

You see, it's a bit like that when we meditate regularly and intensely. At one point, apparently incoherent things come to mind in the form of images, sounds, visions or even smells.

Yesterday evening, for instance, just as I was arriving at our hosts' house, I heard the words of a song in my head: "*At first we could give the kids to your parents, just till we do what we have to. Of course, I was jealous, it was a blow to my pride...*" It's a French song from the 70s that just sprang into my mind, just like that. I'd begun singing it without even realizing. So I said to myself, 'This couple's either already separated or they soon will be.' For me, it was clear—I knew it. This information had been communicated to me without my asking or even wishing to know about the state of their relationship. Later I was able to validate it. Whenever we have truly stabilized our conscience, we receive information in this manner. We become a little like children, who sometimes say things which seem irrelevant to the situation. One day, we understand that life responds to one of the most coherent structures, to a highly mathematical structure.

If Up Above, They decide that such and such a person will be directly involved in an accident and they'll survive, you can be sure it will happen exactly as planned. Here on Earth, if we wish to receive a pair of boots by mail, we simply order them, specifying style, color and size, and then we either pay the mail service delivery man, or simply have them debit our credit card. The same goes for Up Above: They can create any event whatsoever, because They have all the information and all the resources.

Yes, madam? (Dreamer: Recently I've had several dreams about moving. One of these dreams really made an impression on me. In my dream, *I had just moved into a really big apartment in a four- or five-storey apartment building with great big bay windows. It was really nice; there were magnificent landscapes with rivers. I came out of the building and went down to the village. Then there was a change of scene: I was in a restaurant. The people there were drinking and smoking, and I didn't feel comfortable because of that. So I left. Then I saw a huge navigation lock, and a little farther out, the sea.* I woke up with this dream.) Ok, I understand. Thank you.

The fact that you'd just moved in the dream indicates that you've been in a very particular state of conscience for some time now. Moving symbolizes changing inner worlds, changing on the inside. It is very common to dream about moving when on a spiritual path, because spiritual Work leads to inner transformation.

Sometimes, we live in a house in concrete reality and we dream we live in an apartment. An apartment evokes the idea of sharing—

or learning to share—because, in a way, we live closer to and are more involved with neighbors: we meet them in the hallway, we hear noise through the walls, etc. So, even if an apartment symbolizes intimacy and the inner world, it also concerns our relationship with others and, from an inner point of view, the relationships we have with various parts of ourselves.

We need to consider the outer world as a reflection of our inner Universe. Everything moves in accordance with our spirit. We are created according to this fundamental principle that the outer world manifests itself according to what we are, with our states of conscience and our memories. We are plunged into experimentation scenarios that other people also have to go through, because they have similar apprenticeships to do.

Since the first element of the dream was the awareness you'd just moved, that was the theme of the dream. Hence the dream was about a change that is taking place within you.

The fact that the apartment building was high and had lots of big bay windows, through which you could see beautiful landscapes, shows that when you are all by yourself, without direct contact with others, you feel good, you have beautiful thoughts, like a monk living up in the mountains. But the rest of the dream shows that this isn't the case when you are in the outside world, in society. Contact with others awakens lots of negative memories.

That's why you felt annoyed when you were in the restaurant. The people there were drinking alcohol and smoking and that bothered you. The restaurant, the people, the alcohol and the smoke all represented parts of yourself—even if you do not drink alcohol or smoke.

We can see that you still have dependencies on the emotional level. As alcohol is a liquid, it symbolizes affective, emotional dependency. As for cigarette smoke—which belongs to the element air—it represents confusion on the thought level, confusion due to an inner rebellious attitude and a dependency on erroneous thought systems. You aspire to an expansion, to freedom in your life on the intellectual level, but, given the limits, certain erroneous concepts have a negative influence on you. Smoking is also related to a lack of love; people are searching for warmth, tenderness and affection throughout this experimentation. In your case, because your dream shows you as a person who smokes in a restaurant, it is social warmth. You also nourish yourself sometimes with the behavior of others, without any discernment, and this creates confusion in your program. So you still maintain thinking, thoughts and concepts that cut you off from the Light, from understanding. We can add also that sometimes, you stress too much and you go into certain places to find relaxation, which you do not find, of course. We all do this at the beginning of our spiritual journey. We go through many discrepancies.

Cigarette smoke doesn't only pollute the body and the environment; it also pollutes the mind, our spirit and the metaphysical environment. If we are to experiment with such dependencies, then we experience them, experiment and move on to other experimentations once we have cleansed the memories linked to a lack of love, of warmth, and we find good ways to eliminate our stress instead of nourishing it. So you were being shown these aspects of yourself — aspects you need to rectify during the process of inner change.

But you must remember that you're not only that; you also have beautiful aspects. The fact that you felt annoyed by the behavior of the people in the restaurant indicates that you are aware of the negative nature of these dependencies. And the fact that you left because of that shows that you wish to cleanse these distortions. On the conscience level, you are moving and you don't want to bring these dependencies with you. That's very positive.

However, the fact that you left because of those people also indicates a puritanical attitude toward people who have emotional dependencies and who adhere to erroneous thought systems. Of course you can be really bothered by smokers and drinkers in concrete reality, but cigarettes and alcohol are merely symbols of psychological attitudes, which essentially bother you because they are still part and parcel of your personal memories. We can be a non-smoker and still have a smoker within us, in the form of memories and ways of thinking that have long kept and still keep us mentally confused. Everybody has such memories. It takes time to cleanse all of them.

At the beginning of a spiritual path, it's normal to be a little rigid, a little puritanical when we encounter other people's distorted behavior. I've been through that stage, my wife Christiane went through that stage, we all go through a stage of puritanism. We so want what's beautiful, right and good that we reject people who don't correspond enough to our ideals. But it's just a stage, because one day we manage to remain calm in the presence of any sort of behavior and feel compassion for those people because we understand what they are going through.

When we visit someone in hospital who is ill, we don't feel aggressed and we don't become aggressive. We feel love, we listen and we have compassion for him. We should have the same attitude toward a person who doesn't behave right. They've got certain things they have to experiment and go through and that's OK for them. It's their reality and we should respect it. One day, we will live in this tolerance and love which allows us to understand, with our heart, that each experience has its place, that each person follows a path of evolution. That is what respect for other people's conscience is. Unless, of course, the judicial system has to intervene because other people can be hurt.

This dream about the inner changes you are going through indicates that you are trying to develop healthier life habits. You recognize the forces you need to transform and that, of course, is very positive.

The puritanical attitude you were shown can be worked on. We need to manage these forces consciously because they can lead to quite destructive behavior for our friends and family as well as for ourselves. The most efficient way of moving on to another stage is to refer back to ourselves, to tell ourselves that whatever annoys us in others represents parts of ourselves that we are being shown. The deep reason why we cut ourselves off from everything that seems distorted at the beginning of a spiritual path is that we seek — even unconsciously — to concentrate our energies, to cease scattering them all over the place. We are trying to discipline our instincts. Then we come back to the world, so to speak. It's as though we went up the mountain in search of Knowledge, and then we came back to the material world to apply it.

Several of you may recognize yourselves in this image, having been monks or nuns in other lives. In this life, you are attracted to the study of dreams, symbols & signs as well as meditation and

206

prayer, and you are now trying to marry spirit and matter. So we come down from the mountain to learn to apply Knowledge in our daily lives so as to achieve this synthesis.

It's easy to be spiritual in a mountain monastery. The birds sing, we've only got little repetitive tasks to do and everything is fine. Such a life is not negative in itself—on the contrary! By doing this, a person has the opportunity to concentrate on his spirit and on trying to improve himself. However, afterwards, he has to rediscover his creative power. He's got to return, get a job and take on responsibilities—family or otherwise—in society once again. These will provide him with the opportunity to manifest and to put into practice the spiritual knowledge he's acquired. AH! That's a whole different experience—because when we do nothing, we seem spiritual and everything seems to be correct. Except that we don't do anything, we don't materialize. It's when we are active, it's through action and via our actions that we can test our capacity to remain wise, calm and attentive.

That's what Up Above wanted to show you in this dream—that you are in the process of coming down from your own little monastery.

Whenever I lecture in Paris, I say to the people attending the workshop, "You take part in spiritual workshops, but the most beautiful workshop you can attend is to take the ring road at rush hour. Once you're stuck in a traffic jam with a 2-hour delay, you have a perfect opportunity to work on your patience. (*laughter*) Meditate, pray, analyze the signs and symbols around you, and that will help you. You'll feel everyone around you is impatient, while you are trying to stay calm and in complete harmony. That's a wonderful workshop! And what's more, there isn't even a toll gate on the ring road of Paris; it won't cost you anything and it will bring you spiritual abundance." (*laughter*)

People laugh when I say that, but it's true. We sometimes forget to apply Knowledge. We leave a workshop where the atmosphere and ambience was beautiful and as soon as we're back in traffic, we start to complain and criticize others. We should say to ourselves, 'It's as if I were in a dream. The other people represent parts of me and by being nice to them, I'm being nice to myself. If someone wants to overtake me, I let him.' It isn't important to be at the head of the line, out in front, first. Whenever we place Qualities and Virtues in first position, we attain the Highest levels of conscience. That completes the interpretation of this dream.

Yes, madam? (Dreamer: Last night I had two dreams. In the first one, *I was in a shop and a very wealthy lady I know came along with a box in her hands. She offered me the box and I said to myself, 'Oh! This box probably contains jewels.' When I opened it I saw that it contained pairs of glasses. I said to the lady, "Gosh... erm... well, I don't actually need these glasses, I've already got glasses." She replied, "You'll see, you'll need them." So I accepted the box. The lady left and I examined the glasses. There were round ones, square ones, oval ones, etc.* In my other dream, I was also with other people. I always dream I'm among a lot of people. Anyway, *I was with other people and I left them. I found myself in front of a staircase leading to a door. I climbed the stairs and opened the door. Behind the door, there was a dazzling sun and a beautiful tree-lined path. Right at the bottom, a multitude of birds took flight. My heart soared; I felt happy.*) That's a very beautiful dream.

First of all, the fact that you have multiple birds in your dream explains that great forces in your thoughts are taking flight, expanding. This is very positive because quantity symbolizes a multiplication of the forces represented. When we see multiple aspects of a symbol, for example, a lot of people, in a dream, it means it is related to our social life, our collective consciousness and it also means that we have abundant, strong vital energy. A large quantity of people appearing in a dream can signify either positivity or negativity. The negative aspect would be that we are scattered all over the place, lacking focus or a center, as if a person had a variety of ways of being, doing, living, and lacked true coherency. Such a person would have no social cohesion in terms of conscience. However in your dream, of course, it was the positive aspect that was manifested: you have great vital energy and multiple possibilities on the level of your thoughts.

What does the wealthy lady represent for you? (Dreamer: She's a former neighbor who is very wealthy. We've more or less remained in touch. That's all.) Have you good feelings about her? How do you consider her? (Dreamer: She's a nice person.)

208

Ok. I understand.

In the dream, this woman symbolized your feminine polarity and a part of your inner world that is drawing close to you. It's a part that is full of potential, because the woman is very wealthy on the material level.

She brought along pairs of glasses in a box. A box represents structure, because of its cubic form. It also expressed the idea of a present, because it contained something that was offered to you. Cosmic Intelligence is offering you a gift. You said that you already had glasses but those glasses are going to help you see differently.

What are glasses for? To correct our eyesight and help us to see better. So the glasses you were offered will allow you to view life in a new way and, because there were several pairs, on a collective level as well. You had this dream last night, and here you are today taking part in a workshop that is opening lots of doors for you on the conscience level.

It's as though you received a great treasure, a capacity to see things with new depth. Since the woman represents material wealth for you, you'll apply this new capacity of seeing things on the material level, in the field of material things. This will allow you to make enlightened choices, for example, when it's time to make concrete decisions.

The fact that the glasses were geometrically shaped — square, round, oval — indicates that this vision will help structure your life, on the concrete level once again.

In the second dream, you were being led to an opening on a different level. It's very interesting. You went up a staircase, which means you visited a more causal level, that is to say, the thought level, because of the birds. Let's have a look at it in detail.

When you opened the door, you saw the dazzling sun. Of course, the Sun is the representation of God, the Divine, the Spirit, because without the sun that lights and heats the world, nothing would exist, no life could manifest itself on Earth. When we tell someone they are a real ray of sunshine, we are referring to the Light and Love they radiate.

A flock of birds flew up in the air. This flock represented a multitude of thoughts taking flight. This shows that you are really experiencing a great opening on the level of concepts and ideas.

Hence you are acquiring and receiving great wealth and great riches in a new vision of life. You are here today and, over the coming months, you'll experience other openings of conscience. You'll be able to better understand aspects of yourself. Because for the moment, this vision isn't natural yet — this needs to be pointed out. You are being given help, but you'll have to work deeply for it to become natural, for it to come from your soul. You'll need to integrate it on the physical and emotional levels.

It's good to remember that glasses represent a sort of handicap regarding our ability to see. A person who needs glasses has developed a distorted way of seeing and observing. Eyesight problems appear after a long period — sometimes an entire lifetime — during which people exhausted themselves considering details with a rigid attitude that caused them to lose sight of the essence of things. Such people experience profound insecurity because, although they ardently wish to know people and things, they only look horizontally, with a concrete, rational, non-spiritual approach. Or it can be the other way around: by not being precise enough, by not seeing in depth, the person develops a difficulty to see and understand.

Both of these dreams are important for you. They're working on correcting your sight, your vision, so that you can better perceive and understand your experimentation on the material level. (Dreamer: Thank you.) You're welcome.

Yes, madam. (Dreamer: I received a dream after I'd asked a question. One of my daughters is always dissatisfied. She always feels she never has enough, etc. The evening before, she'd been aggressive and jealous. So I asked for a dream that could help me. In my dream, *I was near the house where we — the whole family — had lived for 17 years. I was near the house. There were roses along the street and opposite the house, the church and the town hall. On the sidewalk in front of the church, I saw a man who looked like a Jew dressed in olden-day clothes and he was kicking and beating a woman.* I can no longer remember what the woman was like. *I witnessed this scene, which was really very cruel. I opened my mouth to shout at him to stop, but my voice didn't work—only a tiny little sound came out. So I went into the house because I saw I was completely blocked.* I know we always dream about ourselves, and I wonder if there's any connection with the question I asked.) Thank you for sharing this with us. It's sure to help many people.

First of all, we need to understand that our children represent parts of ourselves. And each difficulty that manifests in our relationship with them serves to help us understand things about ourselves. This is also true of all those near and dear to us: family, friends, colleagues — they are mirrors that reflect facets of ourselves. So when our children have difficult behavior — whether it's aggression, escapism, dissatisfaction, jealousy, whatever — it means we need to cleanse similar memories within ourselves. Our child is an important mirror of our unconscious.

Through her aggressive, complaining behavior, your daughter finds herself in the role of the aggressor and you in the role of the victim. But, we cannot be a victim if we haven't already been an aggressor, if we haven't had the same kind of behavior — in this life or in another life — as that which we are now being subjected to. And as in this case, the victim is necessarily more evolved than her aggressor. Therefore, if you manage to understand and cleanse the memories linked to your difficulties with your daughter, you will end the associated karmic cycle; you'll close the circle, so to speak.

So you ought to say to yourself, 'Ok, this is what I need to work on; I've got to solve this within myself. I need to learn to feel satisfied with whatever life offers me. I need to learn to deal with my little frustrations, my anger impulses.' You use this as your starting point. And when you refer this back to yourself, you need to be careful not to over-dramatize, because you aren't only this; this isn't all of you. You're simply focusing on this particular *file* so as to be able to understand it deeply.

In this dream, you received a very precise reply to your questions about your daughter, about her behavior. The choice of a village is a key clue. You were shown this village so as to attract your attention to your family life, to your family links and to what connects you to the heart of this issue. And you were deliberately not shown your daughter so that you could recognize your own, personal karma in the difficulty you are experiencing at the present time.

The scene of cruelty with the Jewish man occurred in public, in front of the church and town hall. Such a location refers to community life and exchanges among people living near each other. We can easily recognize the scenario in your family relationships, where your daughter's behavior could be described as cruel—her dissatisfaction, her difficulty living with the family, the pressure she puts on you to get what she wants.

The Jewish aspect, like every other nationality, can be very positive, but in this dream, it was a negative symbol. The positive aspect of Jews is their capacity to pick themselves up and get back on their feet after great ordeals and hardship. These people went through great suffering and managed to rebuild themselves. Economically, Jews help each other within their community and this has allowed them to become one of the greatest financial powers on the planet. They are at the head of the biggest companies, the most influential corporations. Moreover Jews are very involved in politics in both the United States and the world.

As for the negative aspect of Jews, it's related to ideas of persecution and a refusal to share wealth. Jews are often accused of wanting to keep money and resources for themselves, of not caring about anyone outside their community. Well, someone who wants to have a lot of material things for himself is usually prepared to use violence to achieve his ends. This is how a cycle of persecution is engendered. In other lives, if a person persecuted or dispossessed others, in his present life, he is therefore persecuted and is so afraid of losing what he possesses that he cannot have enough for himself and his family and always wants more. He finds himself in a cycle of violence due to his needs—need for money or self-centeredness. It is no coincidence your husband is a Swiss banker in his present life and your daughter is greedy for material goods and social acknowledgment. You share a family karma regarding money and social acknowledgment. The fact that your family is involved in the world of finance shows that you have come to learn how to manage resources well, in every sense of the term.

Hence the image of the Jew assaulting a woman in front of the church and town hall expressed something very powerful regarding these attitudes. It shows that you have memories of persecution and fear of lacking money, which cause you to attack the inner world of others, since it was a woman who was attacked.

So in this dream, you were given a good idea of the kind of memories you need to cleanse so as to improve your relationship with your daughter. You weren't told what to do with her; you were shown the deep cause of the problem — and, consequently, the solution — which, at first, resides within you. When you have cleansed these memories, the situation is sure to solve itself, one way or another.

When you wanted to cry out and stop the man, you had no voice left and you went into your house. This is a good reflection of the fact that you have no voice left to confront your daughter when she behaves in a distorted manner. You find it difficult to direct or guide her. You can't manage to put her in her place and you let her do what she wants. When a child creates difficulties, we have to make him understand that he can't go on behaving like this. Of course we need to take into account the level of the problem, but, to use a metaphor, if we leave a rotten apple in a bag, it causes the others to rot too.

We need to use our pedagogical sense with the child in order to help him understand things, and, if he doesn't want to know, if he refuses to listen and learn, then we need to take other measures. We can even envisage sending him to live elsewhere.

(Dreamer: My daughter is already 24 years old; she could be independent. But since she's still studying, she lives with us. Except she doesn't appreciate it — she's always dissatisfied about money.) I don't know if you support her financially, for her studies. (Dreamer: Yes, we pay all her tuition fees and expenses, because she studies well.)

Still, at 24, she's already an adult. So you ought to speak to her as you would an adult. You can give her the gift of limiting her — on the very level she'd least appreciate; in the same manner that Up Above does when we don't act properly. It takes away our resources so that the minute we get them back, we'll appreciate them.

This solution may seem hard and not appeal to us at all but, usually, after a few years, once the person has managed to get out of his slump, he tells us, "When you refused to give me such and such a thing—or when you refused to continue accepting my behavior back then—that was the best thing you ever did for me."

If we let them, people will continue to create difficulties. When your daughter has children of her own, they'll behave the same way and the conflicts will continue. You'll continue to suffer the consequences of your lack of strictness for many years. Therefore in a situation like yours, we need to find a solution to manage these energies and put a stop to them.

The fact remains, however, that we need to begin by doing inner work. We have to accept the situation and find the deep-rooted cause of it, its origin—on the level of our memories—and to rectify those parts of us that created the situation. Only then can we speak correctly to the other person and find a concrete, correct solution.

And if the solution means the person is to be limited regarding his liberty or resources, we limit him. Because your daughter won't pray and meditate or call upon an Angel to help her transform herself, will she?

When we don't want to evolve in the world of causes, then we have to do it in the world of consequences. There are two ways to evolve in life: cause or consequence. On Earth, there are police forces and courts of law to deal with delinquents. Up Above too. In the Parallel Worlds there are various systems of rehabilitation that allow people to get back on the right path.

As a mother, then, it's up to you to help her understand that her actions will have consequences—that you'll have to restrict her on such a level, for instance—and discover what could be of help to her. Needless to say, there is no ready-made recipe; you're the one who knows best what could possibly solve the situation.

In any case, you had a truly solid dream! You received very important information that will allow you to understand exactly what it is you need to understand. Simultaneously, the dream has helped you see the kind of energy your daughter bears within her. She's in the persecution field of conscience and she projects this onto the outside—she blames others for persecuting her—instead of dealing with the distortion within herself. She does this because she doesn't feel good. There you are. Thank you for sharing this with us.

And that's the end of this beautiful workshop. Heartfelt thanks for your attention and for all you have shared. May you be conscious that dreaming can elevate our conscience and enlighten our lives.

WORKSHOP

Dreams: Your Spiritual Autonomy

Yes, madam? (Dreamer: I had a dream last night. *I was driving a small car and there were passengers with me. The idea was to park at the station but, to get there, we'd have to go under scaffolding, which left quite a narrow passageway. The others said I wouldn't be able to get through but I did. I arrived in a little square where I couldn't park on the left—there was a door into a hangar with a sailboat inside. I turned around in the little space that was left and parked on the right. There the sea ended with waves crashing against an embankment wall. The sea was quite clear, but there were brown patches or stains in the water. I said to myself, 'It's algae.' At the water's edge, on my left, there was a man—I don't know him—and he was throwing Medicine Balls into the sea. The balls were about 10 inches (25 cms) wide, and he was throwing them to an incredible distance, out to his right. I said to him, "Ah! Wow! What a distance for such heavy balls!" Watching the balls land in the water, at one point, I realized that the brown marks weren't algae but lions' heads. There were lots of them—a whole line up of lions' heads across the water. Then these lions started coming out of the water. There were also bears. These animals came out of the water and went into a house where there were lots of people. All of a sudden, I found myself in the house too, and it seems that the animals were going to eat the last person who arrived. I was that person. Fortunately, or unfortunately, I don't know—let's say unfortunately, I knocked a woman down. There was a kind of raised bridge, and I knocked down this woman who was wearing a white coat, you know, like a doctor's or nurse's. Everything was quite dark in my dream, but I saw the woman fall into the light. And there was the sound of breaking glass when she fell. Phew! I was no longer the victim! Nevertheless, I still had to escape. There were four other places where I could take refuge. I chose one of them, which turned out to be a laboratory. In the laboratory, there was a little girl that I saw behind me and someone was hosing her up and down, like people sometimes do in spas. I remarked, 'Oh but her woolen jacket is going to be soaked! She can't stay like that—she's all wet.' The little girl just remained there, unperturbed, not making the slightest sound as she was being hosed down. Then the hose was turned off and the little girl came out. Not a single drop of water fell from her.* I have to tell you, though, that regarding the young girl, I had another dream about three weeks ago. In that dream, *I opened up my wardrobe and a little girl's flowery, summer dress was hanging there and it was soaking wet. So I said to myself, 'I can't leave this in the wardrobe soaking wet.'* To continue with last night's dream, *I came out of the laboratory and found myself in the street. There was a sidewalk on the left and lots of people, all dressed in black, were making their way up a hilly street, looking overwhelmed with worries. They were all around me; I belonged to the group.* And that's the dream.) Thank you very much for sharing this with us.

We shall see what a deep dream this is, how revealing it is for the evolution of your soul.

Sometimes we receive quite an elaborate dream like this but in our daily lives, we may also go through situations that resemble these long dreams. We get up in the morning, go to the toilet, have breakfast, get dressed, go to the supermarket and meet a friend who tells us about her aunt who had an accident. This conversation awakens fears in us that our son, who's taken the car for the first time to go away for the weekend, might have an accident. Then we go back home, put away the shopping, drop a jar, the jar breaks, etc.

Such a sequence of little episodes seems really banal, like a daily routine, but it is full of information about our soul-states and our unconscious memories.

Our spirit moves in matter. Whenever we wash, our spirit experiences the state of conscience of purification; when we have breakfast, the state of reception of resources. When we arrive at the supermarket, it bathes us in a feeling of abundance. When we hear our friend talk about her aunt's accident and fears for our son are awakened, this activates memories of accidents that affected our resources—because the conversation takes place in the supermarket and our environment influences us when we talk to another person. Some people may think more about the car they lent their son for the weekend than their actual son. And so on. By analyzing little daily events, we can find out so much about our soul, about our conscience!

Why have I drawn this parallel before beginning the interpretation? Because one day we see our life in terms of states of conscience. We are a spirit that takes on a physical body, and the only reason we are here on Earth is to develop qualities and virtues. Through the situations we experience day after day, via the states of conscience those situations give rise to within us, we are led to encounter our distortions, to cleanse them and to develop the corresponding qualities. Hence we develop our interiority, this spirit that is the source of our being, of ourselves.

Now let's do the analysis. First of all, in this dream, all the elements represented parts of yourself, in the sense that you were on an inner journey, in your own *personal computer.*

As the dream is long and detailed, I suggest we make a list of the elements in it. So, *the Self,* because you yourself were present as a character in the dream. And let's note right away that it was dark, because that's general information. *Dark.*

You were driving a car. Was it your car? The one you drive at the moment? (Dreamer: I have no idea.) Ok. Was it a particular color? (Dreamer: I've got a feeling it was gray.) *Gray car.* There we are.

There were passengers. This is a very important detail. As indeed all the details are because each one gives us information about the field of conscience visited.

Next you had to go under scaffolding so as to be able to park the car. *Scaffolding.* The passengers weren't at all sure you'd manage, but you did. *Passengers doubtful, disbelieving; Self succeeds in getting through.* Next, *wants to park on the left.* There was a sailboat in the hangar. *Sailboat in hangar.* Then you did a U-turn and parked on the right. *U-turn; park on right.* There we are.

You were at the seaside. (Dreamer: Yes. The water was relatively clear but I could see brown patches, brown stains.) Ok. And there was an embankment. *Sea; relatively clear water; brown patches/ stains; embankment.* Then you saw a man throwing... what did you call them? (Dreamer: Medicine Balls.) Ah yes! That's very important. And he was throwing them out to the right, wasn't he? (Dreamer: Yes.) Ok, so, *Man on left; throwing out to right.*

219

Could you tell me what Medicine Balls are? (Dreamer: They are exercise balls that we use a little like dumbbells—you know, like weights for weight lifting or getting fit.) Ok, I understand. Thanks. (Dreamer: But they were enormous; much bigger than Medicine Balls usually are. They were 10 inches wide.) Were you given the figure 10 in your dream or did you just surmise it? (Dreamer: It was my impression. I wasn't actually told 10 inches.) Ok, fine.

Let me open a parenthesis here about this. When analyzing dreams we have to be careful not to add a number—like 10 in this one—if it is not explicitly mentioned or shown. A dream is a mathematical equation. If we add information, even just a tiny detail, we could misinterpret the message.

Here you are talking to us about size—the Medicine Balls were big—but the figure 10 wasn't one of the symbols in the dream. So we'll only retain the idea of size, of their being very big. (Dreamer: The Medicine Balls were brown and the man was throwing them very far; I was impressed.) Ok, so let's note that down: *Enormous Medicine Balls; brown; thrown far; Self impressed.* There we are.

Next you noticed the brown patches were lions' heads. *Lions' heads.* (Dreamer: There were so many of them!) Ok, so we add, *Lions' heads +++.* Then the lions came out of the water and there were also bears. *Lions and bears come out of water.*

Then, they went into a house. *Enter house.* And so did you, you were in the house too. *Self in house.* Then…? (Dreamer: Then, I was told the animals were going to eat whoever arrived last and it was me; I was the last person to come into the house.) Fine. *Info: eat last person in: the Self.* There we are. Ok.

Then you knocked over a woman who was dressed in white, and she fell into a luminous place to the sound of breaking glass. *Self knocks over lady in white; lady falls into bright place; breaking glass.* Ok.

Then, you fled and choosing a way out from among four choices, you hid in a laboratory. *Seeks refuge; 4 possible places; laboratories.* There was a little girl there and someone was hosing her down. *Little girl; hosed down.*

220

Then...? (Dreamer: I said she couldn't stay there like that; her woolen jacket was all wet. But when the hose stopped, her jacket wasn't wet. Then the little girl left.)

Then...? (Dreamer: Then, I found myself in the street among people all dressed in black. The street went uphill and the group of people that was heading up it looking weighed down with worries and cares. *Characters dressed in black; procession going uphill; overwhelmed with worries.* Ok, so there we are.

First of all, when it's dark in a dream, it means we aren't completely conscious of what's emerging from it. It's like in concrete reality: we can see clearly in daylight—in terms of conscience, we understand, we are aware of what's there—whereas when it's dark or at night, we don't see well.

But you used the word dark, not night; you didn't say it was nighttime. When we think about our dark side, we think about regions in our conscience that we do not know or where we don't feel very comfortable or even where there are very negative aspects of our personality. So this symbol tends to be negative in this dream—even if sometimes, it can be positive and represents a concentration of energy, discretion, unknown, mysterious or other unconscious aspects. Moreover, the car was gray. Was it a lovely, silver gray or a dark, somber gray? (Dreamer: I can't really say. I only had the feeling it was gray.) Ok, so these two symbols combined give us a general idea of the positive or negative tone or aspect of the dream. Gray is a mixture of black and white; white symbolizes spirituality and black, matter or hidden aspects, discretion, mystery or fears triggered by negative forces. Hence, when positively presented, gray represents experimentation, the path that leads a person from the material level to a spiritual conscience that leads him toward wisdom. And from a negative point of view, this color represents the nebulous, unclear, a little lax aspect of a path toward greater consciousness. Someone who doesn't really apply himself to developing qualities, but who remains rather lukewarm, without any real motivation. It's this lukewarm aspect that is revealed in the beginning of the dream.

I often say this—it's very important to be gentle, to be kind in our discernment, to feel compassion for ourselves as we gradually discover our distorted zones. Because, although we tend to visit these regions or *departments* in our memories, we are more than these regions. We have a lot of positive memories too. A person can discover a distortion in one area of his conscience and have the same force inverted, therefore made positive, in another region. That is all for the dark aspect.

You were driving a car. We often see cars in dreams. A car represents the way we advance in society, in our social life, the way we advance toward others. We can easily understand this: whenever we drive on the highway, we feel or sense the other drivers around us advancing to reach their goal. When the driver of the car behind us is impatient, if we are the slightest bit intuitive, we can feel it. It's not the car engine that we feel; it's the state of the driver. When we drive a car, it's a little like walking among other people: sometimes we speak to them, sometimes we push past them and, at other moments, we remain in our personal bubble. A car also allows us to reach a destination more rapidly than if we were on foot. Hence it is an extension of our physical body related to our capacity to advance and attain our goals.

As for the color gray, its symbolism can be linked to the dark aspect we mentioned earlier: it shows that you are visiting a zone in your conscience that tends to be lukewarm, lacking commitment, reluctant to make any real effort to deeply understand your life.

You needed to park your car. The negative symbolism of parking is inertia. The person is in a stationary state; he is limited and cannot advance to attain his objectives, his goals, on the social level. However, in this part of the dream, it's the positive symbolism that is present, i.e. the arrival at our destination. Normally when we park our car, it's because we've arrived at our destination. Hence, you reached your destination regarding certain aspects of your relationship with others, and you were preparing to experiment with other things.

You had to go under scaffolding to be able to park. Was it an apartment building that was under repair? (Dreamer: I don't know. All I know is the way past was narrow.) Ok, so we retain the idea of narrowness. The other people in the car told you that you wouldn't be able to get through.

Those characters are parts within you that can undermine your self-confidence when you go toward other people. Doubt arrives and says, "I'll not manage; I won't succeed." Then another part of you, one you identify with more easily—because it is the Self—asserts itself, asserts your capacity to attain your goals. That is very positive, because, if we transpose this idea onto the social level, we can see that you are in the process of rediscovering and regaining confidence in your capacity to advance and be less influenced by what others might think.

The force that usually makes you doubt yourself may manifest itself in the form of your husband or someone else who doesn't have full confidence in you and who limits you. However, the fact remains that the capacity to assert yourself and say to that force, "I can do it; the car can get through here," is now present. The fact that several people doubted that you could get through shows that this tendency toward self-doubt and this lack of confidence is quite strong. You are beginning to re-educate these parts of yourself and to be able to go toward what is right for you. That's a very important point in the dream.

You wanted to park on the left. The left represents the inner world, inner action, whereas the right symbolizes the outer side and action in the outside world. That's why the left symbolism includes mediumnity, clairvoyance and spiritual powers in general. In the past, most Catholic educators forbade writing with the left hand. In French Canada, it was customary to punish children who wrote with their left hand. There are positive aspects to all religions and spiritual philosophies, but this was clearly wrong. It shows a lack of Knowledge. Forbidding people to write with their left hand symbolically prevented them from developing their inner powers and becoming like Jesus, following the same path as him. What a paradox!

You couldn't park on the left because that would have blocked the entrance to the hangar containing the sailboat. What does a sailboat represent? First of all, it goes on water so it concerns the emotional world. A sailboat is also like a car, because it allows us to advance. So there is the idea of advancing on the inside, on the emotional level. A sailboat is also like a house, in the sense that we can live on it, and it's like a car, because it allows us to advance. A sailboat also represents emotional stability due to good mastery of our thoughts—because of the sails.

However the sailboat in the dream was in storage; it wasn't in use. So you have a whole emotional potential set aside, unused, either because you haven't got an emotional, sentimental relationship, or — if you have — because it's stationary; there's no movement in it. In any case, there's a latent emotional force within you and, given the fact that you chose not to park in front of the hangar, it is clear that you don't want to block access to this force nor prevent it from emerging.

Next you did a U-turn. This shows that you are in a state of seeking, of searching for the right way to advance and behave. We saw earlier that it's the positive aspect of parking that is present in this dream. This is because you wanted to park in the right place; you looked around for a correct place to park the car. In terms of conscience, you are seeking to stabilize yourself, to establish a way of advancing that will allow you to get through the next stages.

You were at the seaside. The sea represents the emotional unconscious. You are encountering your emotional memories, positive as well as negative ones. However, your emotional, sentimental life is rather stationary — we saw this with the sailboat stored away in the hangar. You have unawakened potential and being at the seaside indicates that you are going to encounter this potential. In the rest of the dream, you were shown why you cannot use these stored away forces just yet.

The man was on the left and he was throwing balls out to the right. Once again there is the idea of left and right. Often, when we tell a dream, we don't think of specifying whether an element was on the right or the left or sometimes the scenarios appear in such a way that these aspects aren't apparent. However it is really noticeable in this dream.

The man, who was on the left, represented your emissivity toward the inner world — emissivity because it was a man, and toward the inner world because he was on the left. And the fact that he was throwing balls out to the right represented your emissivity toward the outer world. So your will to get better, to heal — symbolized by the name Medicine Balls — has been activated, and one day this allows us to bring to light a collection of emotional memories that dwell in the unconscious.

It's an interesting dream because it indicates both an activation of inner forces — through the will to get better, to be healed — and an outer activation, symbolized by the man throwing out to the right. At the moment you are going through a concrete situation related to this activation — you can probably identify it.

The Medicine Balls were very big, and the man was throwing them out far, with great strength. This indicates that you are really taking things in hand but perhaps a bit too aggressively. You say to yourself, ' I'm going to make those distorted, emotional memories that prevent me from experiencing happiness rise to the surface.' You are determined to heal yourself, to cleanse the memories that prevent you from using your emotional potential but because you throw the Medicine Balls so far out, we see by this gesture a sort of frustration, a discouragement of not having healed yet.

You saw dark patches or stains on the sea and you thought they were algae. This shows that you underestimate the extent of your problems. Whenever we visit our unconscious, we are always surprised by what we find there. When we think of a patch or stain, we think of something that has to be repaired or cleansed. Therefore, through the emotions you are experiencing at the moment, you are being led to repair or cleanse something that, symbolically speaking, is revealed to be animals. In actual fact the brown marks were lions' heads. What does a lion symbolize? This animal is said to be king of the jungle. The negative symbolism of the lion is a tendency to think we are important, to attract attention to ourselves by talking loudly or in other ways, and by imposing our will so as to be considered the leader; whereas the positive aspect is related to self-assertion.

The lions that came out of the sea symbolized an instinctual force coming from your emotional unconscious that sought to manifest itself in broad daylight. And as there were so many of them, they clearly represented a great force of self-assertion but it remains very negative because the lions were in troubled water, in the middle of dark patches and stains.

Well, what happens when such forces awaken — and we see this in the following scene — is that the person is afraid; he's afraid of being devoured by them.

This is a typical reaction of people who have accumulated a lot of repressed emotions. The person has a spouse who doesn't treat her well—he's not nice to her, or vice versa—and at some point, her lions emerge. Because it was repressed in the unconscious, great anger now manifests itself. From one day to the next, you who have always been so gentle, say to yourself, 'Goodness me, I wasn't like this before. I'm really abrupt and when I say no, it's "NO! I DON'T WANT THAT!" What is happening to me?' And the other people around you say to themselves, 'Gosh! What's gotten into her?' What's happening is that you are in the process of taming your assertion forces. For you it's a case of transcending these instinctual energies and integrating the positive force of the lion.

The same idea applies to the bears; they too represent certain needs, certain instincts. The negative aspects of a bear are the brutish, unrefined, greedy, glutinous aspects that characterize this animal. Hence, as your self-assertion force is activated, you need to transcend both of these attitudes; i.e., rediscover beautiful manners and discipline your tendency to constantly seek satisfaction of your needs—mainly on the emotional, sentimental level, because of their emergence from the sea.

In the course of the next few days, you'll notice a tendency to *roar*, in terms of conscience. Before, you showed tolerance in relation to certain situations that affected you but, from now on, you'll be less tolerant. The idea is to succeed in asserting yourself in a right and correct manner, to learn to master this emerging force. Your family, friends and colleagues aren't used to you asserting yourself and they won't change from one day to the next, so you need to tame this force.

We are actually observing this phenomenon at the moment with our daughter Kasara, who's just entering adolescence. She has always listened to her dad; we've always gotten on really well, and we still do, but sometimes a little lion emerges. Because, during adolescence, the phenomenon of self-assertion occurs. One day, our sweet little beloved cherubs suddenly transform into warriors. They assert themselves, even though what they suggest sometimes doesn't make any sense. They can be like a bear that wants to destroy the Eiffel tower in order to use it as a toothpick. It doesn't make any sense; it's not logical. Their needs are disproportionate.

In our family, we have the advantage of working with dreams. Kasara tells me her dreams and if she loses mastery of her energy during the course of the day, I only need to remind her of her dream for her to check herself. She has the awareness and capacity, on the initiatic level, to evaluate herself and to tame the forces that awaken within her.

During adolescence, the forces that awaken are so powerful, and the phenomenon is so new for teenagers, that they'd like to have the whole planet at their disposal. They lose all sense of proportion — they confuse big and small. When their friends come over, they want space for their activities and, listening to them, you'd think they needed the whole house. The rest of the family should clear out just for them. We all have these forces within us, except we have to master them. Sometimes we see people watch the news on TV, and judging by their reactions, you'd think it was their mission to set the world to rights. They sit there in front of the screen and they rant and rave, insulting the politicians on the screen — "He's just an old so and so... and he's even worse! He should never have been elected!"

Everybody has ideas on how things should be run, and everyone has inner politicians and inner ambassadors, but if we don't get involved in politics or in the community, our armchair debates won't do much good. All we do is shake the furniture a bit and we may even destroy the peaceful atmosphere in our home that day. Instead of improving the world, ranting like this can spoil our intimacy, our home-world! It's important to master our powerfully emerging forces — at all ages.

So, true healing has started within you, and you're aware of it. Of course, you'll be de-stabilized at the beginning. That's normal. Because the awakened forces are very powerful — a lot of animals emerged from the sea. When we receive a dream like this, we can better understand why we married a man who has lion or bear attitudes. This may not necessarily be your case, but you may have had such people in your life — your father, mother, brother or others. This is because we have these very characteristics, these attitudes within ourselves, in the form of memories. And the idea is to recognize the fact that we have strong resonance with these people.

Then the animals went into a house. This means that these instinctual forces will manifest in your intimacy, in your private life. Needless to say, when a lion or bear enters a house — that doesn't happen every day, though, does it? (*laughter*) — it's good to know beforehand so we can prepare and be ready for them. So just imagine a whole pack of lions and bears! You should expect to be quite de-stabilized in your intimacy, because of repressed emotions that are beginning to resurface.

You knew that the animals were to eat the last person to arrive, and you knew that person was you. This means that needs and instincts will lead your life for a while. They could manifest directly in your behavior — for instance, you could be devoured by an obsession related to unsatisfied needs and be quite hard on yourself — or, they could be manifested in others. Through the intermediation of others, we bring our inner forces to light, without even being aware of it. It's the Law of Resonance — we attract what we are. Hence, others may have more demands than usual and you'll feel *devoured* by life and responsibilities, so to speak. Sometimes we find ourselves saying, "Ah! I always do everything for others but I never get anything in return." We feel frustrated, because we're under the impression that we don't get our due. At times like this, we literally feel devoured by life. In reality, it's because we haven't yet mastered our inner animals and we maintain a thought system that is erroneous.

This process probably won't be a conscious one, especially at the beginning, because it was dark in the dream, but, over the forthcoming weeks and months, it will become clearer and clearer that that's exactly what is happening. You'll feel these forces. In the dream, when you heard these forces were going to eat you, you were afraid. So, you are afraid of these forces that are emerging from your unconscious. But you shouldn't be afraid of them, because their activation is part of the great movement of your inner healing. Of course, this movement will only be fruitful if you choose to educate your inner animals.

At the moment, you are stirring up the waters of your unconscious — that's exactly what happens when you are working consciously with a dream — and you need to learn how to tame and master these forces that are being awakened.

Then you jostled a woman dressed in white. Because of her being dressed in white, this woman represented your spiritual side, as it is expressed within you. You have a tendency to jostle yourself on the spiritual level; you want to advance faster than the natural movement sees fit.

The woman fell into a bright, luminous place. This indicated that from now on, you'll better understand that your misactions wound your spiritual parts. Whenever you lose your balance, when you lose your inner stability, it will help you know yourself better.

You heard the sound of breaking glass. When we think of glass, we think of transparency. Among other things, glass serves to make recipients — like bowls, dishes, cups — and that's why it also symbolizes a capacity to receive. The sound of breaking glass indicated that whenever you lose your footing, your authenticity and receptivity will be greatly affected. In actual fact, this whole scene announced periods of great instability, which usually accompany an opening of the unconscious.

This dream is rich in information; it describes in detail the process that has been set off.

Then you chose a hiding place, which turned out to be a laboratory. What kind of laboratory was it? (Dreamer: Pharmaceutical. I should tell you that in concrete reality, I work in a pharmaceutical laboratory.)

It's no coincidence that we work in a laboratory. Everyone who works in a laboratory — whether it's medical, pharmaceutical or whatever — all have experiences in their lives that will lead them to heal their souls. It's part of their Program. Likewise, doctors, nurses, researchers, pharmacists, therapists, in short, all those who work in the medical field, in the broadest sense possible, have something to understand about illness or ill-being. They need to integrate the Qualities that correspond to their specific job. If they deal with patients first hand, their experience will lead them to understand the meaning of suffering. When we understand the meaning of suffering, we stop over-dramatizing it and we develop deep compassion and great love for those who suffer!

In the dream, you hid in a laboratory because you wish to find a way to heal yourself. You need to discover your emotional potential—which is immense—and to realize it in all its power and in its whole dimension, taking care that it does not become a destructive force or cause you to fall ill.

When you went into the laboratory, you saw a little girl in the back, who was being hosed down. The back is always related to the past, to memories we have recorded in the past. The water-hose represents emotions once again but this time they were directed. It's not very pleasant to be hosed down, unless, of course, we're having fun with children and then it is generally positive. Otherwise, to be hosed down indicates, for example, that someone is sending us emotions that are not very nice, that are not right. We feel all wet in terms of conscience; we don't feel good.

Usually, when we are hosed down, we react, whereas the little girl in the dream didn't react; she remained completely passive. She represented your inner child who tends not to express himself, who doesn't talk when you are going through emotional difficulties.

In the dream, you were all three of these: the little girl, the water-hose, and the person who hosed her down. So, in the past, you sprayed others with your emotions, and, in this life, in a way, you have lost your capacity to react when people soak you with their negative emotions. So you were shown the cause of your tendency to repress emotions. This is an important element. It is the key that will allow you to understand the cause of your emotional outbursts. Because by dint of accumulating repressed emotions, we run the risk of having them erupt violently one day.

The little girl was wearing a woolen jacket. Wool comes from sheep. And what do sheep do? They follow. It's good to follow provided we follow what's right—our shepherd needs to be divine. This divine shepherd can manifest in the form of a child, another person, a situation. Personally, I can be guided by my daughter, by my wife. Sometimes a piece of information I've heard on the radio or in a conversation guides me. Anyone can guide us, even people who aren't right; at any given time, they can give us information that goes straight to our heart and we can extract a whole lesson from it. One day, we learn to recognize the Divine in everyone and everything that exists, and we remain open and receptive while maintaining our discernment as to what is right and what isn't.

230

So the woolen jacket represented the attitude of following, of blindly conforming, and this symbolism is reinforced by the procession at the end of the dream — we'll talk about this in a few minutes. We see that one little detail in a dream can take on great importance, just as tiny bacteria can lead to a serious illness.

The little girl went out and there wasn't even the slightest drip of water from her clothes. The symbolism of this image, combined with the dream where you wanted to take the wet dress out of the wardrobe for it to dry, along with the idea of conformity, the following attitude we've just seen, shows us something very interesting. When you are emotionally, sentimentally perturbed, you tend to go out to find some sort of consolation. If someone you know suggests going out as consolation, you tend to accept and follow no matter what is suggested. Let me give you a simple example. Let's say a friend or an aunt invites you to go to the casino, saying, "Aw! Poor you, you're all on your own, you have no boyfriend. Come along with me, we'll cheer ourselves up at the casino. There's a great dance show on, The Macho Men. (*laughter*) And after the show, we'll try our luck with the slot machines." You'll accept and go along with her idea. What is positive is that you'll understand things through the emergence of these emotional forces; the light the woman fell into shows this.

An initiatic path without Knowledge is very dangerous, because we can get lost. If we don't know the Law of Resonance and if we don't understand that everything is a state of conscience, through conformity, through following others, we can join protest movements that lose touch with reality. We can fall into a form of fanaticism whereby we think everyone else is wrong. We think society is running late and the world is lost.

The world is not lost. It is exactly on time — the time that is exactly right for its evolution. Wars have their place in the scheme of things. Everything has its place. One day, we understand that wars exist simply because we all have little wars going on inside of us. We nourish them daily. Everyone has a little bit of war on the inside and at any given moment, these energies condense and war manifests itself on the collective level. When a person starts to cleanse his inner wars, this manifests itself in his relationship with his wife, his children, with everyone around him. It is only by committing ourselves to such a process that we can hope to one day put a stop to war forever and see societies living in peace.

If there is no war in our countries, it's because Up Above, They wish us to live in a peaceful world. Because from one day to the next, if They so wished, They could create certain instabilities and whoops! there could be total anarchy on Earth. Everything could explode at any time.

I'd like to go back to the fact that the little girl wasn't wet after being hosed down. That meant that, by dint of being sprayed with other people's negative emotions, you have become *waterproof*, so to speak. It's like people who no longer feel the pain or hurt that's inflicted on them. Other people are mean to them and it doesn't affect them anymore; they're used to it. Even though that's not yet mastery, not replying to violence with violence is already a step.

Then you came out and you found yourself in the street among people walking up a hill looking overburdened. First of all, the act of going out represented a passage from the inner to the outer world, just like when we leave home and go into the social world. As for the procession of people going up the hill, they represented a way of collective thinking or parts of you regarding the collectivity.

The people were dressed in black. From a negative point of view, black represents a solely materialistic vision of things and a multitude of hidden memories, buried in the unconscious related to abuse of powers. As for their being overburdened, bowed down with cares, this represented ordeals, sadness and a feeling of despair.

One day, we understand the meaning of difficulties, hardships and ordeals. We consider them as springboards to something new. Everyone who goes through difficulties eventually discovers their meaning.

The Guides of the Parallel Worlds program the situations we have to go through in accordance with our Life Plan. Of course we keep our free will, but as soon as the orientations we take diverge from those planned in our Program, the Guides intervene to bring us back onto the right track. It's as if we were piloting a plane and as soon as we slipped off our planned route, then

232

the automatic pilot system took over. The Work of the Guides ensures that perfection is always present. This implies that no one can be a victim of assault, theft or rape — or whatever the ordeal — if there isn't something for him to learn through that very ordeal.

(Participant: We get what we deserve, don't we?) That's right.

The Guides aren't up there saying, "Oh! I've nothing to do today, I think I'll send so and so an ordeal or hardship to deal with." No, not at all. To be sent difficulties, we must have prepared, organized and arranged for them ourselves on the metaphysical level — during the course of our other lives and this one too — and this idea also applies to beautiful situations.

So, if a difficulty turns up, we should accept it and ask ourselves, 'What am I to understand here? Why has this happened to me?' And we analyze its symbolic meaning. And if our difficulties last a long time, well then, they last a long time. We use these periods to deeply cleanse and purify ourselves.

If we don't feel well and we just complain and whine about our lot, we blame others for our misfortune. It's the fault of society, our parents, our brother who made us do such and such when we were young and our mother who didn't defend us. It's always other people's fault.

We must come to understand that our parents and our brother represent important parts of ourselves, that there are reasons why we were born into this family. When we refer back to ourselves, one after another, we drop all our weapons; we lay down arms. Because we say to ourselves, 'If I did it, it's normal that it's done to me. I didn't know I had this or that in my memories, but now I know. So I accept it. Thank you for not being nice to me. You've helped me understand what I needed to understand.'

Of course, that doesn't stop us from changing things in our life. We mustn't stay where we are beaten and say, "Thank you, hit me more." If we've married a violent man, at one point, we say to ourselves, 'That's enough of physical and verbal aggressions. I'm putting a stop to this; I'm leaving him. But I'm going to work on myself. This wife batterer exists in me. I've got to re-educate him.' If we don't do so, we attract another violent man, or, on the

233

other hand, we may end up with a man who is far too soft, who's weak, indecisive, lacks initiative and who is of no help or support to us at all.

At one point, we get out of such situations. We understand that it was we ourselves who engendered the situation and we change it. And in doing so, we don't need to be violent. Instead we feel compassion for the other person since we know what he'll have to go through himself later on. Because life sees to it that people get exactly what they deserve. The person who abused us will attract someone who will resonate with him and he will be subjected to the violence he made us suffer.

When we work with positive Energies, we integrate Good and so we emanate the Forces of Good. We remain aware of evil—we know it exists—but it isn't manifested through us. It is manifested through people who nourish evil. These people encounter each other and are led to evolve together—they give each other mutual lessons.

Once we have integrated this understanding, we are no longer perturbed or negatively affected by the sight of others in difficulty, in the sense that we don't feel upset. When my daughter was a little girl and I told her the story of Cinderella. I didn't feel sorry for her. I didn't say, "Oh! Poor Cinderella, her stepmother is so mean to her!" Instead I told her Cinderella had something she needed to understand, to work on, cleanse and transcend and that her stepmother represented a part of herself that had acted in the same way in another life, and that one day, she'd be subjected to the same difficulties she made Cinderella suffer. I taught her the meaning of ordeals and hardships, of their teaching role in our evolution.

Yesterday—the first day of this 3-day seminar—I met a woman who told me about her situation with her mother-in-law, and when I saw her earlier today, she told me what happened to her when she went home yesterday evening.

Her mother-in-law lives with them and she's been putting her down, crushing her, for over 20 years. She even calls her a vulture, a turd, etc. So, when she went home last night, she was feeling all sorts of emotions related to her mother-in-law's attitude. She arrived home, parked the car and, before locking it, she said to herself, 'Ok, I'm going to close this door and lock the car as if it were me so that she — her mother-in-law — can't affect me.' She wanted to make a symbolic gesture to exorcize her mother-in-law's negative influence. So she slammed and locked the car door very angrily. She told me, "It was stronger than me. I really slammed it hard." And looking through the window, OOOH! She saw her keys swing back and forth! (*laughter*) It was lovely to hear her, because she said, "It was as if the keys were taunting me, saying, 'Hey, you! You're going to have to change your attitude, the way you think about your mother-in-law.'" (*laughter*) Up Above, They had just given her a whole lesson. They were telling her, "Listen, you mustn't close yourself off from your mother-in-law. Your mother-in-law is you. You acted the same way in another life."

We talked a lot about this. I said to her, "Now you can understand that that's not the way to solve the problem. If you don't manage to fuse with your mother-in-law, with the memories that correspond to her, she'll come back in your next life. You could even marry your mother-in-law. (*laughter*) Now that's something! Better settle it correctly right now; otherwise it will last for lives and lives. If you end up in an igloo with your mother-in-law reincarnated as your husband, she could be even more tyrannical than in this life. She could even sexually abuse you and you'd suffer all the pains of your soul. By working with this dream, you can dislodge your memories of tyranny and transform them rapidly."

When this woman caught sight of her keys swinging inside the locked car, she said to herself, 'Oh my goodness, what have I done?' (*laughter*) In actual fact, she was being told, "It's not by closing off spaces, by compartmentalizing things and blocking or repressing them; it's not by shutting your heart that you'll settle your problem." It was really beautiful to hear her tell her story.

To go back to the dream, the procession as it was staged — going uphill, overburdened, black clothes — showed that you haven't yet integrated the Law of Resonance concerning issues that relate to the collectivity, to society, although this may not be the case for more personal relationship issues. You have some journeying to do on this level. To conclude this interpretation, you were being told that openings of conscience would lead you to do serious work on the emotional level and to understand the meaning of ordeals on both the individual as well as collective levels.

(Dreamer: Thank you very much.) You're very welcome.

(Another dreamer: I've got a dream I'd like you to interpret, please. In my dream, *I was in the woods with a friend when all of a sudden, night started to fall. I called my friend but she didn't answer. Then I heard a noise in the trees. A bad guy, a malefactor, someone who meant no good, a criminal, was coming and I moved off from where I was because I was looking for the fence you had to follow to reach the lake. I found the fence, climbed over it and I saw a whole group of very friendly German women. I walked along with them for a while; then I reached the top of a mountain. At one point I had to go under a cable car and it was very difficult for me—I couldn't. A minute later, I was inside the cable car and I could see where I should have gone. At the bottom of the cable car there was a very nice cashier. I had to pay and I gave her a tip because she was very nice. Then I arrived in a Swiss mountain resort and I looked for the office my friend worked in, because, since she hadn't answered me, I wanted to know if she'd gotten back safe and sound. I saw her from afar through the window. She was there, in an architect's office, at reception. And somehow, I was a little jealous of her, because— I don't know—she seemed happy, she seemed to be doing well. I was a little jealous of her situation.*) Thank you very much for such lovely sharing, for your beautiful humility. It's so beautiful!

In initiatic science, the most important quality for a spiritual path is said to be humility. It is the capacity to tell the truth about ourselves, about what we discover when we explore our conscience. Some people are not authentic with themselves; they turn away from their distortions, they don't want to see them. So this humility that allows us to be authentic is really beautiful.

What does your friend who was in the dream represent for you? (Dreamer: What does she represent?... erm... oof! She cleans toilets for a living; that's her job.) Ah! That's a beautiful job, much more beneficial than being a salesperson in certain companies where the products are unhealthy for humans or for the environment. This is a very interesting dream. Let's analyze it.

First of all, we need to remember that all the elements of this dream represented parts of yourself, aspects of your conscience, and that you are not only these aspects.

You were in the woods and night started to fall. From a positive point of view, the woods symbolize emotions and feelings while a person is regenerating forces. Why? First of all, because plants and their green color are great symbols of the emotional world. Then, because vegetation renews the soil and provides oxygen — which represents the physical body and the world of thoughts. We only need think of the state of conscience a beautiful walk in the woods leads to. We breathe deeply, renew and regenerate ourselves, because the intensity of life in the woods has a vibratory effect on all our cells. From a negative point of view, the woods represent negative aspects in our capacity to materialize our life and the deep intimacy of negative instinctual forces related to animals, which are hidden in our unconscious and can destroy us, or emerge at any moment. Because of the presence of the bad guy, we'll retain the negative symbolism.

In your dream, it was dark in the woods; it was night. So you are going to encounter instinctual forces that up to now have been unconscious and will remain so for a certain length of time.

Given the presence of your friend from the beginning, your dream concerns a part of you that is committed to a process of purification, because of the fact that her job is to clean toilets. But I'm sure your friend brings to mind other aspects. Does she have a positive connotation for you… or a negative one? (Dreamer: It's so-so.) Let's go further. Why? (Dreamer: Why?) Yes. (Dreamer: Well, she's rather bossy.) Bossy. Ok, that's fine. So, in your dream, you visited parts of yourself that are on a purification path, but which are still rigid, authoritarian, and bossy.

The fact that your friend didn't answer when you called her indicates a lack of communication with the part within you that's working to purify itself. It's as if you sometimes refuse to admit you have work to do on this level, because of a certain image you have of yourself that you want to maintain. Indeed, it's your attachment to this image that makes you rigid.

Then you saw a bad guy in the woods. This bad guy, a malefactor, a criminal, represented another part of your conscience. Everyone has inner criminals, wrongdoers, malefactors, bad guys, until they have been transcended. These are the parts of you that are not right, that are aggressive and assault or attack others to satisfy personal needs. Criminals are a bit like fierce animals. Their needs are so strong, so powerful, they don't think about others. If we examine the dreams of people who have committed criminal acts, we see that they harbor a lot of aggressive animals in their unconscious. Sometimes, they say, "I don't know what came over me, it was stronger than me. I saw nothing of what happened."

We see just how important it is to cleanse our memories of anger and aggression. When we think of the woman I mentioned earlier—the one who violently slammed the car door—we can't help imagining that at some point she could push her mother-in-law down the stairs. And maybe not even deliberately. She could be holding onto her while walking and with an involuntary gesture, she could cause her to lose her footing, lose her balance and fall. Unconscious memories can go as far as making us commit criminal acts.

If we don't know how to manage the negative forces present in our unconscious, the accumulated memories will manifest themselves at one time or another, sometimes very destructively.

The fact that you wanted to get back to the fence indicates that that day, you sought a threshold, an opening onto another territory that would allow you to change moods, to change your state of conscience. And you found this opening. The symbolism of the German women will show you what you are headed for.

The idea of encountering German women is very interesting. These women represented parts of you that manifest the characteristics of the German people on the inside. The positive aspects of the Germans are structure, discipline and a lot of rigor. The Germans have beautiful structure in their language, in the way they act, in their behavior, etc. We can learn a lot from these people on that level and on the level of discipline and rigorousness. We see this in what they build or manufacture; the structures are always very solid.

And the negative symbolism is all that a poorly integrated structure engenders, i.e. rigidity and authoritarianism. Moreover, when

238

the Germans have a drink, they aren't very restful. (*laughter*) They become a little like bears—loud and rough—because when a person conforms, a lot of forces are repressed.

Nearly everyone can recognize themselves in this description. We behave in a certain way because we were taught to behave like this, without understanding why, and, as the years go by, we accumulate a lot of repressed forces. So on the slightest occasion to relax—for instance, when we drink alcohol or take drugs—these forces emerge and manifest themselves. That's why people who usually behave correctly and seem as meek as lambs can suddenly become violent. We don't recognize them. These excessive sides are present in them, but they usually manage to control them by continually repressing them.

Someone who, in this life, has developed rigidity because of a badly integrated structure, will reincarnate in a country and in a family where they will have an opportunity to work on their emotional problems. Hence they'll have a chance to rediscover balance and harmony.

So by seeking the fence that led down to the lake, you wished to get closer to some of your emotions that are better structured than those that characterize the atmosphere, the ambience of the criminal, the bad guy. These are the emotions represented by the German women. When you are in a situation that awakens your fears, your conscience activates a process of inner restructuring that allows it to get back in order, so to speak.

This aspect of the dream is very interesting. We see that we can change atmosphere and ambience within ourselves, just as when we move from the kitchen to the bedroom when we are at home, or from our workplace to the canteen or cafeteria when we are at the factory or in the office.

Then you walked along with the German women and you reached the top of a mountain. So you left a place where there was a bad guy and you ended up in a higher, more elevated place. In terms of conscience, you contacted parts of yourself that are structured and they allowed you to raise yourself above and beyond the bad guy, the wrong-doer, the criminal, that part of you that tends to ignore others to satisfy its own needs.

Then you had to go under a cable car and you couldn't. And then you found yourself inside the cable car. Through this scene we can see you had difficulty raising yourself up but that you eventually succeeded. Then you saw the cashier, you thought she was very nice and you had a generous impulse. This shows that you are generous toward people who are nice to you, especially when things go well, when they are there to serve or help you.

Then you found yourself in a Swiss mountain resort, and you looked for the office where your friend worked to see if she had arrived safe and sound. And, from afar, you saw her through the window, at the reception desk of an architect's office.

The fact of finding your friend at the end of the dream takes us back to the beginning in a way; it's a way of closing the circle. It's as though you had settled or solved something, as if you had found a solution to a question or difficulty you were going through at that time.

Your friend was in an architect's office in a Swiss mountain resort. Once again there's the idea of structure here—because of the architect's office—combined with the idea of an elevation of conscience. These two elements provide you with the key, which allowed you—or will allow you—to solve your difficulty: an elevation of conscience engendered by a structured but not rigid way of living.

Then you felt jealous of your friend, of her situation. By having you feel this sentiment in your dream, you were being put in touch with a tendency you have to envy people that you think are in a better situation than yours. This also shows that you are still unstable in your desire to purify yourself and structure your spiritual path. Through this sentiment, the field of conscience represented by the bad guy shows up again. Why? Because a criminal is someone who envies others, other people's lives, other people's situations.

This dream shows that even though you can control your inner criminals for a while, the problem hasn't really been solved. To succeed in cleansing these petty criminals, these little malefactors, we need to understand that limitations are part and parcel of a spiritual path, that we shouldn't envy others, that we receive what's due to us.

240

If we don't understand that — if we continue to envy others — we probably won't steal in this life, but the frustrations and envious thoughts will continue to accumulate and all it will take is for us to find ourselves in a precarious situation and whoop! we'll start stealing. People can record such memories for two or three lives, until at one point, they get hurt, can no longer find work and they start scheming all sorts of things to improve their material situation. Let's imagine someone experienced this in another life — let's say he lost a leg — and his children were crying from hunger. He used to see fat rich people disdainfully throw him some bread and he envied them. This is how he accumulated thoughts that one day would turn him into a thief or swindler.

And why are we afraid of bad guys? Some people walk in the streets at night and they are afraid. Yet nothing happens or has happened to them — they aren't assaulted. Their fear comes from their own memories because they harbor little criminals within themselves. A person who hasn't already assaulted someone else in a public place cannot be assaulted like this — it's impossible. If a criminal really is in the area, he won't encounter this person or he'll be deviated one way or another. He won't be able to commit his crime; something will prevent him — maybe just a little inner voice within himself. Or maybe the person at risk will sense danger and decided to change his route. It is so easy for Up Above to block a criminal.

As a spiritual person, we can truly rely on the idea that Divine Justice is absolute. Up Above, everything is passed through the finest filter, nothing is let through that shouldn't be. If a person isn't to be assaulted, he won't be assaulted. If he has assaulted others, he will be assaulted in turn. Jesus said, "If you live by the sword, you'll die by the sword." This image explains the idea of karma.

(Participant: And yet Gandhi was assassinated. Does that mean he had already killed?) Ah! That's interesting too! Whenever a person has a mission to accomplish for the good of the evolution of mankind, of a society, his difficulties, ordeals and death serve a Divine purpose, serve Up Above; their experiences serve as an example, to teach us and help the whole of humanity to evolve. Of course, these people are very evolved. Jesus is one of the greatest examples.

Gandhi probably knew he was going to be killed that day. No doubt he was sent a dream informing him—like Jesus. And he didn't do anything to avoid being killed. Because he'd been told that his death was going to put an end to the civil violence that was threatening his country while it was being restructured. It was also his time to leave and inspire this world.

Very evolved people receive everything in dreams. Hence they know why they have to go through certain things. And they are capable of total submission to the Divine Plan. Jesus knew very well what was going on before they came to execute him. He had dreamed about it. During the Last Supper that he shared with the apostles, the evening before his death, he spoke to them of imminent danger and betrayal. He knew that Judas was going to hand him over to the Roman soldiers. He said to them, "I won't be with you much longer, my friends." And he told Peter, "Before the cock crows, you'll deny me three times." And he did.

Like all great initiates, these people continually submitted to guidance from Up Above. They *tuned in* to Heaven and asked, "Is it right to do such and such a thing? Does it correspond to the Divine Plan?" So by being killed, Gandhi simply served as an instrument of peace. He used this event to continue his evolution.

Yes, madam? (Participant: What's the symbolic meaning of a bracelet, please?)

A bracelet represents a link or an allegiance with whatever the bracelet represents. The link can be positive or negative, in the sense that it can be inspiring or limiting. Indeed, a woman came to see me recently and she said, "I've lost my bracelet and I'd like to know what that means." I asked her, "What does this bracelet represent for you?" She replied, "It was a present from someone I like very much, someone I feel deeply for."

So I calmly began to explain, "Well, it could mean that something related to this feeling has to stop. Maybe there's something not right in what you are experiencing with that person." She looked at me slightly embarrassed and admitted, "For sure there's something that's not right. You know, he's my lover; I'm involved in an extra-marital affair. He's the one who gave me the bracelet."

Then she added, "It was a silver bracelet and a month ago, I broke my chain, which was also silver. I know that silver is associated with the Moon and receptivity." "Madam," I said, "There's your answer. You are being asked to understand something concerning this relationship. You are being shown that you won't find happiness as long as you are torn between two relationships. You'll never be completely with your lover or with your husband. At times like this, we have to make a choice, and we have to face the consequences of that choice. You need to find the way that is right for your evolution. I can't tell you what to do. But one thing is certain: you have a choice to make, because, otherwise, in another life, you will attract a spouse who will do the same thing. In this life, you might maintain the status quo in your marriage — keep the material goods, the house, the boat, the cars, etc. — and have your lover on the side, in a hotel room from time to time."

It comes down to this: in this life, we think we've created a little holiday oasis for ourselves. (*laughter*) But in another life, we'll find ourselves living with someone who tells us lies and we won't feel good at all. There we are with three or four children but our spouse is having an affair and, at some point, he goes off with his mistress and we are left poor and miserable. We experience the pain that we ourselves engendered through our lies and lack of fidelity. If our infidelities were numerous, such karma can pursue us for several lives. And all that will have begun with our first infidelity, as with this woman.

I said to her, "If you choose to stay with your husband, it's simple: you'll have to communicate, you need to try and change things. It won't happen overnight, of course, but you need to begin the process. You need to open up to each other. You don't need to tell him about your experience. Sometimes Wisdom counsels us to say to ourselves, 'I didn't know, I apologize to his soul. I've experimented and now it's over; I've turned the page. From now on, I'm going to work on my relationship with my husband.'

We behave as if we had experienced the other relationship in a dream. In doing so, we must be honest with ourselves and not use the request for forgiveness to his soul as an excuse to start again at the very first opportunity, like a compulsive gambler who keeps apologizing to his spouse but bets again the very next day because, in reality, he has no intention of healing himself. Because the more unfaithful acts you commit, the greater the chances the truth will come out and your life may be destroyed. If, on seeing your sincerity and changed attitude, Heaven grants you Its Divine Grace, then you will be protected and nothing will be found out. Even the wind will help you get rid of proof of your misactions." Of course, in some circumstances, it is right to confess our infidelity to our spouse. But, normally, if the person does that, it is almost certain that the true relationship will be destroyed forever. There we are; that's all for this subject.

Yes, madam? (Dreamer: I had a dream last night. *I was on a little motorboat with my husband. He was on the left and I was on the right. He was going very fast; he was driving. At one point, he turned sharply and he banged against another boat. He caused an accident. I was under the impression he didn't realize and that he had no intention of doing anything. But I wanted to go back and see if anyone needed help. I didn't feel good about this.* So after the dream, I asked myself, 'What is it I don't want to see?') Good, that's a good question to ask ourselves in such a case.

We talked about the symbolism of boats earlier. A boat is a little like a car since it represents the way we advance, the way we behave or conduct ourselves, but on the emotional level. It can be considered as a house for emotions. It all depends on whether it's a houseboat, a yacht or just a craft for leisure activities. (Dreamer: It was a little leisure boat.) Ok, so your dream was about the way you behave emotionally and what that gives rise to on the emotional level.

Your husband represented an important part of your inner man. He was on the left and he was driving. Consequently he represented an inner part of yourself that is emissive. And he was going very fast. This means that you tend to go very fast on the emotional level, and sometimes you can hurt others, bang into and jostle them, so to speak. When this happens, you don't take time to see if you caused any damage or, if there is any, to try and repair it.

The fact that you didn't feel happy with this attitude in your dream shows that you are beginning to become aware that this is not good, that it's not right to behave like this. From now on, when you hurt or bang into someone on the emotional level—your husband or someone else—you'll say to yourself, 'Ah! I didn't behave or act well there; that wasn't very nice of me; that wasn't right.' Whereas in the past, you did not notice it all—or, at least, not as clearly.

(Dreamer: Yes, that makes sense. It's true I always go fast. I dash from one activity to the next.)

Let me show you a sign of that. Look, you've got a picture of a frog on your sweater. It's no coincidence that you wear a sweater with a frog on it. (*laughter*) (Dreamer: Oh my! I've got lots of frogs at home—I collect them.) (*laughter*) You see how interesting it is? (Dreamer: I need to work on my inner frogs, right?) Yes, that's right. (*laughter*)

The fact that you surround yourself with frogs shows that frog behavior is very present in you. (*laughter*) When you have transcended the negative aspects of the frog, you won't need them in your house any more. And you'll develop the positive aspects. We are greatly influenced by our surroundings, by what's in our personal environment. In a way, we identify with it, and this process of identification isn't necessarily conscious.

So it would be important to think about what you are nourishing within yourself by having all those frogs in your home. At some point, you should do a good frog clean up (*laughter*) and, one day, when you look back on this, you'll wonder, 'Why on earth was I so fond of frogs?' (*laughter*) Like when we think about an ex-boyfriend or spouse and wonder, 'How could I ever have been in love with that person?'

Thank you very much for sharing with us, because it can help several frogs in the hall today. (*Heartfelt laughter from the participants*)

Yes, madam? (Dreamer: I received a dream last night and when I woke up this morning, I'd forgotten it. Then, later on when we did the yoga exercises, it came back to me. In my dream, *I was at the North Pole; it was all white, it was magnificent. There was a research station and scientists were digging in the ice. They were drilling, you know, when they sink pipes deep into the ground to study past climates. Then they withdrew the pipe and, as they did so, I felt as though the pipe was being withdrawn from my body. And there were different layers of ice of different shades and colors—gray, white, blue, etc.* This seems awful to me, because that would mean I had been frozen for centuries.) (*laughter*) In a way, you've already understood your dream. Except you haven't only got the North

245

Pole in your conscience. You've also got Antarctica, America, Europe and many other warm regions.

In this dream, you visited your frozen emotions that have been put on hold — because of the ice — hence your emotional potential. Here the ice in the ground plays the same role as the sailboat stored away in the hangar in the first dream we analyzed this evening. Studying the layers of ice symbolizes an examination of old memories buried deep in the emotional unconscious.

We can see the Work that has been done for you over the last two days of this seminar. Yesterday we discussed climate change, and in your dream a related theme was used to help you understand things about your emotional world.

This dream gives you a guideline; it shows you what you need to work on. For this lady, it's to transcend frog energy and for you, it's to study what has been accumulated over various lives on the emotional level so as to liberate your emotional potential. That means you need to meditate on this, by continuing to work with other dreams you will eventually receive.

If you do this, you'll bring about major changes in a very short time. When we deeply analyze our dreams and signs, we are on a highway: we cleanse our karma and we advance very quickly. Because, with dreams, we accelerate our karmic level. Often the very fact of experiencing things in our dreams exempts us from having to go through them on the material level — especially if we understand them. Better to have a nightmare one night and feel anxious — even anguished — the next day than to have a father or mother who tyrannizes us for a whole lifetime. With deep inner work, we can avoid whole lifetimes full of difficulties.

It is generally believed that spiritual work is very abstract. But one day, when we use symbolic language, we understand that it is very concrete and practical. Earlier, we established a link between this lady's dream and what's printed on her T-shirt and what she has at home. It's fantastic to see just how clearly our conscience continually manifests itself through symbols.

Yes, sir? (Dreamer: My wife and I spoke to you yesterday about our wish to have another child by adopting one and how we wanted to be sure our intention to go ahead with the adoption procedure

246

was right. So as you suggested, we asked for signs and dreams about this. We meditated on that question — it was completely new for us to meditate — and we asked our question before going to sleep. Last night I received a dream and I'd like your opinion. In my dream, *we were on holiday — the whole family, in a hotel at the top of a mountain. There were several children jumping from quite a height down into a pool of water, and I was afraid for them. Then a little girl went under. Then the phone rang in my hotel bedroom and I went to answer it. It was the social worker calling to tell me she had a child for us.*) Bravo! Congratulations! Well done!

(Dreamer: I don't know…this is all new to us: should I ask for a sign to see if it's that…?) (*laughter*) You've got a whole reply there!

Let's analyze the dream. First of all, you were on vacation. Vacations are a time for renewal, to rest, a time to think about our life, where we're heading, and the direction we're taking or would like to take. Sometimes we make important decisions while on vacation, because we have time to think deeply. That's the positive aspect of holidays. When we don't spend them drinking tequila, they allow us to do all of that.

The fact that you were in the mountains indicates that you had the possibility of seeing things from an elevated point of view. You were given this possibility because you asked if it was right to adopt a child, if that's what you needed to do for the evolution of your souls.

Children were having fun jumping into the water. Generally speaking, children represent our works, because we conceived and gave birth to them. They also represent our future, what we shall or can become. Hence they can also symbolize a project — in a company, to study, etc. — as well as new inner development, our apprenticeship. When we speak of our inner child, we refer to the potential for development and learning we all have within us. Children represent all of that.

The pool symbolized your emotions, of course. Children were jumping from a height down into the water and you were worried about them. The height symbolized your thoughts, first of all because our head is situated at the top of our body and

247

also because thoughts are relatively high up in the causal chain. Jumping—moving from high to low—indicates an incarnation or a rapid accomplishment, in this case into water, which showed that you move from thought to emotion. Such a movement engenders a hope, a wish. Then you were afraid. So you were being shown that certain fears may cause you to have doubts about your adoption project. These fears may even prevent you from having another child.

Then a little girl went under. This confirms the fear you felt in the dream—you were submerged by fears and troubled emotions. You were afraid of not being up to it, not being good or capable enough. In reality, these can be all sorts of fears: fear that something might happen to your children and that they could hurt themselves; fear of lacking resources, of the future; fear of not having enough love; fear that your children won't accept the new child.

Then the telephone rang and it was the social worker. When we receive a phone call in a dream, either another soul is trying to communicate with us, or our unconscious is transmitting some information to us, or Heaven Itself is sending us a message. Because via the phone, we communicate from one place to another or from one soul to another.

In this dream, Heaven answered your question. There is certainly a child somewhere on Earth who's waiting for you to start adoption procedures. The dream is quite clear about this. The fact that the person on the line was a social worker confirms that there's a child out there waiting for you.

You really asked a question with all your heart, with a sincere desire to do what's right. Indeed, I felt your sincerity when we spoke yesterday. I understand why you received an answer so quickly.

This message didn't come from a memory or a need. It came directly from Heaven. I offer you this interpretation and you can choose what to do with it. The decision you'll make will have an important impact on you and your family. You can even ask for other dreams and signs should doubt return. Up Above, They'll understand.

Yes, young lady? (Dreamer: Well, it's a nightmare I had about a year ago. *I found myself in a town. There was a great big building and it was dark. Then, all of a sudden, my head fell over to one side, but it was still hanging on by a thread. And after this, I had a look and I saw there was blood. Then the thread broke and my head fell off. I found myself just beside the Seine River, in a cloud, and I started to cry. Then I saw The Lord and I woke up.*) Ah! That's an intense dream for a young girl like you!

I understand now why you've remained so still throughout the whole workshop. How old are you? (Dreamer: I'm 11.) 11. Ah! That's wonderful. And you received this dream last year, is that right? (Dreamer: Yes.)

You shall see just how interesting it is. You know, my daughter Kasara sometimes has dreams like this.

On becoming an adolescent, you'll notice that new spaces open up inside of you. You have new ideas and you feel a greater need to discover things, to go through new experiences. And it's often more than your mother would wish you to do or to become. There are all sorts of ideas about things you'd like to do, that you'd like to experiment with. All of this emerges and, confronted with this, you experience a sort of duality; sometimes there can be so many influences from outside that you can no longer think for yourself.

What's more, when we become adolescents, there are often inner forces that aren't easy to manage or master and that can create despair and discouragement. That's normal. It is absolutely normal because ancient memories from previous lives are added to those you've recorded in this life.

Ok, so let's analyze your dream in more detail. First of all, you were in a town. A town represents a form of intensity: lots of ideas, lots of projects, and lots of options, possibilities. This is what occurs at the beginning of adolescence: the young person finds he is in a situation similar to being in town, where there are so many possibilities that he doesn't know what direction to take. He'd like to take them all as he wants to try out everything.

Your head fell over to the side and was held on only by a thread. Our head represents our post of command, our rudder, our steering wheel; it contains the thoughts that allow us to make decisions about where to go. Well, when our boat has no rudder and our car has no steering wheel, we let ourselves be affected, influenced, pulled in all directions by everything around us and we follow trends, fashions. That's what that means. If you didn't have your head, other people would do your thinking for you. For example, your friends could tell you that a spider tattoo on the face was beautiful and so you would want one. Or you'd listen to a certain kind of music that isn't necessarily good, just because your friends do. It's like the first time we try smoking. At first, no one—absolutely no one—likes the taste of cigarettes, and everyone coughs and chokes first time round. We keep trying to be like everyone else, to feel important and to nourish our rebellious side and it becomes a habit. It is a very bad habit and it is not at all natural to smoke.

The fact that your head was held on only by a thread means that, at the time you had this dream, you were hardly thinking for yourself, and you didn't know which direction to take. You were going through a great initiation. And we can see this especially when your head falls off, when the thread that is holding it on snaps. You really and truly had no more post of command, no rudder or steering wheel. An initiation is a transformation that is part of our Program and can lead to difficulties we will need to surmount—and we can see you had such a difficulty. There was blood, which means you suffered energy losses.

Then you found yourself beside the Seine. The Seine is a river in France that flows down to the sea; hence it is related to water, to the world of emotions. So, this disturbance, this perturbation that you were experiencing particularly affected your emotions.

A cloud is related to the world of air, so to thoughts, and it is made up of water droplets, so to elevated emotions. The cloud and your crying indicated sad thoughts. That day, you probably broke down and cried—it was all too much for you. You didn't feel good not being able to think for yourself, following just about anyone, friends, parents, anyone, and your ill-being created an opening on the emotional level.

Crying in a dream is very good, as indeed it is in concrete reality too, because it denotes a capacity to call oneself into question, to bring to light a painful emotion. Once we've cried, we feel good afterwards. It's important to learn not to hold back our tears, to let them out—in the right place and at the right time, of course. And goodness knows how much we cry at the beginning of our spiritual path!

I cried so much during my initiations; I really suffered, it was so intense! With time, things calmed down. The more we work on ourselves, the less we cry from pain and sorrow, because we truly understand the Divine Laws—we understand the meaning of all ordeals—and nothing more saddens, pains or grieves us. One day, tears become subtle, like a flower blossoming, releasing its fragrance. It's beautiful when that happens. I feel this when I feel something beautiful, something truly beautiful. Whenever I see people who radiate inner beauty or who, with all their heart, wish to transform themselves to become better souls, that makes my soul vibrate and brings tears of deep, soul-joy to my eyes.

What's wonderful in this dream is that you saw the Lord when you were on the cloud. This scene shows that life's spiritual dimension is part of your life and that you had an elevated point of view. You'll find strength and depth in spirituality. You'll find Knowledge therein that will allow you to find your direction and make the right choices. What is happening is that you are experiencing a great opening into spirituality. You are 11 years old and already you're attending a workshop on dreams & signs. That's wonderful! I'm moved to tears, it's so beautiful. Your example represents hope for humanity because when we seek tools to improve ourselves, we truly evolve in the right direction.

Walking a spiritual path like this, you and your mother can share your experiences, your discoveries. That's the most beautiful thing that can happen to you. How many people would just love to share their spirituality with their family? It's the greatest gift that exists to be able to share what we experience on the inside, to be able to express what we are going through and be understood on a deep level.

Sometimes, my daughter Kasara, who is a teenager, says to me, "Dad, sometimes I have negative thoughts, even about you. I love you, but, you know, when you said no to such and such a thing, it was stronger than me, I could have exploded." And at times like this, I say to her, "It's good to talk about these feelings, Kasara." I don't tell her she's mean or naughty or bad. Not at all. On the contrary, it's so beautiful she can speak to me so openly! I say to her, "If you are able to meditate on it, you'll start cleansing and healing that negative force." And she does pray and meditate and afterwards she tells me how much it helped. She agrees that it transforms her and helps her grow and mature. She is aware of the change in her mood, in her soul-state by asking for help from God. She activates this change herself, through her spiritual willpower.

Oof! I'm moved just talking about it. Because it is this kind of spiritual autonomy that will lead to the greatest changes on the planet.

Knowledge of the symbolic language and the capacity to decode dreams and signs will allow mankind to break through to a new stage in evolution. The integration of this major aspect or *department* of Knowledge will allow us to change our interpersonal relationships and the way we live in matter. Because everything is symbolic—the physical and the metaphysical are one. One day, millions of people on Earth will live like those in the other dimensions, guided by dreams & signs.

You see, your dream means all of that. It shows that you are heading toward spiritual autonomy, that you are a pioneer of a new way of living on Earth.

GENERAL COMMENTARY ON THE
DREAMS SHARED IN THE WORKSHOPS

What better way to see the path the soul follows as it evolves than an overview of the dreams analyzed in a book like this? The collection of dreams we've analyzed herein allows us to see various dynamics that are inherent in the process of spiritual evolution.

Initiations: de-structuring and self-revelation

During initiations, we are de-structured on several levels before we rebuild ourselves an identity or an essential, central Self and during this process, we have to encounter our unconscious memories. Thus initiatic dreams reveal intense de-structuring of the ego and the existence of numerous mostly unconscious personalities.

A state of bewilderment was clear for the participant who frequently dreamed that she was lost, seeking her way among people who were indifferent to her (*cf. In Dreams, Symbolism is very Precise* workshop). Indeed, the dreamer admitted that sometimes she no longer knew who she was.

The dream about returning from a journey and being on a station platform (*cf. Repressed Memories* workshop) is another powerful initiatic dream. The scene where the dreamer saw a man steal her handbag and where she begged him to leave her her identity cards revealed an important de-structuring of identity. Other details in the dream show just how destabilized, disorganized and vulnerable the dreamer felt. She too admitted that sometimes she no longer recognized herself.

De-structuring dreams sometimes concern more limited, less central areas of the self.

In the dream with the vein of rust around the rocks and steps descending into the sea (*cf. In Dreams, Symbolism is very Precise* workshop), the dreamer—who worked as a sales representative in the towns of Nice and Montpellier—was being shown that she was losing motivation for her work and that she needed to re-structure on that level.

253

The dream where the Self lost its head and saw the Lord (*cf. Dreams: Your Spiritual Autonomy* workshop)—the young girl's dream where her head fell sideways and, at one point, fell completely off—indicated that the dreamer was experiencing typical initiatic bewilderment, especially on the level of ideas and orientations, choices.

Here are a few examples of initiatic dreams that reveal unconscious personalities.

The woman, who in her dreams, was frequently lost among people who seemed to ignore her (*cf. In Dreams, Symbolism is very Precise* workshop), was actually being shown her own indifference—her lack of acknowledgment of others, of herself and of her own spiritual path.

The woman who dreamed about the female baker and her own irresponsible father (*cf. In Dreams, Symbolism is very Precise* workshop), who saw herself being offered a sandwich attached to a chain, was being shown distorted aspects in her way of communicating with others: her own tendency to use seduction to obtain what she wants as well as the self-interested, non-detached aspect of the way she gives.

In the dream where the husband causes a boat accident (*cf. Dreams: Your Spiritual Autonomy* workshop), the dreamer was seeing her own tendency to create emotional accidents.

The woman who assisted a person who was assaulted in a public place and who, after a series of nightmares, dreamed she had a great, big heart that was being shot at (*cf. Dreams are Parallel Worlds* workshop) was being shown that she had a lot of memories of aggression in her unconscious.

Different reactions and attitudes

People don't all react in the same way to the revelations they receive about themselves during initiation periods. Some dreams show hesitation, doubt or avoidance tactics. It is good to remind ourselves that such reactions are perfectly normal.

The woman who dreamed she was wearing pantyhose under a pink bikini (*cf. Inner Beauty* workshop) was blocked on her spiritual path by her preoccupation with looking good on the spiritual level.

In the dream about the passageway in the plane bound for Canada (*cf. Dreams are Parallel Worlds* workshop), the dreamer's hesitation when she had to cross over the glass porthole in the floor represented the dreamer's fear of the great opening of conscience that she was undergoing.

Generally speaking the attitudes people have along their spiritual path also vary.

The man who dreamed about the car race through a stable (*cf. Soul-States* workshop) maintained an attitude of spiritual competitiveness that prevented him from advancing when alone, without the stimulation provided by the presence of others.

A puritanical attitude is also common at the beginning of initiations and this is highlighted in the dream of the Self going down the street after moving into a beautiful apartment (*cf. Repressed Memories* workshop). The dreamer's intolerance of people drinking and smoking in the dream revealed her own resonances relating to these distortions.

Initiations are often accompanied by ordeals, hardships and difficulties. It is not rare to see a person react negatively to a stage he has to go through. In the dream about separation and selling the house (*cf. Soul-States* workshop), the dreamer was asked what she intended to do about her cupboards. She was about to begin a new stage in her life but she was resisting sorting out the past and tended to persist in feeling bitter toward her husband, thereby committing herself to a difficult path.

Awakenings of conscience

Awakenings of conscience usually occur in us on one particular level rather than another and often via means that involve certain levels more than others.

In the dream featuring the guided meditation and the three babies (*cf. Flashback* workshop), the dreamer was being shown that her meditation practice had begun to help her edify herself and develop her spiritual autonomy.

In the dream of the blue Angel and the woman floating in the air (*cf. Flashback* workshop), the dreamer was being shown that his spiritual potential was being awakened through understanding and spiritual communication, and that this awakening would later lead him to understand the outside world, to consider it from a spiritual point of view.

In the dream where the wealthy lady gave the dreamer a box full of glasses, and she saw a flock of birds take off and soar into the sky (*cf. Repressed Memories* workshop), the dreamer was being told that she was acquiring a new vision of life, a new way of considering life — a more causal vision — that would allow her to make enlightened decisions on the concrete level. The dreamer was going through a great opening on the level of concepts, especially in relation to material abundance.

The participant who dreamed of three women flying with kite wings (*cf. Soul-States* workshop) was also experiencing an awakening of conscience on the level of ideas — because of the element air — and this was through her willpower and desire for purity — symbolized by the red and orange colors of the kites.

In the dream of the big heart being shot at (*cf. Dreams are Parallel Worlds* workshop), the awakening of conscience occurred on both the intellectual and emotional levels, and it was being carried out through purification and the development of compassion.

The dream of the car race through the stable (*cf. Soul-States* workshop) showed that the dreamer's opening of conscience was motivated by his intention, by his strong will to learn.

Hence by examining dreams it is possible to validate the opening of conscience that is taking place within a person and consequently to evaluate the effectiveness of the steps he is taking, will take or has taken.

Discrepancies

A person who hasn't attained Enlightenment — who hasn't fused and united with his central Self or essence — is a combination of numerous personalities that have been created over several lives, some of which were more evolved than others. When powerful

256

openings of conscience occur, we experience discrepancies or rifts between our various personalities. Sometimes a discrepancy between the inner and outer worlds can be felt.

The best illustration of such discrepancies is the dream where the dreamer jumped into the void, walked on water and entered a magical garden (*cf. Events Planned in Advance* workshop). On analyzing this dream, we noticed the deep discrepancy that had been established between the person's newly awakened potential and certain distorted attitudes that she hadn't yet rectified. Hence her profound feeling of being cut off from and out of kilter with the world, which was actually a reflection of her own inner division.

Seeking balance

As a person experiments, he is led to commit acts that distance him from the Source, from his Divine nature, and create a form of imbalance within whereas in its Great Beauty, balance is a prime factor of the Universe. Hence the spirit seeks to compensate for the distorted forces recorded in its soul by developing complementary tendencies, which are manifested, more or less consciously, via his inner attitudes and his behavior. Furthermore, this search for balance is part of the application of the Law of Karma. Several of the dreams analyzed in the workshops illustrate this.

One of the most frequent and most obvious returns to balance relates to power. Whenever a person has used power unjustly — in this life or in others — he ends up losing it, becoming powerless or impotent, in the field concerned.

The woman who dreamed of a man hassling the pope to go faster (*cf. Events Planned in Advance* workshop) counterbalanced her tendency to push others — and herself — on their spiritual path with a tendency to give her spiritual power to others.

In the dream where the sister insists three times on Anna reading the book (*cf. Soul-States* workshop), the insistence and forced smile represented the dreamer's tendency to insist on others following the same spiritual path as herself. In concrete reality, this woman had lost the ability to communicate with her sister, which reflects a certain loss of power on the communication level.

257

In the dream about the engineer uncle and decorator wearing make-up (*cf. Soul-States* workshop), the decorator incarnated both the person who created the violence and its compensatory aspect, that of a man who was manipulated by others and who'd lost his masculine polarity–his de-polarization, was represented by his wearing make-up. The *attacker-attacked* and *victim* relationship was also manifested in the scene where the Self shot two people. A second compensatory effect is shown in this dream: the dreamer's tendency to clown around and have fun, to create crazy, zany situations in order to mask her potential violence.

In the dream where a person beats up a woman (*cf. Repressed Memories* workshop), the victim and the aggressor are shown as different characters, but both of them represent parts of the dreamer. She herself mentioned her difficulty exerting authority over her daughter because she was afraid of her own potential violence.

From another perspective but also an example of the search for balance, the dream about the friend working in an architect's office (*cf. Dreams: Your Spiritual Autonomy* workshop) illustrated the fact that rigidity becomes necessary—at least for a certain length of time—for whoever hopes to master his inner malefactors, wrong-doers or petty criminals. Too much of anything serves to compensate a lack and vice versa.

In the dream where the Self goes downtown after moving into a beautiful apartment (*cf. Repressed Memories* workshop), the dreamer's intolerance of drinkers and smokers—as we've already seen—revealed she had the forms of dependence such behavior symbolized within herself. Moreover, since her soul still harbored such memories of dependencies, in her search for balance, very interestingly, her spirit tended toward puritanism.

Managing vital energy

A great example of the natural tendency of the spirit to regain its balance is the outburst, the unleashing of destructive emotions following a long period of inhibition.

The dream about the lions and bears coming out of the sea (*cf. Dreams: Your Spiritual Autonomy* workshop) shows that such an unleashing usually occurs when instinctual forces haven't been expressed or transcended for a long period of time, and they awaken during an opening of conscience at the beginning of the initiatic process. This example leads us to consider the importance of transcending negative forces that awaken gradually as the unconscious opens.

Let's do a quick review of the dreams that concern the action of un-transcended instincts and good management of vital energy, challenges which become particularly important during the awakening of the kundalini.*

Three dreams deal specifically with the influence of un-transcended instincts on the expression of vital energy, a theme that is easily recognized by the presence of animals in dreams.

The various energies of the participant who shared the dream about the little rodents (*cf. That's the First Key* workshop) were being eroded by instinctual parts that haunted her conscience.

The person who, as a child, dreamed she'd had her head crushed by an elephant fleeing a fire (*cf. That's the First Key* workshop) and who said she suffered from great fatigue has, from a very young age, had powerful energy that frightens her.

The man who dreamed about the car race through a stable (*cf. Soul-States* workshop) repressed his instincts in order to appear — and to believe himself to be — spiritually evolved. This prevented him from having access to the source of his vital energy.

Guidance

By analyzing our dreams, we can get to know what attitudes we need to rectify to continue our journey. Some of the dreams we've examined remind us of certain attitudes that it is essential to develop on our path: discipline and depth in our approach, humility, detachment, compassion or gentleness with ourselves.

In the dream of the Self naked in the abbey park (*cf. That's the First Key* workshop), the dreamer was reminded that a spiritual path is serious, that it's not right to lay oneself bare, psychologically-speaking, simply to amuse or entertain people.

---

* *The dream of snakes down the back (cf: Awakening of Vital Energy workshop) illustrates an awakening of the kundalini.*

In the pantyhose-pink-bikini dream (*cf. Inner Beauty* workshop), the dreamer was being reminded that it is important to be authentic in the process of purification, to accept and see ourselves as we are so that Work can continue.

Similarly, in the dreams of the horse half rising out of the mist and the woman half out of the water (*cf. That's the First Key* workshop) — both elements in these dreams appeared to be at a standstill, as though frozen — the dreamer was being reminded that she lacked discipline on her spiritual path, that she wasn't applying Knowledge and because of this, she wasn't making progress; she wasn't advancing.

In the dream of the car race via the stable (*cf. Soul-States* workshop), the dreamer was being reminded that a spiritual journey is not a competition, that it is work that must be carried out day after day, and that he should try and be kinder, more gentle toward himself.

In the dream with the broken high heel (*cf. Flashback* workshop), the dreamer was reminded that her old way of advancing, which included a feeling of superiority, no longer worked. She was also invited to go deeper by learning to master solitude.

In the dream about traveling toward happiness (*cf. Inner Beauty* workshop), through the image of the puppet, the dreamer was reminded that she needed to rediscover her spiritual autonomy and to become detached from the false pleasures and conscience-less activities that were preventing her from applying her spiritual principles and values.

Markers and beacons along the way

Numerous dreams clearly indicate the stages of spiritual development a person has come through, is going through, or will go through later. These dreams are precious beacons for anyone on a spiritual path.

This is the case for the first three dreams examined in this book (*cf. That's the First Key* workshop) — childhood dreams where the dreamer fell down a ravine, fell from an elevator into a hole, or saw a wall collapse to reveal a dragon. The first two of these dreams showed the difficulties she was going to encounter in her family life throughout her childhood. The third one was a forewarning of the de-structuring that would occur during her adult life, while simultaneously revealing the cause of her difficulties.

The announcement of situations through dreams is sometimes accompanied by elements such as the night, darkness or sleep to indicate that the person won't be immediately aware of the ongoing process. This idea can be found in the dream of the blue Angel and the woman floating in the air (*cf. Flashback* workshop), where the dreamer was asleep and it was night. It can also be found in the dream about the friend working in an architect's office where night fell at the beginning of the dream (*cf. Dreams: Your Spiritual Autonomy* workshop).

At other times, the announcement of situations is accompanied by elements such as geometric shapes or numbers, to indicate that the dream describes the very first stages of the materialization of a situation, *setting the tone*, so to speak. This is the case in the dream about the guided meditation and the three babies (*cf. Flashback* workshop) where the very beginning, the earliest stages in the spiritual construction of the person were being announced–because of the number 3, among other things. The same idea is expressed in the dream of the three women flying with kite wings (*cf. Soul-States* workshop), because of both the number 3 and the triangular shape of the kites.

When we start learning how to interpret dreams it isn't always easy to determine whether the dream solely relates to the dreamer or whether the dreamer has visited another person's soul — in other words, whether the dream is of the first or second type. In the interpretation of the grandmother in the shopping center (*cf. In Dreams, Symbolism is very Precise* workshop), for a moment we thought it was a dream of the second type, but, since the dreamer made a decision in the dream, we considered it to be a dream of the first type.

The dream about a separation and sale of the house (*cf. Soul-States* workshop) can become a dream of the second type. If this is the case, the dreamer will go through a separation in concrete reality.

The Beauty of Dream Work

Dreams are an unlimited resource for our evolution. They represent one of the most intimate connections with our conscious, concrete life and, day after day, or rather, night after night, or indeed, night and day (*laughter*), they show us various scenarios of our evolution in the Metaphysical World. By analyzing them with the help of symbolic language and by deepening their meaning through meditation, we remain connected to the motions made by and for our destiny and to what it is we've come to learn in this life. The understanding of dreams is truly the key to our spiritual autonomy.

LECTURE AND SEMINAR

To organize a lecture or a seminar with Kaya
on Dreams & Signs Interpretation,
please contact us at: org@ucm.ca

INDEX

Table of Contents

BY THE SAME AUTHOR

GOLDEN ● WISDOM
RECORDS

airgomusic

DISCOVER KAYA IN MUSIC
WITH HIS UNIQUE INSPIRATIONAL ALBUM

«BORN UNDER THE STAR OF CHANGE»

**Produced in New York, Los Angeles and Nashville
by Russ DeSalvo (Paul McCartney, Carlos Santana, Celine Dion, etc.)**

13 Inspirational songs that will touch your mind & soul...

Included a 36-page booklet
explaining what inspired Kaya to compose
these amazing songs.

CD available in stores and on MP3 Digital format on
 iTunes
and on our website:
www.kaya.fm and **www.ucm.ca**

Join KAYA on Facebook:

f

KAYA (official)

277

WWW.UCM.CA
PUBLISHING@UCM.CA

THE BOOK OF ANGELS
The Hidden Secrets
Kaya and Christiane Muller
ISBN 978-2-923097-54-1
e-Book version ISBN 978-2-923654-05-8

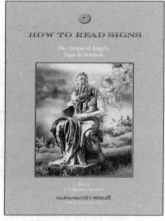

HOW TO READ SIGNS
The Origin of Angels, Signs & Symbols
Kaya and Christiane Muller
ISBN 978-2-923097-61-9
e-Book version ISBN 978-2-923654-06-5

ANGELICA YOGA
Introduction
Kaya and Christiane Muller
ISBN 978-2-923097-63-3
e-Book version ISBN 978-2-923654-07-2

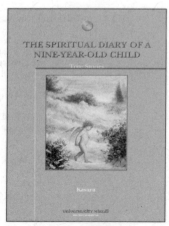

**THE SPIRITUAL DIARY OF A
NINE-YEAR-OLD CHILD**
True Stories
Kasara
ISBN 978-2-923097-66-4
e-Book version ISBN 978-2-923654-08-9

278

UCM

IN THE LAND OF BLUE SKIES
Gabriell, Kaya and Christiane Muller
ISBN 978-2-923097-65-7

THE 72 ANGEL CARDS
Dreams, Signs, Meditation
Kaya and Christiane Muller
ISBN 978-2-923097-60-2

**STUCK IN INSECURITIES:
CHANGE YOUR INNER CLIMATE**
The Traditional Study of Angels
Kaya and Christiane Muller
ISBN 978-2-922467-26-0

**ANGELICA MEDITATION
COLLECTION**
CD 1: (Angels 72 to 67)   ISBN: 978-2-923097-68-8
CD 2: (Angels 66 to 61)   ISBN: 978-2-923097-69-5
CD 3: (Angels 60 to 55)   ISBN: 978-2-923097-70-1
CD 4: (Angels 54 to 49)   ISBN: 978-2-923097-71-8
CD 5: (Angels 48 to 43)   ISBN: 978-2-923097-72-5
CD 8: (Angels 30 to 25)   ISBN: 978-2-923097-75-6

ANGELICA MUSICA COLLECTION

CD 1: (Angels 72 to 67) ISBN: 978-2-923097-80-0
CD 2: (Angels 66 to 61) ISBN: 978-2-923097-81-7
CD 3: (Angels 60 to 55) ISBN: 978-2-923097-82-4
CD 4: (Angels 54 to 49) ISBN: 978-2-923097-83-1
CD 5: (Angels 48 to 43) ISBN: 978-2-923097-84-8
CD 6: (Angels 42 to 37) ISBN: 978-2-923097-85-5

CD 7:   (Angels 36 to 31) ISBN: 978-2-923097-86-2
CD 8:   (Angels 30 to 25) ISBN: 978-2-923097-87-9
CD 9:   (Angels 24 to 19) ISBN: 978-2-923097-88-6
CD 10: (Angels 18 to 13) ISBN: 978-2-923097-89-3
CD 11: (Angels 12 to 7)   ISBN: 978-2-923097-90-9
CD 12: (Angels 6 to 1)   ISBN: 978-2-923097-91-6

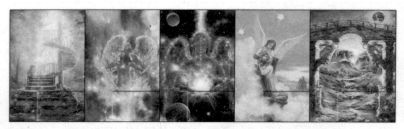

GREETING CARDS
EXPOSITION ANGELICA
Artist: Gabriell
A collection of 65 greeting cards